Just *Lassen* to Me!

A First-generation Son's Story: Surviving a Survivor

Book Two: Survivor Teachings

Harvy Simkovits

Just *Lassen* to Me!

A First-generation Son's Story: Surviving a Survivor

Book Two: Survivor Teachings

Second Edition

Copyright © 2018 Harvy Simkovits

Published by Wise Press

ISBN: 9781723116889

Memoir Series by Harvy Simkovits

Just *Lassen* to Me!
Book One: Survivor Indoctrination
(An Amazon Kindle Bestseller)

Just *Lassen* to Me!
Book Two: Survivor Teachings

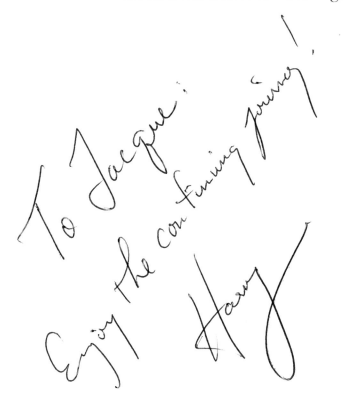

To Jacque,
Enjoy the continuing journey,
Harvy

Praise for

Just Lassen to Me!

Book Two: Survivor Teachings

Though this book series is a memoir, taken from real life events and conversations, it could easily have been a novel, made up of characters and stories shaped by the author to be so real. You can't wait for the next page, the next chapter. The patriarch, Johnny Simkovits, is a sly, ruthless, and often beyond-the-law businessman who strives to become somebody in his world thru his financial successes. He is practically willing to leave his family behind to support his live-for-today ways. Our narrator, Harvy, Johnny's second son, desperately wants his father's approval, and he closes his eyes to his father's shenanigans so that he can obtain his Dad's love and approval. The many characters in this intimate and warmly written tale may come and go, yet each feels real and complete. If this book were written for TV, it would be a much-watched program. It is written with such warmth, so much honesty and affection, that the reader cannot but hope that our narrator Harvy may someday feel his father's love.

~Steve Shama, MD, MPH, Retired Physician, Professional Speaker on topics of empathetic communications, Former Board of Trustees member of the Creative Education Foundation.

Harvy effortlessly weaves together his role in the growth and development of his father's business with his growing awareness of his large-living father's questionable practices. With candor and poignancy, Harvy writes of his struggles to find himself, caught as he is between a desire to please his charismatic, double-dealing, womanizing father by looking the other way, and his distress over the unhappiness of his neglected and ultimately abandoned mother, brought about by that same father. Further complicating his life is his conflicted relationship with his volatile older brother, who deals with their father's forceful personality with anger and defiance. In the end, amidst all the clamor and angst of his family, Harvy must choose between standing up for what he knows to be right with the painful certainty he will lose his father's favor or live his life dragged through the wake of the full-throttle passageway of his scheming father. A terrific read!

~Pamela Moriarty, author of *What Happened to My Mother: A Story of Family, War, and Reconciliation.*

A well-written book that is difficult to put down. Character development is excellent, enabling the reader to get to know each of the principals intimately in the story.

~Dave Ehlke, Founder and Former Owner/CEO, Geek Housecalls

Harvy Simkovits masterfully captured the reality and dynamic tension that can exist between love and shame, respect and disappointment, in his honest, moving, and deeply introspective book, "Just Lassen to Me." The creative weaving of family ties, history, emotions and thought creates a web into which the reader is captured both by fascination and unavoidable personal inquiry. This book is indeed a dedication to the story that exists in all of us. Bravo!"

~Robert J. Broudo, M.Ed., President and Headmaster, Landmark School

There are no saints in the second volume of Harvy Simkovits' memoir series, Just Lassen to Me! Rather, there is a group of fascinatingly flawed relatives, friends, and employees orbiting around Harvy's charismatic and corrupt father, Johnny. The candor and detail with which Harvy portrays his participation in his father's wheeling and dealing and ultimate disavowal of it are truly memorable. In Harvy's Book 2: Survivor Teachings, he weaves a complicated and compelling story.

~Marion Kilson, Ph.D. in Social Anthropology from Harvard University, retired Dean of the Graduate School at Salem State University.

With uncompromising candor and wonderful cinematic detail, Harvy Simkovits has written a powerful memoir of culture, character, family dynamics, triumph, and trauma. In Just Lassen to Me, Book One, the author views his father—at once brilliant and generous, and cruel and deeply flawed—through the eyes of a boy, teen, young man, and mature man. Book Two is a deeper dive into Harvy's journey toward adulthood and the often conflicting agendas of success, his father's approval, self-preservation, and healing his family, body, and psyche. I feel deeply moved, as many will be, by this story of uncommon courage through pain toward truth and personal integrity.

~Lawrence Peltz MD, Psychiatrist, author of *The Mindful Path to Addiction Recovery*—a practical guide to regaining control over your life.

Dedication

This memoir series continues to be dedicated to sons and daughters who have had to both live up to great life promise and confront deep family shame, and to my mother.

Contents

Praise for *Just Lassen to Me!* Book Two
Dedication
Welcome Back to *Just Lassen to Me!*
Note to U.S. Readers & A Personal Note

Book Two: Survivor Teachings

Part V. Fatherly Enticements

Part VI. Patriarchal Disenchantments

Part VII. Homecoming

Excerpt – Book Three: Survivor Learning

Acknowledgements

About the Author

Welcome Back to

Just Lassen to Me!

Is it possible to admire a man's accomplishments but abhor what he stands for, to seek his blessing but spurn his legacy? What if that man is your father?

"Live for today, for you never know what could happen tomorrow," was the life motto for Johnny Simkovits. He drank like a Russian fish, smoked like a Subarctic chimney, sang like a Hungarian songbird, worked hard like a Canadian beaver, kicked out his feet to gypsy music like a Cossack soldier, and kissed the hands of swooning women like a French balladeer. When he was riled or didn't get his way, he swore and screamed like a Slovak compatriot. His stories about conquering "sexy broads," besting colleagues and competitors, and screwing the government, could make you howl to the ceiling with laughter or cry into your bowl of borscht.

Johnny was a strong-willed military man who survived WWII. He had fought on both the Hungarian (Axis) and Russian (Allied) sides, connected to four militaries. In post-war Czechoslovakia, he became a tough-minded capitalist before the Soviet communists seized the country and confiscated his budding electronics business. He then escaped his homeland accompanied by my Jewish mother, and they immigrated to Canada. There, with $50 in their pockets, they started a new life.

Within a few years, Johnny founded the Canadian record player and console stereo business that he operated in Montreal during the rise of the Quebec separation movement. His dogged determination had him stop at nothing to build his dream and become somebody in the new world, even requiring him to fend off unionization in his successive Quebec factories.

For the next thirty years, Johnny grew his Canadian manufacturing company and real estate empire, not only through shrewd business instincts but also via under-the-table gifts and cash kickbacks. He kept supplier prices in check through belligerent shouts. He serenaded his associates via the sweet perks of everyone's favourite nighttime vices. Johnny worked as hard with his colleagues during the business day as he played hard with his friends into all hours of the night.

Colleagues admired him; employees looked up to him; women were charmed by him. Many became cast-asides, recipients of his barefaced anger and pointed finger of blame, or beneficiaries of his fists to their chest or foot to their backside. I, his second son, both revered and feared him, down into my quivering bones. For way too long, I wanted to become just like him.

Johnny's wife, Anna, had sacrificed everything in her life to come to Canada with her "true love." She had survived WWII in Budapest, her Jewish family hiding in broad daylight with false Christian papers. The misery of those war years became replaced by the continual grief that she received from her husband. She gave up her family, her country, her profession, and her religion to come to Canada with him and raise their children.

In making their Canadian home, Johnny had Anna keep her Jewish heritage hidden, even from my brother and me. After Dad had left her for a second time, when I was eighteen years old, she revealed to my brother and me her family's Judaic history and their traumatic war survival.

While Anna washed and ironed her husband's clothes, prepared and put his food on the table, and took care of the children, Johnny gallivanted with his comrades to fancy Montreal clubs and womanized at every opportunity. It led to nighttime living room screaming matches between them while my brother and I, as kids, shivered under our covers in our upstairs beds.

Anna's closest brother tried to protect her from Johnny, but my uncle was no match for my mom's blind adoration for her husband. I too failed to protect or defend her from Dad during their nighttime inquisitions. With absolute loyalty to my father, I mentally made my mother the instigator of the turbulence in their marriage. I still regret my choice today.

Dad showed my brother and me his business ropes and moneymaking tricks. Unlike Steve, who continually questioned and fought against our father's underhanded ways, I gained Dad's trust so I could be first in line to his fatherly favours and financial fortunes. In exchange for my allegiance, he revealed to me his tax-skirting shenanigans and offshore cash havens.

In the summer of '72, when I was 17 years old, my father took me and not my brother to a Swiss bank to open up his first hidden offshore account. Many times, he leaned into me and said, "Just *lassen* to me, son. You need to protect yourself because you can neither trust the government to protect you nor depend on your friends to look out for your best interests."

In my quest to remain my father's favorite, I kept his money secrets and shenanigans concealed for decades, not only from my mother, brother, and the government but also from my conscience. My father's ways, both charming and brutal, gave me sleepless nights and pangs of guilt and shame.

This no-holds-barred second volume in the "Just *Lassen* to Me!" series continues my tell-all tale of reconciling, repudiating, and rectifying my dad's dubious legacy and of my working to survive my tumultuous family and survivor father.

Other than immediate family members and my father's closest company employees who have given their permission, this memoir works to maintain the anonymity of individuals and entities that surrounded my father's illegitimate business ventures and reckless personal pursuits.

Harvy Simkovits

Note to U.S. Readers

This memoir series continues to use Canadian English spelling and writing conventions.

A Personal Note

No less than fifty percent of the profits from the sales of this book will go to support non-profits (like Jane Doe, Inc. and the Urban Ministry) that work to help victims of domestic abuse and violence.

Book Two:

Survivor Teachings

Part V:

Fatherly Enticements

22

Trade Trickery

Mechanical hums, swishes, bangs, rumbles, whirls, and whizzes filled the air nearly nine hours each day in my father's Montreal Phono console stereo plant. Factory foremen rushed about and yelled over the noise, "Come here!" . . . "Do this!" . . . "Do that!"

The acrid odors of melting solder flux wafted from the electronic amplifier department. There, a wall of women sat in hard metal chairs while they prepared the electrical connections for what Dad calls "the guts" of a stereo unit. An electromechanical wire cutting and splicing machine *CLINKED-CLINKED* in the background as these "girls" (what my father and the foremen called them) sat tirelessly for the whole workday. They repeated the same intricate hand movements every few minutes until their work was complete.

Their job was to make ready the myriad wires and connections among the Asian radios, cassette and 8-track players, and British changer-turntables that would be placed and wired together within each console stereo box. They chatted in what Dad called "*vimen* talk." He allowed them to gossip away, even listen to the radio, as long as they got their wiring and soldering quotas done well and on time. They always met their mark.

I was among the men positioned along the electronics assembly line. We installed, secured, and connected these staged electronic components into the empty carcasses of vinyl covered, particleboard cabinets. We pushed the simulated hardwood beasts in single file down the 60-foot conveyor.

Every four to six minutes, a unit passed from one manned station to another. We didn't talk much, except to point out a problem we saw in a previous guy's work, or if we needed to warn the next guy down the line about something to which he needed to pay attention.

These pressed wood stereo cabinets, up to sixty inches long, were composed of as much industrial glue as they were of wood chips. The cabinets had been stacked two-wide and three-high on pallets that were rolled in from the factory's cabinetmaking and wood finishing departments.

All day, employees breathed in the fine sawdust particles of freshly cut pressed wood. They inhaled the full fragrance of the white glue that bound the cabinet together. They smelled the bouquet of toxic spray paint that lingered on the molded-plastic grill that decorated the front of the barren units.

I thanked the stars that I worked here only for short summer stints. I didn't have to take in these toxic odors for fifty weeks a year and half a generation.

I glanced toward the front of the electronics assembly line where two muscular, minimum wage male labourers loaded a stack of cabinets onto the electronics assembly conveyor. I helped out at that station when I wanted upper body exercise.

But today I was filling in for a guy on the line who hadn't shown this morning. Hopefully, he would have a good excuse, like a doctor's note, if he was to avoid an inquisition from his foreman, or worse, from the big boss, my father.

Each stereo unit was handled with care to prevent bangs or scratches that would beget a foreman's shout. Once, while my father had been standing nearby, a worker dropped a console box accidentally onto the floor—perhaps the labourer had been nervous about the boss watching. Fire rose in my father's eyes, and his fist rose as he bellowed at the perpetrator "I *dun't* know *whaat!* I *looose* my *shhert!*"

The foreman immediately removed the lackadaisical employee from the production line to an area requiring less strenuous work—like flattening used corrugated boxes for refuse or resale. Being the boss's son, I stayed focused on my job to avoid an angry outburst from my father.

Today, like any day on the production line, pneumatic screwdrivers hummed in random succession, *WHIZ...WHIZ...WHIZ.* My assembly-line compadres were securing turntable motor boards and other electronic components under the cabinet's hinged wooden lid.

A fellow further up the line firmly fastened sets of Czechoslovakian-made Tesla speakers on the back side of the unit's fabric-lined front grill. Down the line, the necessary internal electronic connections would be made, giving life to the modulated current coming from the set of sound equipment when plugged in and powered on.

The veterans among us kept an eye pegged to the office entrance door. We watched out for the big boss who might walk through the plant unannounced.

The other day, my father had caught a Slavic guy smoking on the job. He subsequently motioned crotch-high with his flat hand, and shouted at the worker in mixed English and Ukrainian, "I'll cut off the *yaytsya* [eggs] from between your legs if I catch you doing that again."

Typical console stereo units from the early-1970s (previous page),
the mid-1970s (top) and the late-1970s (bottom).

The employee stomped out his cigarette quickly and turned his focus back to where it belonged. Though I was doing my job further down the production line, my dad's unpredictable ire sent shivers down my spine.

His outbursts were like a lightning bolt or volcanic eruption. They came with little warning and dissipated as quickly as they flared up, but not before doing their damage. I kept my eyes on my production-line work and was grateful that I wasn't a target.

It was the summer of 1976. I was here on a college break between my MIT bachelor's and master's degree programs. I worked side-by-side with low-wage, Eastern and Southern European, Vietnamese, Middle-Eastern, Pakistani, Haitian, and French Canadian workers—as diverse in background as the imported components that constituted the console stereos. Though most of these folks spoke English or French, the electronics foreman might employ makeshift sign language to show newer immigrants what they needed to do.

Many of these employees had recently arrived in Canada, seeking a better life in a free land. Dad had once told me, "Immigrants know better how to work." He smiled. "You can get good, hard workers right off the boat, as I was when I came here in '49."

From this mélange of ethnicity, many of the men stood on pedestals as they looked down on the console on the production conveyor in front of them. Others crouched down from behind the unit as they performed their recurring routine. It wasn't every day that I got to sit in a chair—like to plug in the many wire connections inside the bowels of each console carcass as it passed by in monotonous succession.

As I did, every worker repeated their same choreographed procedure a hundred times a day, day after day, week after week, until a 500- or 1000-unit order was complete. The next console or record-player-model run followed right behind.

Some employees here barely eked out a living—perhaps still living with parents or a relative, or crammed into a cheap apartment or boarding house. They were ready to jump jobs at a moment's notice for better pay, if and when it came along.

But others stayed. There was the quiet Greek papa who sat off to one side of the conveyor while he screwed down speakers, *ZZZ...ZZZ...ZZZ*, onto the front grills of the wooden speaker-boxes. Another was the short, thin, muscular Basque senior who pulled the pallet truck, *RUMBLE-RUMBLE-RUMBLE*, down the factory aisles to replenish production-line materials. A third was the Lebanese single mother who sat the whole day soldering wires, *Shh...Shh*, with her fuming soldering gun. All of them would live out their careers as Montreal Phono's own.

Working side-by-side with these long-timers, I got to know them during work breaks. I heard about their immigrant voyages across an ocean, their overseas families they rarely if ever saw, and their children who were the first generation in their family to go to college or even to finish high school. They told of their difficulty in adjusting to our cold and bilingual Quebec, but they saw it as a small price to pay to be able to speak openly about the government without fearing for their lives. They told me, "Your father has been good to me; he gives me work and pays me okay."

I appreciated their loyalty, work ethic, and quiet character. Being twenty-one, I thanked God for being the boss's son, having to do this kind of factory work only part-time. I was planning to complete my MIT master's degree within a year, then secure a more prosperous and prestigious future in electrical engineering by working elsewhere.

One of the transient workers disrupted the assembly-line monotony with his antics. He was a bean-thin, late-twenties, long-haired, Ukrainian-Canadian, rock-band guitarist. We called him by a nickname, Johnny Guitar.

Johnny's rock career had yet to take off. Having few other skills, and needing to support his rock 'n roll habits, he screwed down radio chassis on the electronics assembly line in between nighttime band performances.

Besides bellbottom jeans, Johnny Guitar wore a big smile. My father once told him, "Johnny, you look like a Beatnik."

Johnny retorted, "Better me than you, Mr. S."

My father laughed, for he saw a bit of himself in that always upbeat guy.

Johnny Guitar might come to work weary-eyed and tipsy from a late-night gig. His tiredness might cause him to place his screws crooked or in the wrong hole within a stereo cabinet. Nevertheless, my father enjoyed bantering with him (before or after work of course) about "screwing other things, like young chicks."

Johnny Guitar and I sometimes worked side-by-side on the assembly line. We talked and joked while we stood at our stations screwing radio chassis onto the console's motor board.

I don't recall what Johnny said that had provoked our fun one day, but Dad unexpectedly walked into the plant from the office. The boss looked our way as he overheard us laugh and snicker.

Johnny and I clammed up quickly, but I could tell my father was not amused. He stood at the front of the line and called over the electronics department foreman. As predictable as the punch clock, Dad raised his fist and screamed his signature shout. "Why are the people playing around and not working? It's *une*-believable! I *dun't* know *whaat!* I *looose* my *shhhert* with the stupidity that's going on here!"

Chills went through my spine. The factory floor became quiet except for the humming of pneumatic screwdrivers, the banging of rubber mallets, and the crunching of staples that sealed the packed cabinet boxes. I kept my nose pointed to my motor board screwing and didn't say a word. The foreman stood with a long face and took in my father's tirade. After the boss fireworks, Dad turned and headed back to his office.

The foreman came over to Johnny and me. "You guys are getting me into trouble. Stop your screwing around!"

"Sorry," we both said. Johnny Guitar's face looked sincerely apologetic. I suspected he was thinking, *Cool your jets, man. Screwing is our job,* referring to what we were doing with the motor boards. I snickered inside, but my face stayed serious and still.

A moment after the foreman departed, Johnny chuckled softly. He sang and swayed his head to a rock tune. "I *dun't* know *whaaat....; I looose* my *shhhert....,ya babiee...*"

I smiled and tried to ignore him, and then double-checked from my vantage point to see whether his chassis screwing was straight or crooked.

* * *

Over the factory intercom, the office secretary's voice blared out. "Harvy, office please; Harvy, come to the office."

Ever since I started high school, I had worked part of my summer breaks in my father's factory. Now, with my MIT engineering bachelor's degree under my belt, I continued to act as a swing person on the production line. I took over an open position when an employee arrived late or needed to leave early, or helped out if anyone was behind in their work.

I also performed special projects, like testing and repairing electronic components in the electronic staging area. That job gave me practical experience in applying a minuscule amount of my engineering education.

I had been relieved of my assembly line job by the usual worker who manned that station—after he got a talking to by the foreman for being late. I had begun an electronic repair job when I heard Helen's call.

I knew not to keep her waiting. If it was my father who wanted me, and I didn't get to the office quickly, he'd look at her sternly and ask gruffly, "Where is Harvy? Call him again!"

I walked briskly—but didn't run—toward the front office. There my father spent most of his day, at his desk. If he wanted privacy for a business call or one-on-one meeting, he'd retire to his back office down a hallway.

No partitions separated my father's roost from the six other large, heavy, oak-wood desks situated in that big office. My brother Steve, the company's purchasing agent, sat right behind Dad. He faced the wall where a blackboard hung to track merchandise shipments. He was talking on the phone.

Opposite Dad, facing him, sat the production planner, Herb. He had his head down as he looked at production schedules. Beyond Herb, right near the office's front entrance, Helen sat at her L-shaped secretarial desk and was typing away on correspondence. She too faced my father. To my father's distant right sat the shipping clerk, Danny, his head down on transportation documents. Though Danny was at the far end of the room, he was still within sighting and hailing distance of the boss.

The company bookkeeper, Jane, sat across the room from Danny, on the other side of the office entrance. She was a slender, middle-aged woman with a shapely body. Dad placed her slightly around a corner to afford her a bit more privacy for her detailed bookkeeping work, and perhaps to keep his roaming eyes away from her well-formed figure.

The remaining desk, next to the factory office door and facing the shipping clerk, was left open for a salesman or truck driver who needed to complete paperwork or make a phone call. Employees could use that phone too for a personal call, but only during lunch breaks.

When I walked into the office, Helen saw me, raised her hand, and presented a cheerful smile. She pointed Dad's way, and her face turned serious. "Harvy, your father wants to see you," she said.

Dad was on his phone. He looked at me, nodded, and held up his hand—a fuming cigarette between his fingers—to let me know to stay put.

I looked at Herb. He glanced up from his work and nodded at me. I nodded back. He then quickly put his eyes back on his production planning sheets. I could tell he didn't want to be disturbed.

I glanced at my brother. He hardly noticed me. His black phone receiver was cradled between his right shoulder and ear as if it were a permanent fixture. His left hand was writing a purchase order as he spoke to a supplier.

I thanked the Lord that I didn't work in this congested office. My butt would get sore from the sitting; my neck would get stiff from continual phone calling; I'd choke on Dad and Helen's cigarette smoke. I'd go crazy with the all-day chatter and get nervous from being in the same room with my father.

I looked around the office as I waited. Prominently displayed on the walls and counters were RCA logos and memorabilia. A picture above the filing cabinets showed RCA's white Nipper dog sitting next to a black phonograph. "His Master's Voice" was the caption. A brass model of the phonograph sat on Dad's desk. These things reminded everyone for whom they were working.

Dad once told me that the RCA head buyer had given him a gold Cross pen and pencil set, with the original round RCA logo attached to its clip. Dad cherished that set and kept it for years in his inside suit pocket. He told me he used those writing instruments at every business meeting he had at RCA's Montreal head office.

The RCA picture that hung on my father's factory front-office.

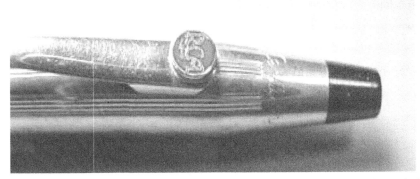

Sometime in the 1960s, the head buyer at RCA gave my father a Cross pen and pencil set with the RCA logo attached to its clip. Years later, after RCA's logo changed to its more modern form, Dad told me that one of his contacts at RCA picked his suit pocket while it hung in a closet there. Dad never recovered that pen and pencil set.

Even when he was out of the office for a meeting at RCA, Dad called in at 4:45 to check in with his secretary and foremen. No one dared leave the premises a minute before the factory buzzer rang five o'clock. If they did, they'd later get a penetrating eye and a "Why are you running away? Do you have a better place to be?" from my father. Unless there was a hospital or family emergency, no one escaped Montreal Phono on Johnny Simkovits's time.

Dad finished his call and turned to me. "Hi son; can you please come with me to my back office. I have an important job for you concerning our recent European trip."

Dad picked out a half dozen red, blue, and black pens from a metal cup on his desk. He also grabbed a pad of notepaper. He gestured for me to follow him and escorted me into his private domain where he had another desk.

From his top desk drawer, he pulled out a small stack of papers that were clipped together. He put them on the glass desktop and pointed. "These are our cash receipts from our hotel stays, restaurant meals, and gas station fill-ups during our recent trip to Czechoslovakia and Hungary." The receipts had been handwritten—credit cards charges were not possible in either communist country.

We had been on another two-week family trip to my parents' homeland. From the time of his first trip back to Czechoslovakia in 1968, Dad had established a business relationship with Tesla, a Czechoslovak supplier of acoustic speakers. My father bought Tesla speakers by the tens of thousands to use in Montreal Phono's console stereo units. That business arrangement allowed him not only to enter his communist homeland more easily but also to deduct a portion of our overseas trip as a business expense.

Dad spoke calmly. "Son, please sit here at my desk."

He remained standing next to me. He demonstrated what he wanted me to do. He took his pens and scribbled vertical lines from each onto the pad. He picked up the receipt on the top of the stack and placed it next to the pad. "First I want you to match the ink colour on each receipt with the right pen colour."

A handwritten restaurant supper receipt showed "93 Kcs" (Czechoslovak koruna). That was about $9CAD at the official exchange rate we had received when we converted money at those border crossings.

Dad retrieved the pen that best matched the colour of the ink on the receipt. He practised writing the number "1" on the notepad. He then placed a

"1" in front of the "93," changing the total to "193." He was careful to match the handwriting of the server who had created the tally.

"See what I'm doing," he said. "I want you to do the same with the rest of the receipts. Find simple ways to change the numbers so you can at least double the total." He showed me another example. He altered a "381 Kcs" supper cheque to look like "881 Kcs," again being careful to match the ink color and handwriting that was on the receipt.

He looked at me. "You see how I'm doing this?" He had a soft yet serious look on his face. "I could use your help on this, son."

My eyes opened wide, but I didn't say a word. It occurred to me that what my father was doing was not legit. I nodded and said, "Yes, okay, Dad." I gave his request no second thought. I figured that Dad knew what he was doing and I was learning his trade tricks.

He continued. "Good! And when you have finished, add everything up on a separate sheet, separating out the different types of expenses: hotel, restaurant, and car."

He put a pad of lined paper on the desk in front of me. "To make your accounting easier, keep Czechoslovakian korunas and Hungarian forints separate. And, if any of the receipts are typewritten—like some of these hotel receipts are—leave those alone. Just report those amounts as they are."

I nodded again. Dad continued to speak matter-of-factly. "Then convert the koruna and forint into dollars by using the official exchange rate of 10 koruna and 100 forints to one dollar U.S., as you see here on these currency exchange receipts we received at those borders." He pointed to our border bank receipts. He then looked at me. "Don't worry about converting the results into Canadian dollars; our bookkeeper will do that later."

Those Iron Curtain countries had forced us, as they did with all tourists, to convert some hard U.S. currency into their local money when we entered their country. It was at a measly one-third of the exchange rate that Dad could obtain from illegal money changers on the streets of Košice, Prague, and Budapest.

Dad didn't give a second thought about using the more meagre exchange rate for my calculations. That way, our Canadian government would pay for a larger part of that communist foreign-exchange enterprise through a bigger business tax deduction.

As a young adult, I didn't question my dad. I admired his shrewdness and was glad he was showing me his business ropes.

An hour later I called my father into his back office. I presented a proud smile. "How's this?"

He examined my work, both the doctored receipts and the neat spreadsheet of expense calculations I had created. He responded, "That's good son." He grabbed the receipts and my tally and headed out the office door. I followed right behind as he walked to his bookkeeper's desk.

Jane watched as Dad pointed to my spreadsheet. "Here, Jane. Harvy has made the expense calculations for you. You can enter this as one amount into your books, and then write me a cheque for the total U.S. dollars you see right here."

She nodded at my father and then looked at me. "Thank you, Harvy, for your work."

Dad turned back to me, a slight smile on his face. "Thanks, son; you can go back to the factory now." I could tell he liked having the Eastern European portion of our family's vacation cost him nearly nothing.

Though Dad's blatant deceit and my part in it sour my stomach today, I had been pleased to do my part to make our European trip a little more cost effective. Little did I realize at the time what his survivor teachings would cost me.

* * *

A buzzing sound, ZZZZZZZ, came from the row of bright fluorescent fixtures hanging over the electronics assembly line. It tired my eyes and ears during eight-and-a-half-hours of factory grind. To offset the buzz, gentler sounds of Frank Sinatra and an Italian *Bella Bella Bella* filled the room.

The music came from the finished goods testing booth. The melody provided a recurring, monotonous rhapsody to offset the machine-driven din that permeated the place.

The sound-insulated plywood booth sat atop an eight-foot conveyor section. That "testing cabana" (as Dad called it) had a big opening in the front for human access. It provided large square holes on both sides to let completed console units pass through as they sat on the conveyor.

The semi-isolation cubicle offered my Edo *bácsi* (Uncle Edo)—Montreal Phono's long-time quality-control inspector—sound insulation as he inspected every function of every electrical component under every console's lid.

Not having much of an ear for music, Edo played the same few records, cassettes, and 8-tracks over and over, up to 100 times a day, for many months or years on end. He rarely asked his big brother for replacements, unless a record had become unbearably scratched or a tape badly worn. He probably thought that he was saving the boss money by continually reusing those accessories until what they played could no longer be considered music.

To Edo's credit, his strategy of continually using the same music might allow him to discern audio variations from unit to unit. The growing hiss and crackle from those albums and tapes told me otherwise.

Over the years, Dad had talked to Steve and me about his relationship with Edo. "My half-brother is eleven years younger than I am. After the war, I gave him his first job in my Prima Radio shop in Košice." Dad smiled. "Back then, I even hired our father to be a watchdog in my store when I couldn't be there."

He went on. "After I escaped from Czechoslovakia in '49, Edo found himself a cushy job in Košice. He worked for the power company that ran the town's electrical trollies." My father smirked. "Sometimes, a power surge caused one of the giant circuit breakers to open in the relay station. Edo was the guy who took a big ten-foot rod and pushed the circuit breaker shut."

Dad lifted his arms and pushed his whole body forward to mimic his brother's task. He smirked. "Other than that, your uncle sat on his ass all day and played cards with his station buddies. He was entrepreneurial only in that he could trade shifts with the other technicians who babysat those electrical panels sixteen to eighteen hours a day, six days a week."

In 1968, soon after Soviet tanks reinvaded Czechoslovakia to signal the failed Prague Spring of Alexander Dubček's regime, my father called Edo and urged his only brother to leave his country. "You'll have a much better life in Canada," Dad had told him long-distance. "I'll help you as much as I can."

Edo took his elder brother's advice. He escaped with his cousin, Alex, and two of Alex's friends. The latter three were teammates who played on the Czechoslovak national water polo team. They abandoned their team and fled communist Europe after playing an international match in Yugoslavia.

My father had not only given Edo a job in his Montreal Phono factory but also a place to live. He provided Edo and his compadres several one-bedroom apartments in one of the buildings he owned. (In addition to his industrial buildings, Dad owned and managed several residential buildings totaling hundreds of units.) The apartment building even had an outdoor pool in which Edo and his friends could play water polo in the summer.

When Edo later got his driver's licence, Dad bestowed him a company station wagon. Dad told me, "I promised Edo's mother that I'd take care of him when he came to Canada." He added, "But I don't want Edo to sit on his *arsh* all day as he did in Košice."

As the one-man commander of Montreal Phono's electronics testing cabana, Edo repeated his checklist "from A to Z" (as Dad instructed him to do) for every function of every unit that came down the production line. Edo might have done the same at his big brother's Košice shop where Dad sold radios he had smuggled in from Western Europe.

Edo faithfully manned his Montreal Phono testing cabana, complete with Playboy pinups and provocative Florida postcards that said, "Wish you were here big boy. Come play in the sand with me."

Edo regularly received letters from his mother. They echoed her ongoing sentiments: "*Megházasodik, fiam!* [Get married, my son!]" Dad got similar letters saying, "Help your brother find a wife."

Dad replied to his stepmother, "You can lead a horse to water, but…"

Even my brother and I got into the act of practicing that *megházasodik* word whenever Edo joined us for Sunday dinners. He responded with a smile and a chuckle, saying, "Yah, Yah."

During his life in Canada, Edo *bácsi* remained a bachelor. Maybe he was playing it safe, perhaps worried that his mother, and his big brother too, would never quite approve of his choice of spouse.

Once in a while, Edo stayed home nursing a beer hangover from a night out with his Slovak-Canadian buddies. On those melancholy days, Dad went to his brother's apartment and got the superintendent to unlock Edo's apartment door. He dragged his sibling out of bed, made him strong coffee, and drove him to work. In the car, he gave Edo a talking-to.

I once overheard Dad tell Mom that he had gotten furious at his brother. He said, "I told Edo that he was an irresponsible bum. I said to him that if he kept on drinking, then he'd never amount to anything." Mom nodded her agreement but added no verbal fuel to Dad's sizzling fire concerning his closest kin.

Maintaining his promise to their mother, Dad never fired Edo—even when he totaled the company's station wagon and relinquished his driver's licence for a year. No matter what was happening between Edo and Dad, Edo *bácsi* continued to come with us to family gatherings and on family vacations. On holidays, he led us in kicking around a soccer ball or playing shuffleboard—though he might stay in his room for an evening to down a brew or three.

In Montreal, Edo came to our many summer barbeques and holiday parties. Dad picked up his brother on Sunday morning to go to mass and dinner with our family. He told his sibling, "Edo, you need to make something of yourself. And, you need to control your drinking and know when to stop." My father never considered that his putting drinks into his brother's hand at parties and during vacations encouraged Edo to become what Dad hadn't wanted.

At one party, after a couple of drinks, Edo became bleary-eyed and loose-jawed, and he put on a skewed smile. He stood, teetered about, and pointed to himself. He winked and loudly proclaimed, "C'mon, c'mon, let's go! I'm the big boss now!"

Dad noticed Edo's tipsiness and steered his brother into the kitchen where he or my mother brewed a strong coffee for Edo. They sent Edo home an hour later, alert but wobbly—perhaps a wide-awake drunk.

I liked my svelte, round-shouldered, all-muscle uncle. Edo's Slovak Canadian and Montreal Phone colleagues called him by his nickname, "Mr. Brazil," referring to his deep bronze tan attained while vacationing.

Edo responded to that call with a big grin, shouting back "Pelé! Pelé! Pelé!" He crouched down and demonstrated a soccer move with his feet, or mimicked the bouncing of a soccer ball in the air with his head.

Even though I was an adult, Edo called me, "My pick-me-up boy." It reminded us of the perhaps hundred times he had picked me up as a child when I had seen him in Czechoslovakia.

Edo and I knocked around a soccer ball in our home's backyard or when we were on a family vacation. He had an endearing smile and a hearty laugh. He rarely raised his voice (unlike my parents), and I never heard him say a harsh word about anyone or anything, at least while he was sober.

I could tell that something was a little amiss with that uncle of mine. During parties, as our family and friends chattered incessantly, Edo could sit for over an hour with an empty glass in his hand and a blank look on his face. He only spoke when spoken to, and he provided short answers. He fetched plates, glasses, and cutlery for his brother or my mother without having to be asked twice. But he might put out the wrong glasses or place the cutlery on the plates rather than beside them.

If my father wasn't clear with his instructions, Edo bungled the task. Dad then became both irritated and religious, saying, "*Hesus Maria*, Edo; can't you think?"

Edo threw up his hands. "But Johnny, you told me to do it this way. What do you want from my life?"

Dad came right back, pointing at his kid brother's face. "To use that head that God gave you."

My father once told me that his stepmother had said, "Edo accidentally fell on his head when he was a child." Perhaps Dad worked to find more between his little brother's ears than both God and his mother had given him.

Every day during my college summers, I saw my Edo *bácsi* at Montreal Phono, except for those days when he was "sick" at home. This morning, I had greeted him with a hearty "¡*Cuba sí*" and added a fist pump. It was a reminder of a previous Christmas vacation when Dad had taken our family to Cuba.

Returning my greeting, Edo smiled, chuckled, and came back, "*Hallo* MIT."

It didn't matter to me that Edo was a bit limited, or his drinking a bit worrisome. He remained my dark-skinned, strong hugging, soccer ball bouncing, pick-me-up uncle for always.

* * *

After Edo had tested each console unit, the finishing crew covered its guts (as Dad liked to call them) with a large, dark-brown, Masonite back-panel that was screwed, ZZ..ZZ..ZZ, to the back of the cabinet. The power cord was rolled into a neat bowtie shape and placed in a plastic bag that was staple-gunned, BANG, BANG, onto the Masonite.

One fellow taped plastic-bagged instruction books under the lid. Another guy affixed a model and serial number sticker to the back, giving the console unit a unique identity. A Canadian Standards Association sticker (CSA approval was like UL approval in the USA) indicated the model had been tested and accepted by that government agency.

Several times each day, my father walked into the plant from his busy office, leaving behind the myriad administrative documents and correspondence that crossed his desk. He liked to be involved in everything and to check on the day's production progress. Before the punch-clock buzzer sounded the factory's 4:30 quitting time, Dad passed by the end of the production line. He looked on the back of the last unpacked unit.

The sequential serial number told him how many units the electronics department had produced this day. A small frown appeared on his face because that number was smaller than his production forecast. Had production been way off, he'd shout at the foreman, "What's been the hold-up here?" He rarely offered congratulations or even a smile when the number was higher than what he had expected.

At the end of the line, the finished units were put into corrugated boxes and sealed, CACHUNK-CACHUNK, with a large, pneumatic staple gun. I enjoyed helping out at that station. Stacking those heavy boxes onto pallets provided good exercise for my soccer physique. I played junior varsity at MIT and found that I was most fit when my six-foot frame carried the weight of fewer than 168 pounds.

Our resident Basque, Nick (short for Nikola), whisked away each stack of finished units as soon as a 2-wide by 2-high pile was stacked. He'd take them to a storage area where they awaited distribution papers and shipping labels, hand-typed by the shipping clerk. Shipments were subsequently loaded onto 45-foot trucks and transported to dozens of RCA, Philco, Admiral,

Fleetwood, and Westinghouse retailers in every major metropolitan area from Halifax, Nova Scotia to Victoria, BC.

Sometimes I got into a truck with other labourers to lift, heave, and stack the boxes that could weigh up to 75 pounds. I enjoyed my shipping-and-receiving workouts at Montreal Phono. But no matter how I tried, even down to a low of 162 lbs., I still sported squeezable love handles—a souvenir from having been weaned on Mom's Hungarian cooking.

For Montreal Phono employees, moments of liberation from repetitive assembly-line drudgery came from fifteen-minute midmorning and midafternoon respites. A piercing mechanical buzzer, *BRRINGGGG,* sounded those welcome reliefs.

That same buzzer trumpeted a thirty-minute lunchtime lull that had everyone enjoying the quiet of stopped machines. Edo *bácsi* tuned a console's radio to an English pop station and turned up the volume. Workers pulled out their lunch boxes or made the mad rush to the drive-up canteen for thirst, hunger, and monotony quenching.

During one morning break, while some of us sat having bitter coffee and oily sponge cake for which the canteen was known, I heard from Johnny Guitar about his latest virile advances. In seeking romance, this high-octane assembly line worker told me about his short-lived conquests.

He pointed down the line and boasted, "I made out last week with that French *blonde,* Chantelle, in the finishing department. She's quite something in those tight jeans."

Johnny smiled. "We were walking between stacks of merchandise." He made fists with both of his raised hands. "I grabbed her and gave her a big smooch." He slapped his knee. "I think she liked it because she didn't slap me."

He nodded toward the electronics preparation area. "Harvy, that Sylvie is pretty loose." A boyish smirk came to his face. "You should have a go at her." His head tilted in a different direction. "But watch out for Kate; she's a ball buster. She'll whack you one where the sun doesn't shine if you dare breathe on her."

I shied away from Johnny's fooling around but enjoyed the rush through his recollections.

Over a cold sandwich later that week, I sat with Johnny again. He winked at me. "At Montreal Phono, you know if you are doing a decent job if the foremen or your father don't yell at you."

He showed his toothy grin. "Many of the younger guys here leave for better pastures, or they go home to collect unemployment cheques after they get your father to lay them off." He smiled wide. "Even I do that when your father lets me."

After work, I asked my father about that employee practice. He told me, "Some employees want to leave on their own. They collect unemployment for some months while doing some cash business out of their house."

He pointed toward the factory. "I let the good workers do that, especially if they leave during our quieter times. But they need to promise me that they will come back when I call them during our busier times, like the run-up to the Christmas holidays." He grinned. "It doesn't cost Montreal Phono any more or any less if our workers go on unemployment—the government pretty much pays for it. So it works out well for everyone."

Thursday was payday. At 4:29 p.m., workers lined up to receive a cheque from their foreman. At precisely 4:30, they punched out one-behind-the-other on the factory's time clock that sounded as if it were sneezing, *CURCHEW*, *CURCHEW, CURCHEW*.

Johnny Guitar winked at me as he took in his cheque like a fullback taking a pigskin handoff from the quarterback. A few days in the factory were enough to drive guys like him to the closest sports barroom for psychic relief. As he turned to rush toward the door, he said, "You know, Harvy, the foremen place bets on who's going to call in sick tomorrow."

I wondered if Johnny is the one on which they bet. Certainly, Monday mornings would be a toss-up as to which new workers would continue to show after tasting a few weeks or months of factory grind.

During my next summer work stint, Johnny Guitar was no longer working at Montreal Phono. I asked my brother about him. (Steve had been working for the company full-time for a couple of years.) He offered, "Johnny had asthma;

he couldn't take the factory dust." He chuckled. "Johnny once gave himself so many shots of his inhaler that he then couldn't stand straight. We had to drive him home to sleep it off, and he's not come back since."

Steve grinned at me. "Maybe Johnny's band made it big. He certainly can't make it big working here." He chuckled again. "You know, we don't pay people that well." He winked. "We give them only sixty minutes an hour."

I recognized my brother's quip, something I had heard my father say in jest about how much he liked to pay employees. In Dad's case, he'd sarcastically tell a worker seeking a pay increase, "How much more are you expecting? Are you saying that sixty minutes an hour is not enough for you?"

Though I hoped my brother was right about Johnny's rock 'n roll success, I was sad that my assembly-line chum was no longer there to help me pass the production hours a little more quickly.

* * *

Dad preferred that I work for his electronics foreman, John Baptist, in the electronics assembly department. John was a short, thin, Christian Jordanian. Dad called him "Baptist" because he could never remember or pronounce his real name, which sounded like Hadjian Megurdeech.

The story went that, during Hadjian's job interview, my father had asked him about his background. The recent immigrant said that he had worked for a radio station in Amman, Jordan. He also offered that he had been a childhood friend with King Hussein.

Later in the interview, Dad asked him, "What does your first name mean?"

"Hadjian means 'John,'" the Jordanian said. "You can call me that if you like."

Dad's eyes lit up. "Okay, John, you're hired. And because you are famous for knowing a king, from now on you will be called 'John the Baptist.'"

The nickname stuck with everyone. It morphed to "Batista" at playful times when Dad called the Jordanian by the name of the pre-Castro Cuban dictator. Hadjian was called just "Baptist" when Dad or Helen called him over the factory intercom to come to the front office. My father was never going to call the man Hadjian or Megurdeech.

I worked in Baptist's department because Dad wanted me to become an electrical engineer. He didn't want me to risk losing a finger or hand on a wood-cutting machine, or to damage my lungs in a greasy spray-paint booth. That's what he told me, though he may have masked his real reason. The factory's woodshop was an overly testosterone world, run by an Italian stallion, Guido.

Once, on an errand in the woodshop, Guido showed me a magazine with pictures of heavy-set naked ladies having sex with pigs and sheep. My stomach turned upside down, disgusted by the acts those women and animals were conducting and to which they were abjectly subjected. All I could say was, "Guido, where did you find this awful stuff?"

He presented a pompous smile. "I'm Italian. I have my sources."

Guido showed me around his department. Along with provocative female pinups, he proudly pointed out his industrial-sized, semi-automatic cutting, edging, routing, and drilling machines. He talked about them as if they were his children. "This baby, she can cut a stack of six pressed-wood boards at one time. Isn't she something?"

Guido was known for his supervisory coaching quips, like "Can't find the hole (with your screwdriver, knife, finger, etc.)? Then put some hair around it."

I don't think Dad wanted me exposed to Guido's language or the pictures of naked ladies that hung both in the woodshop's bathroom and in or on employees' lockers. I was relieved there were no animals in those photos.

I figured Dad tolerated the explicit illustrations because women didn't work in Guido's area, and his gang met their production schedule. I didn't know if Dad ever saw Guido's sex magazine. I certainly wasn't going to be the one to bring it to his attention.

As we walked around the woodshop, Guido grinned with his short, crooked teeth. "I know your father doesn't like dust," he said. He shook his raised arm and hand in the air. "I tell my people to work faster when they see him walk in here. This way, they produce more dust with their woodworking machines."

His grin turned into a chuckle as he pointed to his nose. "The boss sneezes like crazy when there's too much dust. He then turns around, goes back to his office, and leaves us alone."

As I walked around the woodshop with Guido, I wondered if this Italian's lair was the right place for a college student like me. Was this the real world of men and factory life? At that time, I couldn't tell whether Guido or I was the one who had a problem.

Years earlier, when I had visited my father's factory as a kid and went to his Montreal Phono Christmas parties, a young and energetic Hungarian forewoman, Edit, supervised the amplifier department. Her boss was a big-bellied Pole named Walter, Dad's electronics foreman before Baptist.

Dad had told me that Edit was beloved by her group of women who soldered radio and amplifier wiring the whole day. Sometime later, my father mentioned that she committed suicide. The news shocked me because I remembered her patting my cheek and giving me a big, cigarette-stained-tooth smile when I saw her at Dad's factory. When I asked my father, "Why did she take her life?" he looked away and said somberly, "I don't know." He never talked about it again.

As for Walter, Dad told me that the foreman had had a penchant for Polish sausage and Russian vodka—drinking the latter medicinally out of a coffee mug throughout the workday. I had heard from others that my father occasionally drank with Walter to celebrate the end of a busy workweek.

Alas, Walter's habits had put him underground in his early 60s. I wondered if that might be the fate of some men who worked many years at Montreal Phono.

Other than Dad's biblical electronics foreman and his Italian woodshop steed, there was a French Canadian supervisor, Georges, in the finishing department. Of all Montreal Phono's employees, Georges had been with the company the longest, having started the year I was born.

Georges was mild-mannered; he rarely screamed at an employee, though he might speak firmly, like a school principal to an unruly child. Like the other foremen and forewomen who had worked at Montreal Phono for many years, he became accustomed to Dad's barks.

Georges was married to Dad's secretary, Helen. They had met at Montreal Phono. Helen once told me, "I was sixteen when I started working part-time for your father. Your father liked my work, so he asked my parents' permission for me to remain with the company. He offered to put me through secretarial school at night." She smiled. "My parents agreed, and so did I. Your father liked that I could speak both French and Slovak, and I learned English while working for him."

Her grin widened. "After Johnny hired Georges, it took Georges nearly a year to ask me out. But once he did, we have been together ever since. I only stopped working at Montreal Phono when my kids were born. But your father kept on pestering me to come back to the company, and I eventually did."

Helen hesitated for a moment, her smile leaving her face, then she continued. "Your father once got very mad at my Georges because of poor cabinet-finishing work. In the middle of yelling something about—excuse my French—'these fucking shitty cabinets,' your father picked up one of those things with his bare hands and smashed it onto the floor in front of Georges and his employees."

Helen's eyes were piercing, her face tight. "My Georges then got mad too. Without saying a word, he picked up another cabinet and threw the unit, *BANG*, on the ground." Helen mimicked her husband's motions by flinging her hands toward the floor. "Georges then stood there with an angry face, not saying a word."

I was astonished that Georges had raised Dad's console cabinet poker bet with his own.

Helen's grin came back. "Without saying anything, your dad turned around and marched back into the front office, disappearing for the rest of the day. Neither of them ever said anything about it again."

She shook her head. "That's one of the reasons I came back to Montreal Phono after I had my children. Though I respected Johnny, he could be a very hard man. I wanted to do what I could to protect my Georges. He's developing high blood pressure from working here all these years."

Not only did Georges' sudden anger surprise me, but I was also amazed that my father had backed down. I didn't think my son-of-the-boss blood could rise to such angry heights, and I feared coming up against my father's violent anger. I wondered what I was afraid of.

I never asked my father about that "shitty cabinet" incident with Georges, and he never spoke about it.

* * *

Every Tuesday afternoon, immediately after the factory shut down for the day, Dad held court over his weekly production meeting. The foremen and my brother sat in a semi-circle around Dad's office desk. Dad set the pace as he reviewed the past week's production, the current week's progress, and the following week's plans. Occasionally, I sat across the office and listened while waiting for Dad or Steve to drive me home.

One time, Georges and my father argued about the production schedule. Dad said, "I need production out by this date."

Georges thought for a moment and then countered, "That impossible! I don't have the people."

Dad came back loudly, "I don't care what you'll do, but it has to be out by then."

Georges later told me that it was no use arguing with my father when he was behind his desk. This time the mild-mannered Frenchman stood up and walked out of the meeting and slammed the office door behind him.

Dad shouted, "Son of a bitch!" and ranted, "Georges can't walk away from me like that. Who does he think he is?"

I sat stunned but said nothing.

After quieting down, Dad turned to Baptist. "John, go run after Georges and bring him back to the meeting. Tell him we'll work out the schedule."

Baptist left the room. He returned a few moments later with Georges. The foreman had his coat on as if he were ready to leave for the evening.

Dad took a puff from his cigarette and pointed to the schedule in his hand. "Okay, Georges, I thought about it. How about we make this change with the schedule?" He and Georges went back and forth for a moment. Soon they agreed, and I found myself relieved.

At the end of the meeting, Dad and the foremen chipped in a couple of bucks each for Georges to buy lottery tickets for the group. I later asked the foreman, "Do you guys ever win?"

He offered, "When we do, it's only a few bucks, and we just buy more tickets with the money." He winked. "We never hit the jackpot. Had we done so, I might have left Montreal Phono a long time ago."

Another time, Georges had a heated exchange with my dad about giving a nickel raise per hour to a couple of his good employees. Red in the face, my father shouted, "There's no raise! I can't afford it."

Without saying another word, Georges turned around and returned heavy-headed into the factory and empty-handed to his employees.

Helen, who had overheard the conversation, looked at Dad and spoke to him calmly yet firmly in Slovak. She later told me privately that she had told him, "Johnny, you need to take better care of the good people that the company depends upon."

After getting a quiet earful from Helen, Dad looked at her, shook his head, and spoke forcefully in English, "You have nothing to do with this. Stay out of it."

Helen went back to her work knowing she had said her piece.

The first thing the following morning, my father called Georges into the office. He told him, "Georges, I slept on it. Tell me again which employees you want to give the raise to." He turned to Helen. "Please log the amounts into the payroll."

Helen nodded and followed Dad's instructions without saying a word.

Years later, Georges told me, "I wondered why your father never fired me." The weathered Montreal Phono man looked at me with a soft expression in his eyes. "No matter how angry we got with each other, we kept on talking. We respected each other, and neither one of us ever remained mad for long."

I don't know if Helen ever told her husband about her role in smoothing things over between the two men. I hoped she'd do the same for my brother or me if we ever got into a skirmish with our father.

* * *

Baptist too had had his regular run-ins with the boss. After a particularly rough-and-tumble confrontation over his salary, Baptist left Montreal Phono and moved to Ontario for a different job.

Over the next couple of years, Dad went through two or three other electronics supervisors. He complained to Mom at home, "Those schmucks know less than my ass."

My father later obtained Baptist's home phone number and called him. Throughout that day, Dad left several messages for his former employee. That evening, Baptist returned my father's call while Dad was home for supper. I overheard their conversation.

Dad offered, "Please come back, John. I need you. I'll give you the money you want. I'll pay for your expenses to return to Montreal. Anything you want, John. Please say yes. I need you desperately."

I was astonished. I had never heard my father speak in a vulnerable and appeasing way to any of his employees, past or present.

Baptist decided to take my father's offer and salary boost. But for the rest of his years working at Dad's company, Baptist never obtained more than a cost-of-living increase. I felt bad for the guy, but I didn't think it was my business to get involved in his and Dad's arrangement.

In the end, Baptist lived out his days at Montreal Phono, never quitting again. Every year, he continued to come up against my father regarding his remuneration. After biting words between them, Baptist walked back to the factory floor with a glum face and nothing to show for his effort.

In Johnny Simkovits's business and factory world, some fared better and others worse.

* * *

Every couple of weeks, Lew the Junker (Dad's name for the fellow) showed up at the factory. He was an old, stout, rumple-clothed guy. For a time, he had been a Montreal Phono office employee, but before my brother or I ever worked there.

Lew pulled up to the shipping doors in his beat-up, beige and brown-paneled station wagon. He walked through the employee's entrance with a meek smile on his stubbled face. He found the shipping foreman and politely asked, "Got anything for me today?"

Though Lew's station wagon was usually full to the brim with used, flattened corrugated boxes, he found ways to carry more within his vehicle or to strap them on top. Today, the foreman, Danny, had something for Lew.

Danny knew to collect the empty boxes from supplier shipments of speakers, radio chassis, record players, and every other component used in Montreal Phono's production. Any used box that remained intact was to be "saved for the Junker" as my father had instructed.

After nodding to Lew, Danny fetched the boss and brought him to the shipping area.

My father and Lew greeted each other quickly. They eyed a pile of random-sized boxes that were stacked helter-skelter on a pallet.

Lew put pen to paper to estimate the number of boxes by size. He then threw out a dollar figure. My father nodded and put out his hand. Lew pulled out a wad of cash and counted out a bunch of bills. He handed them to my father.

When Dad and Lew's business was complete, I watched Lew drive his wagon slowly back out onto the street, with odd-shaped boxes stacked high on the roof. I imagined those boxes scattered over the road at the first sharp turn he took.

Our dad later confided to my brother and me. "I use that cash to give tips to the restaurant maître d at the places where I take our important customers and suppliers. It's a legitimate business expense."

At many weekend family dinners or suppers out, I saw my father slip $5 or $10 to a restaurant host to get a good table. He might slip $20 to get us into a fancy restaurant if he didn't have a reservation.

One day, Dad said to my brother and me, "From now on, you guys take care of Lew."

"Okay Dad," said Steve. "But what's your formula? What's each box worth?"

Our father responded matter-of-factly. "The smaller boxes are worth 5 to 10 cents each, depending on their condition. The largest ones are worth 25 cents or more, again depending on their condition. Brand new cartons would cost between fifty cents and a buck-fifty each." He pointed his finger at my brother. "But the junker has to make money too."

I looked at Dad. "What does Lew sell them for?"

Dad put his hand to his chin. "He probably marks up everything 100%." He pointed. "Up and down these factory streets, he resells that garbage to companies who can't afford new cartons."

Steve and I became systematic in our used-box preparations and negotiations. During breaks or after work hours, we sorted dozens and sometimes a hundred empty boxes into their various sizes. We wielded pliers to remove the old staples. We counted the boxes and bundled them by size. We neatly stored the bundles on pallets and placed them right next to the shipping doors. The next time Lew came calling, we worked to make a more informed deal.

After my brother and I had put a premium price on the pallet of products we had prepared, Lew exclaimed, "What are you trying to do, put me out of business?!"

"No, Lew," Steve and I said. "We sorted everything for you, pulled out the staples, bundled them in groups of ten. Our work will make it easier for you to count the boxes and get them into your station wagon."

We didn't tell him we could load his wagon too. We would do that only if he gave us our price and asked us nicely.

The old man grumbled. "You guys drive a harder bargain than your father."

We looked at him. "But we give you the best service. Aren't the boxes worth more to you and your customers when they're free of stray staples, then sorted and bundled this way?"

Lew looked at us with a skeptical eye and muttered something under his breath, but he acquiesced.

With our extra cash, Steve and I bought lunches and soft drinks at the corner restaurant or from the canteen truck. I saw a proud grin on my father's face every time he spotted Lew walking in and looking for us. His sons were learning the business.

One day, Steve and I grabbed deli sandwiches soon after Lew departed. My brother remarked, "It's nice of the company and Lew to buy us lunch."

I winked at him and smiled. "Yes, it's a legitimate business expense."

We both chuckled.

"I don't know why Dad practically gave those boxes away to that old guy," I said. "I bet he's happy we're getting more from Lew than he ever did."

Steve lifted his can of Sprite. "I'll drink to that," he said.

* * * *

23

Bullshit Business

Dad didn't mind giving Lew-the-Junker's pocket change to his kids. He had better ways of collecting cash for himself.

At the end of every production run, there were a few units or samples left over. "I'd rather have extra units than being one short on a customer order," he once explained to Steve and me. "I always plan for one percent overage in each production run." He pointed toward the factory. "A cabinet could get damaged in the plant or during transport. Sometimes, it's easier to make extra cabinets than to repair a busted one."

My father had other purposes for those spare units. Whenever a friend or business colleague wanted a stereo for himself, he knew to come to Johnny. He sold the fellow a unit at the manufacturing price, without sales tax of course. My father pocketed the proceeds, which amounted to a hundred dollars or more per stereo.

If the purchaser were an important Montreal Phono supplier or business colleague, my father would just give them a console. As a wedding present, he once shipped a 60' console stereo to the president of a major Toronto supplier. Dad even sent the company's repair man to Toronto to fix the unit when it needed repair. He instinctively knew who to keep happy. If my father needed a rush shipment from the supplier, then that president would personally move things along.

One day, the Canadian Standards Association (CSA) representative, Mr. Guy Chevalier, arrived at the factory. As he had done periodically over the years, Mr. Chevalier came to inspect and approve the electrical wiring of an initial production unit. The production run was scheduled to start the next morning, assuming Mr. Chevalier was satisfied with the production sample's wiring.

If Guy didn't like the way the electronics were hooked together, or how a connection looked, or even the thickness of a particular wire, he had the authority to delay Montreal Phono's production. He wouldn't issue the requisite CSA serial-numbered stickers—the government's safety seal—until he was satisfied that the model's electronics were configured properly and completely safe.

The CSA was not an organization with whom to mess. Years earlier, Mr. Chevalier had balked at a turntable transformer that powered both the radio amplifier and the turntable motor. "Too much heat could be created if both the radio and record player were operating at the same time," he had protested, "and that could cause a fire in the console cabinet." Chevalier wanted Montreal Phono to add a separate transformer, at a significant additional product and labour cost, to power the radio independent of the turntable.

Dad thought about the problem overnight. He saw a solution in his dreams. He called the turntable manufacturer, BSR, in England. He asked them if they could incorporate a second, lower voltage coil onto their turntable transformer to power the radio amplifier separate from the turntable. That way, the current used to feed the radio would be independent of the current used to feed the turntable, thus preventing too much heat from building in the transformer winding.

After discussions with both BSR and Mr. Chevalier, everyone agreed to the idea, and Montreal Phono saved a significant cost. Dad's idea worked so well that, from that point forward, BSR incorporated the same dual transformer-winding solution on all its turntables shipped to Canadian manufacturers like Montreal Phono.

I sat within earshot, doing assembly-line preparation work, while Mr. Chevalier inspected the first production unit at the end of the electronics assembly conveyor. The unit's back cover had been removed so that the inspector could place his head and hands into the belly of the console to do his poking around.

Mr. Chevalier and my father had known each other for years and were on a first-name basis. After a few minutes, the inspector said to my father, "Johnny, I'm a little worried about the wire insulation around this backplate." (The "backplate" was where the stereo's input and output wires came together in the rear of the cabinet.) "With all these loose wires around," Guy continued, "one might rub against the metal plate and, in time, lose its insulation. If the 120-volt power wire were involved, it could electrify the plate and create the conditions for a serious electric shock."

My father's face turned serious. He put on his reading glasses, bent over, and looked closely at the wiring inside the stereo. "Okay Guy. What if we secure the component wiring to a tie on the inside of the cabinet, above the plate?" He pointed. "We can also add a sturdy plastic bracket that will isolate the 120-volt line. That way the higher-voltage wiring is separate and secure, and there would be no chance for the power wires to get loose and rub against the plate."

There was another moment of back and forth concerning the best location of the wire tie and plastic bracket. The CSA man then offered, "Johnny, these are nice looking units."

Dad got a bit closer. He calmly and quietly responded, "Guy, I have a fully-operational sample in the showroom. When we're finished here, I can show it to you."

Before they finished, my father called Baptist to come over. In front of Guy, he showed the foreman the extra wiring protections he'd have to arrange for the next day's production. The foreman nodded his understanding and said little. My father and Guy then headed to the office.

After they had gone through the front office door, Baptist took a cigarette from a pack in his shirt pocket and lit it. While the cigarette burned in his mouth, he put his hands into the unit and rearranged the electrical wires going to the unit's back plate. I stood and walked up to him. "So Baptist, what was that about?"

The foreman kept his eyes focused on his work. His hands held onto the wiring while the corner of his mouth hung onto the burning cigarette.

"That Guy is always making something out of nothing," Baptist said with dejection. "Heck if there is any chance of electrical shock here." He hardly glanced my way. "There's nothing wrong with this original wiring and connections. Your father and I designed it ourselves."

Smoke billowed out of Baptists' mouth and maybe out of his ears too. "Now I have to put an extra guy on the line to do this bullshit operation that Guy wants us to do." He sighed. "But at least we don't have to rework anything major and can start production tomorrow."

The foreman put his cigarette down on the edge of the conveyor. "Sometimes that Guy makes us stand on our goddamned heads before he gives us those bloody CSA stickers for these new models."

Ten minutes later, I heard my father's voice over the factory intercom. "Harvy, please come to the showroom; Harvy to the showroom."

When I entered the room, my father looked at me and spoke softly. "Son, please put this sample, as is, into Mr. Chevalier's car." His eyes were reassuring. "Be careful when you lift it; it's fairly heavy."

I nodded and asked no questions. I hoisted the small, maybe 35 lb., unit—worth a couple of hundred dollars retail—into my arms. I carried it to Mr. Chevalier's vehicle. He followed a few steps behind me as if he were a dog following its bone.

Guy hardly looked my way as he opened his compact sedan's rear door. I placed the stereo in the back seat. Without looking back, he nodded and said, "Thank you." He got into his car and drove off.

When I returned to the office, Dad put a pack of CSA stickers into my hand. "Take these to Baptist for our console run tomorrow." He smiled. "Guy was nice to us this time." He raised a hand. "Even though we have to do extra work, that inspection was one of the fastest, new-model production approvals we've ever had."

I walked into the factory and over to Baptist. "Here are the CSA stickers, John. My father gave Guy one of the samples from the showroom." I gestured to the production unit on the line. "He's not worried about the extra work we have to do on this model run."

The foreman looked at me. "This is such a bullshit business. Guy didn't have to cause us trouble on the line to get a gift from your father."

"Yes, Baptist, I know what you mean."

* * *

On another work day, while I was in the front office talking to my brother about a production issue, Baptist walked in from the factory. An unlit cigarette hung from his lips and frustration was in his voice as he blurted, "I'm trying to repair an old unit for a customer." He looked at the boss. "I can't fix it because of this goddamn busted chassis part."

He showed my father a small black plastic piece that had split in two. "The chassis housing won't stay stable without this piece," he complained. "I tried to glue it but couldn't get this old plastic to hold together." He was talking fast, perhaps out of exasperation. "I looked all over the stockroom; we have nothing like it. And we no longer have these chassis in stock, so I can't even swap out the broken housing for a new one."

Dad looked at the broken piece. "I agree with you, John. I would hate for us to scrap the whole console just for this shitty little thing. Give me a minute."

On Dad's desk was a small wooden box, like a manager's outbox for mail distribution. This one was full of odd parts and pieces that Dad has been hanging onto for years. My brother and I had once teased our father, "Why do you keep all that little crap?" He had responded assuredly, "You never know when you might need something."

Dad picked up the box and started rummaging. Baptist, Steve, and I watched in wonderment as Dad pushed small items aside with his index finger. In a moment he grabbed a small grey object. "John, try to see if this will fit. You may have to shave a little off it, but it might work."

Baptist turned it around in his fingers, looking at it half-skeptically and half-hopefully. "Okay, I'll see what I can do."

Twenty minutes later, Baptist came back through the office door with a grin on his face. "Johnny, I was able to make it work with a little filing here and there. The unit is repaired."

Dad nodded and smiled at Baptist. Then he turned to my brother and me and said straight-faced, "You see what I mean!"

* * *

53

My father used his legitimate Montreal Phono dividends and bonuses to invest in several apartment and industrial buildings. He told me, "Good buildings hold their value."

He grinned with confidence. "Everything I own personally sits in one big pool. Gains from one building can offset losses in another. And the annual depreciation from my properties can shield my personal income, deferring income taxes for years." He raised his fist in victory. "I don't have to feed the government for up to twenty-five years, until my properties are fully depreciated or sold."

I was glad that my father was doing legal tax-deferral tricks with his money. Maybe that would have him keep more assets in Canada and not feel he had to hide them offshore. Though I relished what I knew and imagined about my father's hidden holdings in Switzerland, I was pleased that he had a balanced onshore and offshore approach to his investing.

Sometime in the 1970s, the Canadian government closed the pooled-personal-property loophole. Each income-producing property now acted as a separate entity, unless a single real estate corporation owned them, which wasn't my father's case. By then, Dad owned five investment properties: three apartment buildings with hundreds of units, plus two other industrial buildings as big as Montreal Phono's factory.

At the end of one workday, he complained to me. "What a schmuck I was to listen to my lawyer, Mack. He was the one who gave me the idea of buying buildings personally." Dad was irate. "I'm now stuck with these buildings that can no longer shelter my personal income."

His eyes were glaring; his hand formed a fist. "The government screws us business people like it's nothing. You think you are getting ahead, and then they change the tax rules on you. We can't trust those goddamn politicians."

His indignation continued. "I can't even afford to sell some of my properties. With the taxes I'd have to pay on the recaptured depreciation, I'd have nothing left in my pocket." He pointed to the floor. "Those government bureaucrats have us by the *yaytsa*."

He took another breath and repeated one of his business mantras. "And the lawyers, like Mack, have a licence to steal. Whether their advice is good or bad, and whether I make or lose money, they still get paid."

Over the years, Mack had gotten my father into several "can't lose" ventures that went nowhere. He once told Dad to buy shares in a life insurance company that was rumoured to be in merger talks with another big firm. "Their share price will double within a year," the attorney had said.

Dad went along and bought tens of thousands of shares. Months later, the merger didn't go through. The share price halved.

Dad was livid. He repeated his defaming monologue to his business colleagues at the Troika. "That *Schmack* caused me to lose my shirt." (*Schmack* was what Dad called Mack when he was angry.)

I was there listening, but I said nothing while Dad went on and on about his lawyer. He could complain about Mack with gusto, yet he never fired the guy. I never understood why. I considered it might take one *Schmack* to work with another.

At the end of his tirade, my father turned to me. "After finishing engineering and business schools, son, you need to go to law school. That way, you wouldn't have to rely on bad advice from the schmuck lawyers in the world."

All through my years at MIT, Dad had talked to me about going to business school after finishing my engineering degree. *And now he wants me to go to law school too?!* I wondered if I could handle that much education, and if I'd then de facto become my father's Schmack.

* * *

Swearing was a crude art form for many Slovaks and Hungarians. At a restaurant, I once overheard a Hungarian man swear incessantly at his young son for having done something stupid. *"Bassza meg az apád!"* the angry father repeated after every second or third sentence, not realizing that people in the vicinity understood what he was saying. Ironically, what that man repeated to his son was, "F… your father!"

Dad was no exception in such language practices. Though he never said those specific words to my brother and me, he could swear up a storm when riled.

Through the '60s and well into the '70s, Dad employed a manager for his three apartment houses. Andy was a short, thin, chain-smoking, Slovak Canadian. He collected rents, supervised the janitors, coordinated major repair projects, and did the administration for Dad's buildings.

Like my Uncle Edo, Andy worshiped the sun. His skin was dark and leathery from the Florida holiday trips he took in the winter and from the weekend backyard sunbathing he did in the summer.

One time, when Andy was at my father's office, Dad yelled at him in front of the staff. "Andy, what the fuck is going on with those buildings? I'm having terrible trouble with them!" My father banged his fist on the table. "When something needs repair, the tenants will complain to the rental board if we didn't fix it yesterday. On the other hand, even if everything is working fine, those people have no problem giving us their rents late." Dad's eyes were fiery, his face red. "I can't make money with this bullshit."

Andy shrugged and raised his arms, palms open and fingers up. A burning cigarette hung from his thin lips as he spoke. "Johnny; there's nothing I can do. It's the goddamn rental board. They side with the tenants." His voice was discouraged. "Unless the tenants vacate their apartments, the rental board only lets us raise the rents no more than the cost-of-living each year."

The rest of us in the office sat in silence. We dared not say anything, or else Dad might yell, "Mind your f'ing business." He looked at his building manager. "Andy, I don't want you to rent to any more goddamn Haitians. Those bastards stop paying rent and then squat for months. It takes me forever

56

to get eviction notices from the rental board. Those people then screw off and leave their apartment a bloody mess."

Andy shrugged his shoulders once more. "Johnny, you're in a low rent area. You can't discriminate that way; you'll get into trouble with the rental board, or you won't find new tenants."

"What a bullshit business!" my father spewed. He pointed to his temples. "I need these problems like a hole in my fucking head."

He took a breath. "Andy, I want you to do better background checks, so we don't get any transient people." He pointed his finger and bellowed. "I want you to be there and knock on every door on the last day of every month to collect the rent, even if you don't get home until midnight. If you can't do it, I'll find someone who can."

Andy looked even more dejected. "Okay, Johnny. I'll do what I can, but the problem's not me." His eyes lowered to the floor. "There's only so much you can do in that part of the city."

Dad came back strongly. "So let's sell the whole bloody thing. I'm sick of these headaches. Because the goddamned government changed the bloody tax laws, I no longer have the tax advantages I once had with these shitty properties. I can no longer make money with them."

He looked at his building manager, his eyes on fire and finger gesticulating with anger. "Fill the place with half-decent tenants. I can then put these buildings on the market and get out of this shit game." His face was enflamed. "Find me a sucker, and I'll unload the buildings *toute suite*."

Though Dad's new strategy would eventually put Andy out of a job, the cigarette-in-mouth Slovak offered, "Whatever you say, Johnny. I'd be happy to be out of this bullshit business too." He pointed to his head and matched my father's intensity. "It gives me the same fucking headache as it does you."

I wasn't sure if it was my father or the building tenants that gave Andy those headaches, but I wasn't about to ask.

Dad continued to grumble about his "money-sucking buildings" until the time he sold most of them, one by one, over a very long decade.

Sadly, Andy put himself out of a job well before Dad's buildings were out of his hands. Andy contracted lung disease and died within a year of diagnosis, while in his 50s.

For his never-ending smoking and high blood pressure screaming, I wondered and worried if my father would find a similar fate.

* * *

One Friday evening, my father came home with a thick gauze bandage on his left thumb. His face looked in pain. He blurted out *Hesus Maria* every time he accidentally touched something with that hand. Even with the thumb covered, I could tell it had swelled. Without saying much to anyone, Dad went to the bathroom, took pills, and went straight to bed.

I didn't see him the next morning. He rose early and went to work for his usual Saturday morning office stint. When he came back that afternoon, he was in a better mood. I pointed to the big bandage on his thumb. "What happened, Dad?"

He said, "After our bookkeeper had left the office early yesterday afternoon, I had to lock the big office safe by myself." He blinked hard a few times. "I had just gotten off the phone with a supplier about a late shipment. I was still mad when I went over to close the safe."

His voice rose as he put out his thumb and pushed his other hand against his hurt finger. "Son-of-a-gun, I stupidly put my thumb in the bloody door as I closed it." He took a big breath. *"Hesus Maria!* I smashed it in that heavy door."

Ouch!!! My stomach turned upside-down.

Dad continued. "The pain was terrible; I saw stars. I screamed and cried out loud, but everybody was gone home." He took another deep breath. "Luckily, I could tell that I only bruised my thumb badly and didn't break the bone. I immediately put it under the cold water tap, but that didn't help much. Finally, I poured a small glass of vodka and put my thumb into it. I then took a sharp cutting knife and cut out the base of my thumb's nail."

My father used his index finger from the right hand to demonstrate the slicing he had done on his injured left thumb. *Oh my God!*

"When the blood from under my nail gushed out, the pressure was released." He let out a big sigh. "I took aspirin we had in the office, put on a bandage, finished the vodka to calm myself, and then came right home."

I felt nauseous at the thought of what my father had done, both absentmindedly squashing his thumb and then having to do surgery on himself. He may have learned to do such treatments during the war when medics and medicine were not close at hand. *Could I perform such a battlefield procedure on myself?*

"Why didn't you go to the hospital, Dad?" I asked.

He pawed his other hand at me. "The damage wasn't bad enough. I felt better when the pressure was released and after I took 222s [aspirin with codeine] when I got home." He looked at me. "I didn't want to spend hours in the emergency room for such a minor thing."

* * *

Dad told me, "In manufacturing, it's harder to control your labour costs. Where we make or lose our money is with our supplier purchases."

Because the factory started and ended its day a half-hour before the front office did, I got to sit and watch Dad in action with merchandise suppliers. His negotiations were instructive. One afternoon, he and an out-of-town company president, a guy named Jack, were discussing purchases for the following year's production.

As the negotiation progressed, the back-and-forth between the two became heated as they got down to pricing. When the wall clock passed five o'clock, my father, with tongue in cheek, insisted, "Okay, Jack! You give me a good price on these parts right now, and I'll buy you a good supper tonight at the Troika."

Jack paused for a moment then responded, "Okay, okay, Johnny; what if we split the difference we've been talking about? Then we can get out of here."

Dad knew that his supplier friend liked the Troika for more than its Russian atmosphere and fare. My father once told me that Jack had a local francophone lady friend he liked to invite out there for supper.

Mon père stayed straight-faced. "That's fine, Jack. And I'm willing to commit to these quantities right now, but I want another 2% off if I pay your invoices in 30 days."

Jack's face stayed serious. "I can accept 1% and 15 days."

My father stood. His face was stern. He jammed his finger into the desk. "1.5%, 21 days, and that's final." Dad had once told me that the 1 to 2% he saved on paying supplier invoices earlier than their due date contributed a healthy part of his company's profit for the year.

Jack stood and reached out with his hand. "Okay, Johnny. You're a good customer. And that better be a really good supper I get at the Troika tonight."

They both laughed and shook hands.

Sitting across the room, watching these gamesmen play their gambits, I figured that both of them got something worthwhile out of their deal. With smiles having come to both my father's and his supplier's faces, they seemed to be equally pleased with the result, even though it had taken back-and-forth haranguing to get there.

On another day, my father was discussing product pricing with a new vendor who sold cleaning products. Dad demanded, "Okay, Tony, give me *Ivanovich!*"

Tony's face looked perplexed. "What did you say Mr. Simkovits? Who are you asking for?"

Dad kept his face straight and voice loud. "Don't you understand what I'm saying? Is my accent too much for you? I said I wanted *one of each.*"

Tony responded, "Okay, I got it, Mr. Simkovits." The guy made a note in his order book.

Dad looked at the salesman sternly. "And I want those as free samples. Until I know your product is good, I'm not giving your company a penny."

The end of the following day, Dad got riled at another young salesman dropping an MSRP (manufacturer's suggested retail price)—Johnny Simkovits expected discounts. My father's face turned beet red. "Damn it! Are you crazy? I don't have that kind of money to spend on your retail prices." He pointed out the window. "Do you think I ever buy merchandise from the drugstore?"

My father didn't worry about losing a supplier's business. He once told me, "You shouldn't have only one source for anything. You need a few to compete with each other." If my brother ever said that he needed to look for a new item for production, Dad threw the yellow pages phone book on his desk and said, "Here! Call at least three companies and see who could give you what we need for the best price and delivery."

Dad motioned the young salesman toward the door. "Do you think I was born yesterday or in Timbuktu? Go back and sharpen your pencil. Come back only when you can give me a good price."

This green guy said, "Okay, okay, Mr. Simkovits. Let me go back to my manager and see what I can do."

After the rep had departed, my father smiled and chuckled.

Without raising their heads from their deskwork, a few of his office staff smiled and chuckled too. They knew that my father was working to get another hungry or inexperienced vendor to bend.

I wondered what my father would do if he could not wheel and deal.

* * *

Dad protected his plant's profit as a big bear protected its cubs. He gave the foremen lectures on saving money and having little waste in the factory.

At today's Tuesday production meeting, his story went, "When I was in the military, our commander made us go to the shithouse with only one piece of rough toilet paper." My father chuckled with gusto as he demonstrated the technique by putting his middle finger through the center of a toilet paper sheet.

Yuck, I thought, as I imagined the rest.

Raises were few and far between at Montreal Phono; only my father could grant them. One time, as the office staff finished their work for the day, Dad was approached by Leslie, a factory worker. My father had helped Leslie—a Slovak countryman and friend of Dad's half-brother Edo—to immigrate to Canada as the door was closing the 1968 Prague Spring.

In front of my father, the 20-something Leslie stood at ease like a military soldier. He looked Dad's way. "Mr. Simkovits, I've been working my tail off for your company for the last six months. Your foreman will tell you how hard I've been working for you."

Leslie didn't look directly into the boss's eyes but slightly off to one side. "The foremen tell me that you don't like to give raises." He took a breath. "But for the sake of our future together here at Montreal Phono, I want to ask you personally for a raise."

"What are you specifically asking for?" my father asked.

"For now, I'm asking for only ten cents per hour more."

The office staff sat still in their seats. My father pointed his finger toward the factory door and raised his voice. "If I give you ten cents, Leslie, then I'll have to give everybody else ten cents too. I can't afford that."

"I'm not everybody else," Leslie offered.

"I still can't do it," the boss proclaimed.

"Okay, Mr. Simkovits. Thank you for listening to me." Leslie turned around, walked out of the office and left for home.

By the end of the week, Leslie gave his notice and departed the premises.

Years later, during another one of my summer work stints, I bumped into Leslie at my father's office. He came by once in a while to stay in touch with Dad and to see if the two of them could do business.

While waiting for my father to finish a call, Leslie told me, "Your dad gave me my first job in Canada. It was an important experience for me." He recounted the story.

Leslie paused for a moment as he looked back in time. "If your father had said 'yes' to that raise, then I'd still be here working for him. Because he said 'no' to the increase, I left Montreal Phono and invested in my education. I learned the insurance business, and it was a turning point in my life in Canada."

Leslie looked into my eyes and smiled. "I've maintained a good relationship with your father. We've even done business together. I'm grateful that he helped me get settled here in '68." He took a long breath. "He also got me connected to his Slovak Businessman's Association where I found some good sales opportunities. Your father respects immigrants who make something of themselves, as he did."

I was a little surprised by my response. "At least you don't have to live with him." I stopped myself there.

Leslie turned to look at me, but he didn't lose his upbeat tone. "Yes," he said, "that might be a different story."

Maybe there was something in Leslie's approach and attitude for me to learn.

* * *

At the end of a work week, Dad and I had a quiet moment together. He leaned against the edge of his big cherrywood desk while I sat on a simple office chair in front of him. He asked, "Doing anything special this weekend, son?" Before I could answer, he smiled, "Want to come with me to a Montreal Alouettes football game on Saturday?"

Unlike my brother, I enjoyed watching professional sports with my father. At the games, Dad and I shelled and devoured a half-pound bag of peanuts. He let me take sips of his Molson Export beer. When our home team scored a touchdown, we jumped up and down, shouting *hurrah* at the top of our lungs. "Sure, Dad," I said to his offer.

"That's great, son."

Something was not quite right with my father's tone. There was a subdued look on his face, both blank and expressionless. "Something else, Dad?" I asked and then waited silently.

He tapped out a cigarette from his pack and lit it with his gold Dunhill lighter. Usually, he looked me straight in the eye, but this time he looked off to one side. "Mr. Leonard from one of our big customers came to see me early Monday morning. Do you remember him?"

Leonard was the life of the party at Dad's big birthday and Christmas celebrations, or at Dad and Mom's summer backyard barbeques. The guy sported a scotch on the rocks in one hand, a cigarette in the other, and a big grin on his face from the beginning to the end of the gathering. Sometimes I watched him nervously, for when he laughed, he might spill a little of his drink. "Yes, I remember him, Dad. He's a department head of some sort."

Dad looked at me with a blank face. "That's right." He looked down a touch. "The guy came to see me on Monday, at 7:15 in the morning, before any of our office employees arrived. He knows I come in early, so he caught me as I got here."

Dad hesitated a second or two. He looked past me again. "I brought Leonard into my private office. His hands were shaking terribly—as if he had been in an accident. I told him to sit down but he wouldn't. Instead, he begged me to have a drink." Dad took a long breath. "He said he couldn't go to work without one."

My God! I had no idea what I might do in such a situation. "So what did you do?" I asked.

My father looked my way but again slightly off to one side. "I told Leonard he should go home and get rest."

His voice lowered. "But he said he couldn't because his wife would get worried and suspicious. He told me that she removed the alcohol from their house. He couldn't find anything there to steady himself before going to work, and no liquor store was open that early in the morning."

Dad pointed to a long wooden cabinet behind his desk where he kept bottles of alcohol. "The only thing he could think of was to come and see me because he knows that I keep booze in the office."

What a position for my father to be put in! Might I have given Leonard my doctor's number and told the guy to see him? Would I have cajoled Leonard into my car and driven him to a hospital? Might I have called his wife to come and take him home?

"So what happened, Dad?"

My father shrugged, but his voice stayed steady. "The guy was almost crying. His hands were shaking." Dad stared past me. "I gave him a glass and a bottle of rye whiskey. He poured himself a drink and drank it slowly."

He raised one hand. "Within ten minutes Leonard was fine, and he left here to go to work. He was very grateful." Dad's voice hardened slightly. "But I told him that he shouldn't do that ever again with me."

I was at a loss for words. "Gosh," I said. Silence filled the room for a moment. Soon, my curiosity got to me. I asked, "Why did you decide to give him a drink, Dad, and not tell him to go home or to the hospital?"

My father's eyes shifted back and forth, searching for an answer. After a few seconds, he responded. "I didn't know what else to do. Leonard works for an important customer." He took another long, slow breath. "I have to work with the guy. If he went to the hospital, the word could get out, and his job might be in jeopardy. If he went home, his marriage might be in trouble."

It was hard to know what to do on the spur of the moment with someone who had a big say in your livelihood. It was like having to defy your boss. Had my father done more than he did, he might have precipitated the end of his colleague's career or marriage. Dad certainly didn't want to risk his relationship with any of his big-customer colleagues, many of whom—like my father—drank as if there would be no tomorrow. The way he spoke about the situation, I could tell he very much liked Leonard and felt bad for the guy.

Dad and I sat in silence for a few more seconds. He rubbed the side of his nose with his partially closed index finger. "Let's close the place and go home, son."

Years later, during another one of our quiet moments sitting in his back office, Dad told me, "Mr. Leonard died last month."

I looked at him and asked, "How so?"

Dad looked past me again and replied, "He had cirrhosis of the liver."

I nodded and kept my voice calm. "Oh, my! I'm sorry to hear that." I couldn't look at my father's face.

Dad stood from his chair and then offered, "Okay, son. Let's close the place and *foot-scoff*" (his polite word for "get the f… out of here").

I nodded and stood too.

Neither he nor I said another word about it, but I wondered why my father told me such things.

* * *

On this sunny summer day, Dad sat behind his desk with his drugstore reading glasses sitting on the end of his nose. He was working his way through a stack of invoices and purchase orders.

It was ten minutes before five o'clock. Office employees were clearing their desks before leaving for the day. They didn't dare stand and move toward the exit until the factory buzzer sounded, otherwise they'd get a piercing eye and sharp tongue from the boss.

The office entrance door opened and in walked Yasko, my father's commercial insurance agent. He was a tall, rotund Ukrainian-Canadian and Dad's junior by ten years. Because of his girth, Yasko jiggled into the room like a giant bowl of Jell-O. I imagined hugging the guy—my long arms might wrap around his midsection, but my hands wouldn't be able to touch on the other side of him.

Yasko had a big smile on his round face. He said a hearty, "Hello, Johnny. How're you doing?"

My father removed his reading glasses and exclaimed, "Yasko! *Sho yebesch?*"

Dad had once told my younger ears about that expression. He said it was a mixture of Russian and Ukrainian, which are similar languages. Smiling at me, he had offered, "It means, 'Why are you screwing around?'"

Years later, I found out that my father was a little more civil with me. A Ukrainian friend clued me in that it indeed was a mixture of the two languages, but it meant, "What are you screwing?" Maybe to Dad, both of those translations were the same thing.

I was sitting at a nearby desk when Yasko had entered. I was again hanging around until my father or brother could drive me home. I smiled at my father's expression, for I was used to his foul humour. It reminded me of a time when Steve and I had been kids, young enough for me to still suck my thumb and my brother to bite his fingernails. Dad had told my mother, "They'll quickly stop their sucking and biting if you spread some shit on their fingers."

There was no use complaining to Dad about his course idioms. He might apologize and stop swearing for the moment, but he'd start again when it suited him. At least, when in a good mood, he was funny.

Yasko smirked at Dad's quip. He looked my way and said in a half-serious tone, "You know, Harvy, I'm only willing to take that from your father and nobody else."

I shrugged as I looked back at the bulky guy. I worked to convey, *Why are you bringing me into this?*

Dad chuckled. He motioned to his business friend to come closer. "You know I'm always happy to see you, Yasko. Seeing your big build makes me feel better about my waistline."

Since midlife, Dad's girth had enlarged from years of business entertaining. His weight went up and down like a yo-yo. Once a year or so, he needed Mom to let out or take in the buttons of his suit pants and jackets.

"Okay, Johnny," Yasko said. "I see you are in a good mood today. You must have collected money from your customers this week." He pointed at my father. "So then, I can collect a cheque from you for my last invoice."

Yasko pointed around the room. "You know, it's for your building's insurance." His voice quieted, but I could still hear him, "so that you can collect from the insurance company if you ever have a fire or theft." He smirked. "You know, it's us agents that represent your best interests."

Without losing a beat, my father offered, "Good thing it's not Monday, Yasko." He paused, staring at his friend.

Yasko had a confused look. "Why's that, Johnny?"

"Don't you know me already? I never sign cheques on Mondays." He chuckled again.

"Okay, Johnny, I'll play along. So why don't you sign cheques on Mondays?"

"Because, my dear friend, if I sign cheques on Monday, then I'm signing them the whole week." Dad laughed once more.

I chuckled too. Dad always had something amusing to say to his favourite colleagues.

Yasko came back, "Well then, my timing is perfect because today is Thursday."

My father turned his head and called to his bookkeeper. "Jean, please prepare a cheque for Yasko here, for his last invoice to us. But take off one percent of the amount. If I remember correctly, we are paying him in less than thirty days."

Yasko jumped in. "Come on, Johnny, it's been a few weeks since I sent you that invoice. One percent is a big haircut for a service business like mine. I only make a small percentage on these policies."

My father looked at Yasko and then back at Jean. "Okay, Jean. Postdate that cheque for a week from tomorrow and then pay the whole amount."

Yasko said, "Johnny, you are something. For you, every penny and every minute count."

Dad's voice turned serious. "Money costs money, my dear friend. In business, I like to keep it in my pocket as long as I can."

"Yes, Johnny, I know," the agent said with a tone of surrender. He knew that my father's cheques were good; Johnny Simkovits would never stiff a business friend he might need.

Dad went on, and a big grin came over his face. "What if I take you out for a good supper tonight, on me? We can go to that Stache's place you like."

Staches was a Polish restaurant in downtown Montreal. It wasn't as classy or expensive as the Troika, the latter reserved for Montreal Phono's biggest customers and suppliers. Tonight being my father's usual night out on the town, he might have been looking for more company to come along.

"That's nice of you, Johnny, but I got to get home to my family. My kid has a parent thing at school tonight."

"Since when has that stopped you from going out with me for a good *kapusta?" (Kapusta* was a sour or sweet cabbage dish served with bacon or pork, including the fat.) "Your wife can go to school instead of you," my father said. Dad never went to Steve's or my elementary school events or meetings; our mother did that.

Yasko smirked as he grabbed his belly. "I appreciate the offer, Johnny, but my wife has me on a diet."

"You can diet tomorrow, Yasko." Dad winked. "Come and live with me tonight."

"You are such a charmer, Johnny. Maybe we can sneak in a light lunch next week."

"Okay," Dad said. "Call me tomorrow, and we'll make a date. But right now, at least have a drink with me."

My father pointed to a clock on the wall. "It's five o'clock. I know you like Canadian Club; I have some in my office." Dad winked. "It'll put a little lead in your pencil for your wife later tonight." He chuckled once more.

I smiled within myself. Knowing Yasko's bulk, I wasn't sure he could find his pencil let alone put lead into it.

Yasko came back, "I don't know, Johnny. My wife will smell the alcohol on my breath."

"Don't worry," my father retorted. "We'll pour it into coffee for you. There'll be no alcohol smell." My father turned to his secretary. "Helen, get us a couple of coffees before you go. I'll grab the Canadian Club from my office."

Yasko paused and then smiled again. "I guess that can't hurt. Just a short one, Johnny."

"For sure, Yasko; like always."

Dad looked my way. "You want a short one too, Harvy?"

Though I was over 18, Quebec's drinking age, I said, "No Dad, I've had enough coffee for today, and I don't like that CC straight."

"Yes, I know," my father retorted. "You like the sweet drinks, like rum and Coke or vodka and orange juice."

I smiled but said nothing. Dad was right about my drinking. I wasn't the straight man he and his Eastern European friends could be.

A moment later, Dad carefully poured the CC into both his and Yasko's Styrofoam cups of coffee. They lifted them, and my dad smirked. "Here's to keeping your powder dry and ready to fire."

Yasko smiled. "You have a way with words, Johnny."

I was smiling too because my dad usually has his way with everything.

My father later told me, "It's important to schmooze your suppliers as much as your customers." He grinned. "Sometimes I need a guy like Yasko to do something for me. If I treat him well, then he'll more likely do a favour for me when I ask."

I felt concern that Dad's way of "treating others well" was to exploit their vices. Yasko didn't need that end-of-day drink or a stuffing meal at a

Polish restaurant. But count on my father for knowing how to leverage a man's weaknesses.

Though Dad liked to entice even me to join him at his usual haunts or to have a drink with him and the fellas, I mostly avoided the temptations. Not having the stomach capacity he did, I instead offered an adoring son's smile.

My dad failed to add the other side of his explanation. If Montreal Phono didn't get the service he expected from a guy like Yasko, Johnny Simkovits could scream the paint off his friend's office walls, even through the phone. As quickly as he could offer a drink, he could shout, "Your goddamn insurance company is fucking me good! I can't believe you and those bastards are letting me down like this."

* * *

Dad more than once insisted, "Those bloody insurance companies have us business people over a barrel. They charge you coming, when you pay their insurance premiums; then they charge you going, when they take a deductible on a claim."

At 7:50 on a Monday morning, Baptist hurried into the factory office. His face was flushed as he rushed to my father's desk. Because Baptist was a two-pack-a-day smoker, he was huffing and puffing.

He waved his arms and spoke as if the walls were on fire. "Johnny, the trailer full of the Woolco [F.W. Woolworths in the USA] Disco-4 units has disappeared from the yard. It looks like robbers pulled up a tractor during the weekend, hitched up to the full trailer we had sitting outside, and completely fucked off with the whole thing."

"Son of a bitch," Dad said loudly. "I'll call the police right away. There were forty-eight big units in that trailer that was ready for shipment this morning."

My father turned to Helen who had just walked into the office. Before she even removed her coat, Dad told her. "Quick, Helen, get me the police on the phone. Some sons-of-bitches *foot-scoffed* with a whole goddamn trailer of big consoles."

Each one of those large disco units, with high-quality dual turntables, eight speakers, and flashing disco lights, was valued at $500 per piece at their manufacturing sales price, or $999 at full retail.

Helen placed her handbag on her desk but didn't remove her jacket. "Oh, my!" she offered. "I'll get them on the phone right away." She picked up the receiver and dialed, her eyes focused on a sheet of emergency numbers she kept at her desk.

In a moment, Dad was standing while he talked on the phone to the police captain. He spoke politely as a cigarette burned between his fingers. "Good morning, sir. I need to report a robbery." He told the captain what he suspected happened. He added, "Can you send an officer over right away to do a report and to see if we can catch those bums?"

My father listened for a few minutes, repeating, "Yes; yes." He then said, "Thank you, sir," and put the phone down. He turned to Baptist. "The police captain says such robberies have been happening around here recently. He strongly recommends we never leave a full trailer in the yard."

A Woolco salesman with a Disco-4 console stereo at Canada's Consumer Electronics Show in Toronto. The Disco-4 name was because of the four big woofer (bass) speakers located in the top compartment of the unit. The unit had two turntables and flashing lights behind the white Plexiglas grills that were placed right below the turntables and radio chassis. C. 1980.

My father rubbed his forehead as he sat down. "The captain doesn't feel confident that we can catch the robbers or retrieve our product. These guys work fast and are probably long gone. If the theft isn't reported within hours of it happening, then the chance of finding them and the stolen property is negligible." Dad hit his fist on his desk. "Son of a bitch!"

He motioned toward his foreman. "Baptist, we need to get the serial numbers of those stolen units right away so I can give them to the police for their report, and then give them to the insurance company when I file the claim." He grinned a bit. "Go and get me the next two serial number stickers from the production line before it starts up any minute now. We'll work with that."

Baptist ran out to the end of the production line, grabbed the serial number stickers and brought them to Dad. My father took them and did a quick calculation. He offered, "The serial numbers of the units on the trailer are the 48 numbers before these."

Dad wrote down the range of numbers on a pad. He then bent over to reach the trash can under his desk. He tore the two stickers in his hand into unrecognizable pieces and dropped them into the can. He looked at Baptist, "We'll claim that the robbers stole two more units so that the insurance company will cover the $1,000 deductible."

Baptist said nothing. He nodded and grinned as he walked back into the factory.

By nine o'clock, Dad had a police report in hand. He turned to Helen. "Yasko should be in his office by now. Get him on the phone so that I can report the loss."

For the rest of the day, the stolen trailer became the joke-of-the-day around the Montreal Phono factory. Employees smiled, chuckled, and proclaimed, "That trailer of disco units was the fastest sale the company has ever made." Only a few of us knew about the extra insurance bonus my father had created for his company.

A couple of days later, the police found the stolen trailer on a side road a few miles away. It was empty and abandoned. A detective came to tell my father that the thieves had broken through the padlock on the door of the vehicle. Most likely, they transferred the units into an unidentified truck or two that they had waiting.

By then, Dad didn't care because everything was in the hands of the insurance company, and a cheque for $25,000 was on its way to Montreal Phono for the "50 stolen stereos." That insurance payment would get into Montreal Phono's bank account faster than the customer's regular payment would have gotten there.

Dad later told me, "See how good the insurance company is to me when I have a claim."

I bet he wondered, *How can we move more units like that?*

75

Woolco never complained about the loss of that trailer of disco units. Before the year ended, they reordered 500 more Disco-4 consoles.

* * *

Dad had his tricky ways. I once saw him pay our family's two-week Florida winter vacation by putting the whole Holiday Inn Resort bill on a Gulf credit card. At the time, he bragged to a close colleague who had vacationed with us, "The government would never check a gas credit card for a personal expense. My company foremen use the same credit card account to fill up their cars."

I admired my father for his astuteness and deliberateness in finding ways to one-up insurance companies, his suppliers, and the taxman. I also wondered if he was going to get caught by the government tax department. He may have been shrewd and shameless in keeping his money out of the government's coffers, but I worried that a Revenue Canada tax agent might overhear him brag about his deceits while he was downing a drink at his beloved Troika.

Would my father be led away in handcuffs to jail? Would he have a big court fine to pay? If he kept up his business bullshit, he might have to escape his adopted Canada for Switzerland where he had his offshore cash stashed.

Where might that leave the rest of us?

* * * *

24

Midas Man & Oedipal Conflicts

"I have to go," my twenty-year-old brother proclaimed. "My horse is waiting for me." Steve was racing out of the office, his riding boots on his feet and helmet in hand. He glanced at me. "Dad will take you home." He was out the door before I could respond.

It was the summer of 1974, a couple of years before I finished my MIT bachelor's degree. As a nineteen-year-old undergraduate, I was dependent on Dad or Steve to drive me back and forth from home to my summer job at our father's factory.

My father and I were the last ones in the office today after everyone else had rushed out the door at five o'clock, including my brother. I was fine with Steve leaving me behind; I looked forward to time alone with Dad.

From his front-office chair, my father stood and looked at me. "Please follow me to my back office." We walked the few paces into his private domain.

Dad's back office was not big or fancy, but it was the nicest space in the factory building. Burgundy curtains covered the windows to make the room look rich and to conceal the gray-metal factory window frames. Dad's factory people had built the walnut veneer walls and credenza cabinets in the room. A slab of quarter-inch glass covered his large, solid cherry desk.

Under the desk's glass top, Dad kept mementos: postcards from business trips abroad, a business card from the now defunct Hungarian Tokay, and a bar coaster from the Russian Troika. Next to those souvenirs were school photos of my brother and me at different ages. The oldest pictures were of two pudgy-faced kids. I disliked those photos, for Steve and I had thinned out during our boarding school years.

Dad permitted only a few people to enter into his private world. The list included his lawyer and accountant, the company bookkeeper, the priest from my father's Slovak church, and Steve and I when Dad invited us. Mom had never set foot on the premises—wives were meant to stay home.

The only things that decorated the office were oil portraits of Dad and his father that hung on the walls. Mom's photograph was nowhere present here. From my sophomore year in college, she and Dad were separated for the second time; he had left her for another woman. Now nearly two years later, there was no reconciliation in sight.

I was grateful that a photo of my father's girlfriend wasn't present here. Though I had seen her at Dad's country chalet up north, I didn't want to get to know her. Maybe Dad was keeping her at a distance, and I was okay with that.

My father motioned for me to take a seat on one of the metal-framed chairs against the wall. His chair of solid wood and leather was the best one in the room, and it remained behind his desk. Dad, as he always did at these father-son moments, stood and leaned against the front of his desk. "How's it going in the factory?" he asked.

"Everything's going fine."

"Do you have any plans for the weekend, son?"

"Not much doing yet."

He didn't need to hear more. "Want to come and play golf with me on Sunday?"

I liked to hit the links with Dad. If I made a bad shot, he allowed me to hit a second ball from the same spot. On hot summer days, he let me share his cool beer and ginger ale shandy at the 10th-hole turn. And, I had never cracked a club over my knee—something my brother once did after he flubbed an iron approach shot after Dad had tried to give him a pointer. Steve abandoned golf that day, so the sport became Dad's and mine to play.

"Sure Dad," I said. It felt good to do things with him outside of working at his company.

His big blue eyes were on me. "Okay, sweetheart, it's a date."

Dad and I hung out together for a few more moments. I looked over his shoulder as he crouched down and unlocked his waist-high, dark gray, thick metal safe that stood in the corner of the room.

With reading glasses on, he whirled the combination tumbler back and forth, stopping at the numbers he had memorized in his head. He then turned the large handle to open its heavy door. From a bottom shelf, he retrieved papers he needed for his accountant.

As he rummaged, he grabbed a key that he kept hidden in one of the safe's metal drawers. He used it to unlock another compartment where he kept a secluded stash. My eyes widened as he revealed a couple of pieces from his precious collection.

"I want to show you a few things I got recently," he said. He handed me a heavy, all metal watch. "I bought this 14-karat white gold Omega when I was in Switzerland on business this past spring."

The silvery watch had a solid yet flexible metal strap that was integrated with the watch casing, making it a long, continuous piece of gold. My father had once shown me the markings to look for on gold items. I checked the Omega's back and saw it was indeed 14kt.

"Try it on," he said.

I clasped it onto my wrist. The heavy watch hung loosely on my thinner arm.

Dad continued. "Unlike cash, gold watches like this will grow in value over the years." He took a breath. "Son, when you are old enough, I'll get you one."

In his small but growing collection of precious timepieces, Dad's brand of choice was Omega. He had bought his first precious timepiece in the early 1960s during a business trip to Europe. It was a sleek, 14kt yellow-gold watch that he wore every day.

The piece had slender gold hands. Thin, raised gold lines on the white dial marked the hours. Over a thousand tiny, closely packed gold links allowed the band to easily bend to the contours of any wrist, giving the watch ballast without much bulk. Dad wore that Omega in a natural, unassuming way. His friends and colleagues commented on its simple elegance.

Contrary to most people, my father wore his Omega on the inside of his wrist. Initially, I thought he did this to be distinctive. He once told me, "I got into the habit as a reconnaissance pilot in WWII." Dad explained that, when he tracked troop movements behind Russian lines, his small, single-prop German- or Hungarian-made aircraft could be batted about by air currents as he darted in and out of the clouds. He added, "With the watch face on the inside of my wrist, it was less likely the crystal would hit anything and get busted."

Through my college years, I too put the face of my watch on the inside of my wrist. It made me feel distinctive and connected to my father.

Dad had other precious items that were dear to him. He wore a modest, gold St. Christopher pendant that hung on a thin gold chain around his neck. It showed the saint carrying Baby Jesus on his shoulder.

The pendant had been a gift from his parents when, at eighteen, my father began compulsory service in the Czechoslovak military. Dad wore that pendant for most of his life. He felt it helped him survive World War II, escape Soviet Czechoslovakia in 1949, and immigrate to Canada unscathed.

On the ring finger of his right hand was a thick gold ring with a two-carat diamond. He also sported a gold tie clip that had a clear one-carat stone. Those two diamonds had come from an antique gold, ruby, and diamond brooch that his mother had owned.

The brooch was in the shape of three flowers. Diamonds had been in the center of each flower, and dozens of small red and purple rubies comprised the outside of each bloom, with gold lace in between. Dad had told me, "The broach is the only thing I have from my mother after she died of tuberculosis when I was three."

Dad later replaced the original diamonds with zirconium. He used the largest and smallest stones for his gold ring and tie clip. The middle-sized stone, over one-and-a-half-carat, lay secure in his safety deposit box at the bank.

It appeared that my father trusted in precious things more than he trusted in the honesty and dependability of people. He could complain about "damn suppliers" who let him down by being late with material shipments, or about "fucking employees" who cost him money by making production mistakes, or about "bastard brokers" who screwed him in business deals. It seemed that precious metal and jewels were things on which he could rely.

After Dad had left Mom for the second time, he replaced his wedding band with a gold ring that sported a large, flat onyx stone. He wore the ring on the pinky finger of his left hand.

The diamond and ruby brooch that Dad received by way of his mother.

Dad gently handled and carefully placed his watch, chain, ring, and clip onto his wrist, neck, finger, and tie. He appreciated not only the richness of his treasures' look and feel, but also how these things were a sign of his growing status and affluence. He displayed his wares tastefully, never having more than one ring on each hand and one chain around his neck.

While we were still in his office, Dad showed me another item from his safe— a large gold coin. "Look at this 50mm [2" wide] Austrian-Hungarian gold piece," he said. "I bought it in Switzerland when I got the watch."

He explained. "In trying to escape the Germans during the war and the Communists afterward, many European refugees used gold as currency. Gold had value across borders, where one's paper money could be worth nothing. Even today, Eastern European currencies are worthless in the West."

Dad put the piece into my hand to let me feel the coin's nearly 1.5-oz weight. "To hide their gold," he offered, "refugees sewed coins like this into their clothes, or they placed the pieces flat into the bottom of their shoes. They might bury their rings in bars of soap and put loose diamonds into a tube of toothpaste."

I felt not only the weight of the coin but also the weight of life and death. Christian Europeans like my dad, in addition to countless Jews like my mother, must have borne much angst during their daring escapes and dangerous migrations before, during, and after World War II.

My father gathered his pieces and returned them to his safe. "Harvy, remember that you can depend on gold to hold its value, especially during times of economic or political trouble."

I trusted Dad knew what he was talking about.

* * *

At the end of another workday, our father looked at my brother with a stern face. He spoke harshly. "Because of the production-line problems we are having, we should hold the supplier responsible and withhold payment."

Steve raised his voice and pointed to the factory door. "The supplier has nothing to do with our production issues; the problem is in our factory." Steve stood by Dad's desk in the front office. In my brother's left hand were samples of several long aluminum faceplates, designed for a unit that would soon be in production.

Dad pointed his finger. "You always take the supplier's side, Steve, never the company's." His voice was a few decibels louder than my brother's.

It was after five o'clock. Montreal Phono's front office was deserted except for the three of us. Waiting for Dad to take me home, I stood two desks away and leaned against a bank of file cabinets that lined one wall. I watched as my father and brother alternatively stood, sat, and walked around Dad's desk, staking their lion versus adult cub positions.

After a second or two of silence, Steve yelled, "I CAN'T STAND THIS B.S.!" He smashed the faceplates on our dad's glass-covered desk, the force warping the plates badly. As a devout Catholic who went to church every Sunday, this was the closest that Steve ever came to swearing.

Speechless, I moved partially behind a building pillar. An unnerving silence filled the room. During those chilling seconds, Dad's face turned beet red. He grabbed his heavy desk chair and lifted it over his head. "SON-OF-A-BITCH!" he roared. "Don't you *EVER* talk to me like that!" He smashed the chair's leg casters onto the sheet of glass that covered his desk.

The glass exploded into a thousand pieces, jettisoning shards in every direction across the table and floor. Some pieces landed inches from me.

It had been two years since Steve joined our father's business full-time after my brother precipitously ended his engineering studies at Queen's University. When the college told him that he'd need an extra year of coursework to graduate, he decided to leave the university and work for our father.

Over a family supper back then, Dad had asserted, "It's good that Steve's coming into the company. I want him to learn about the real world of building products and doing business, not only the theory they teach in

84

school." He turned to me, "But I want you, Harvy, to stay at MIT and finish your studies." He looked and pointed at both of us. "You boys need to know how to take care of yourselves in business because everybody wants to take advantage."

Dad took Steve into Montreal Phono and trained him to become the company's purchasing agent. "A company is made or broken on purchasing," he told us over that supper. "It's one of the most important jobs in any business. We make or lose our Montreal Phono profit based on how well we purchase merchandise and expedite it for production."

I thought my brother was making a mistake by working for our quick-tempered father. Steve later shared with me, "School's not for me, Harvy. I'm not good at studying like you are. I need to show that I can do something else."

At MIT, I was working toward my bachelor's in electrical engineering and computer science. My summer stints in my father's factory were a way for me to make easy money and obtain work experience until I could get out on my own. I couldn't see myself working full-time for my father.

The shock of our father's explosion and the shattered glass around the office sent chills through my spine. My brother looked rattled too, his eyes staring at the floor. After another short eternity of silence, Steve bowed his head slightly. He raised his right hand in surrender and said, "I'm sorry, Dad, for getting mad."

Now that the top had blown off Dad's pressure cooker, and he saw Steve's remorse, our father quickly calmed down as if nothing had happened. "It's okay, son." He put his arms out to embrace my brother. "I just couldn't control myself when you said those things."

Dad took a breath and looked around at the damage he had created on his desk and over the floor. "Leave everything for now, and let's go home. The cleaners will pick up the glass early in the morning. I'll tell them it was an accident."

We walked out of Dad's office as if nothing bad had happened. That father-son explosion was never mentioned again by any of us.

Over his subsequent months and years at Montreal Phono, Steve continued to challenge Dad. When our father asked him to arrive early to work or to be on time, Steve came in late, saying "I had to do something important at home first." If our father needed him to stay over for an emergency production meeting, Steve offered, "Sorry, I need to go and take care of my horse." If Dad wanted his first son to bring in production merchandise early, Steve contradicted him. "The supplier promised to have it to us in time," but the supplier sometimes let down the company.

If our father asked Steve to squeeze the vendor for a better price, my brother retorted, "I got us a good price already." When Dad called the supplier himself to prove he could negotiate a better deal, Steve called the vendor back and committed to his original arrangement. Whenever Dad said, "Let's go right," Steve countered, "I'm going left."

I was glad I worked in Montreal Phono's factory and not in the front office with those two. When Dad became irritated with Steve, he might take out his frustration by shouting at other office employees. I felt bad for all of them.

Dad even tried kindness with Steve. When our father once perused the shortage list of merchandise that the company needed for the next production run, I overheard him say, "Steve, please be so kind as to call the supplier and check to see if that shipment will be here on Friday. We'll need it for production first thing on Monday."

Steve responded. "I did it already Dad. They promised it to us for this Friday, and it will be here on Friday."

Dad's voice turned a touch terse. "That supplier changes it delivery schedule like I change my shirt. Do you know if it's already in transit? We can't start our new model run without it."

"It's supposed to be on the truck tomorrow."

Dad's voice grew irritated. "Supposed to be or will be?"

Steve's heels stayed Simkovits stiff. "They told me that it would ship tomorrow, Dad. We should trust them at their word."

Dad's voice grew. "If I trusted every supplier at their word, I would have been out of business years ago!" He raised his hand to match his voice and gestured toward my brother. "Can you please call them now? If you don't then I will."

This time, Steve reached for the phone. I was glad he did.

On another occasion concerning a similar situation, Steve stayed planted in his chair and looked intensely at our father. "I don't agree with you, Dad. What you're doing isn't right. We can't be on the supplier's back all the time."

"Son-of-a-bitch!" Dad blurted. "When I ask you to do something for me, I want you to do it." He turned and pointed to his secretary. "Helen, call Pierre at Kruger Corrugated." He turned back to Steve and said angrily, "If you don't talk to him, I will."

After surviving many of Dad's explosions, Steve no longer became fazed by our father's displays. He continued to come to work late for various reasons or to leave early to be with his horse. It seemed as if Steve developed thick calluses to Dad's belligerent barks, though Dad never laid a bloodletting bite on his eldest son. Though our father could get uncontrollably angry, he never fired my brother.

Steve's insubordination didn't endear him to me. Contrary to my confrere, I respected our father and was not combative with him. I watched with disdain from the sidelines as my brother led his first-son rebellion.

Over the years, Dad complained privately to his office staff, to his business colleagues while dining at the Troika, and to me, "Steve is working more for the suppliers than he is for our company."

"Yes, I know, Dad," I once responded. "But other than yell at him or complain about him, you never really do anything." I worked to stay calm and rational. "With any other employee, you'd give them a warning and then fire them if they didn't change their ways."

Dad looked down at his open palms. "I know son, but I can't let your brother go. Who else would hire him without him having a university degree?"

I shut my mouth. I suspected Steve would eventually have his justifiable factory-sawdust desserts if he maintained his continual office defiance of Dad.

* * * *

25

Business in Paradise

Dad's face looked serious. "Son, I need your help again in the factory this summer." It was May 1975, the end of the spring semester during my junior year at college. I was twenty years old.

My father looked at me with his biting blue eyes; I didn't return his glare. He continued. "Our lease is ending at our old Verdun building, and we are moving Montreal Phono to Ville St. Laurent. We are going to a newer, single-floor, 50,000 square-foot facility I recently bought there."

He pointed my way. "I need someone I can trust to help us load the merchandise from the old place." His voice softened. "I can't be everywhere, son, so I need you to help me watch the people doing the loading at our old place."

"What do you mean, Dad?" Did he want me to be an undercover operative or snitch on Montreal Phono employees? Didn't he have people he could trust?

He lowered his voice. "I don't want any merchandise to grow legs and walk away," he confided. "Your brother is helping me move our office, and our foremen are busy getting things put together in the new building."

His face was tight and eyes narrow. "I want you to work with Danny, our shipping foreman and stockroom clerk, to load the merchandise from our old building into the trucks I hired." His voice turned stern. "Danny's a good guy, but he's been working for us only a year. I don't know how much I can trust him. I need you to keep your eyes open for anything suspicious."

I was apprehensive. What if the people figure out I'm spying on them?

Dad must have seen my concerned look. He took another breath. "You don't have to do anything about what you see; just report back to me."

"Okay," I said, trying not to show uncertainty in my voice. Whether it was Dad's untrusting nature, or his knowing that some of his people were untrustworthy, he didn't believe fully in his factory personnel. Merchandise had "walked away" from his plant before. Stacks of components might even "have babies" (as Dad put it) when misplaced goods suddenly reappeared out of nowhere.

Montreal Phono performed manual inventory counts each year, done by eye and paper and pencil. Those counts, done by Danny, Steve, and sometimes me, rarely came out the same twice, which made us scratch our heads. I wondered if a disgruntled Montreal Phono employee was playing tricks on us by clandestinely moving a box of material in and out of a pile so that counts would never be the same.

Those inconsistent counts made my father furious at the ones, even me, who did the counting, but Dad still trusted my eyes and ears.

Dad's Verdun plant was in an industrial district of Montreal that was near the city. Its production operation of three departments snaked through the second floor of several adjoining buildings on a large corner lot. The operation ended at the finished goods holding area that was piled high with completed and packed console stereos ready for transport.

Because most of the factory workers and all the office staff were now at Dad's new building, there were many unattended nooks where a deceitful labourer could hide a box of merchandise. Those goods could be later retrieved and moved clandestinely into the back of a waiting station wagon.

On the third floor, above the company's finished goods holding area, was Montreal Phono's raw material warehouse. Cartons of Korean radio chassis, British turntables, Czechoslovakian speakers, and Taiwanese cassettes and 8-track players were stacked 12-15' high. Every carton had to be placed by hand onto wooden pallets. Some boxes weighed seventy-five pounds, requiring two men to lift and carry.

Each pallet stack then needed to be moved by a hand-pallet-truck— commandeered by Nick, our thin but muscular, smiling but tooth-missing Basque. He transported the merchandise via the factory's snail-paced freight elevator down to the shipping area on the second floor.

I never could understand what that pallet-truck chief said when he mumbled to himself in French or English. He certainly impressed me by whipping a 65-pound container (half his body weight) onto his shoulder with the ease of an Olympic shot-putter gathering his ball. As far as I knew, Nick was a trustworthy guy; he had worked for my father ever since I had been a kid.

At Montreal Phono's shipping area, our merchandise moving project required six labourers. Two of them would work at the second-floor shipping conveyor, two others at the ground floor loading dock, and two more inside the truck to complete the massive, moose muscle, moving job.

It would take weeks of sweaty, shirtless work to lug and load box after box, day after day, down from the third floor via freight elevator and onto the shipping conveyor on the second floor. Then those boxes needed to be conveyed and stack into the waiting trucks on the ground floor. The work would be both strenuous and tedious, and I'd have to keep my eyes open too.

The lugging and lifting didn't bother me. I had done merchandise handling and shipping at Montreal Phono before. The arm, back, and leg strengthening work would keep me fit during my soccer off-season. With this paid exercise, my MIT JV soccer coach might continue to have me lead our team's warm-up calisthenics—a position I coveted proudly. I was now a far cry from the little boy made pudgy by my mother's Hungarian cooking, and that fact made me feel good.

The day before the merchandise move was to commence, Dad met with Danny and me. My father looked the shipping supervisor straight in the eyes and spoke firmly. "Danny, you can't be everywhere all the time, so Harvy is here to work with you and help you watch the people." His voice was loud. "I don't want anybody slacking off or fucking off with merchandise as we finish our warehouse move."

He pointed his finger at both of us. "You need to keep an eye out. If I catch any bum with their hands dirty, I'll cut off his *yaytsa* and crucify them." I chuckled inside of me, for I didn't know if Dad meant crucifying the guy he caught or just their *yaytsa.*

My stomach felt a little uneasy. Even with both Danny and me watching, the two of us couldn't be on all three factory floors at once. *I wonder if Dad wants me to watch Danny too?* If I asked, I figured he'd say, "Son, you need to watch everyone and everything."

Danny presented a glum and anxious face—as if he were "the bum" about which my father was talking. "Yes sir, Mr. Simkovits," he responded like a yeoman to his skipper. He turned to me, a smirk on his face. "If we have to, Harvy, we'll grow eyes out of the back of our heads."

Danny's quip eased the tension. I smiled, and so did my father. Calming down, Dad added, "I'm counting on you two to make sure everything goes smoothly. Keep the people moving; we have to be out of here by the end of this month, a little over three weeks from now." He motioned his finger around the room. "Otherwise, I have to pay for another month's rent on this whorehouse."

* * *

Starting at 7:30 the next morning, our crew of French, Italian, Spanish, and Caribbean labourers (plus Slavic me and our Irish Danny) got down to the hefting, heaving, and hauling.

Because everyone spoke English or French, we could communicate with each other—except maybe for our mumbling Basque. I was amazed that Danny could understand Nick's mumbling. I humorously wondered if, after a few beers, our shipping supervisor spoke the same way Nick did.

Danny and I divvied up where we would station ourselves. Though we switched back and forth, he stayed mostly with the crew inside the building. I stayed with the men at the shipping dock and in the truck. During our hot nine-hour workdays, and five hours on Saturdays, our crew loaded dozens of monster trailers with all sizes and shapes of merchandise-laden cartons.

Sometimes Danny and I needed to whip out a measuring tape to do quick measurements of boxes. We then used a pencil to do arithmetic on the side of a carton—to figure out the most efficient way to stack the boxes to fill the trailer.

The radio, speaker, cassette, turntable, and 8-track boxes from around the world were dusty and as diverse as the immigrant employees who worked in our crew. We strained our arms, legs, and backs in the 90-degree humid weather, which felt like 110 degrees inside the trailer.

Every hour or two, one of us fetched cans of ice-cold Pepsi, 7-Up, and Canada Dry Club Soda for all of us. We got them from the canteen truck or the lunch place next door. Once in a while, Danny bought a round of drinks for everyone. It was so sweltering in the truck that we placed a cold soft drink can under our armpits to cool off a bit before popping it open and swigging it down.

All of us were on a first name basis. Knowing that I was the boss's son, these big bicep guys spoke politely to me. During breaks, they spoke of their lives—so different from mine. Most lived in small, crowded apartments with family or friends, or they resided in row-house Montreal neighbourhoods in which I had never stepped.

None of them had been to college, even though Canadian colleges and universities were a tenth of the cost of higher education in the U.S. Some of these guys hadn't even finished high school. They needed to earn a buck to help their families pay rent and buy groceries. I was here for the exercise and pocket money, and because my father had asked me, but I didn't share any of that.

I was glad that I didn't drive a Mercedes Benz as both my father and brother did. Thank goodness Danny could bring me to and from work in his beat-up Chevy. If I was him, might I feel envy or contempt for a guy like me, a boy born with a silver spoon up his first-generation butt?

I said little about my family and home life. I wanted to be one of the guys, even though we knew I wasn't. What would they think of me if they knew I was here to watch them? Then again, they may have figured that out.

Over our lunch breaks, we sat on what little grass was available outside the property's fence enclosure. Danny once showed up to chatter about the cool, countryside vacation he was planning for the upcoming summer shutdown. The rest of us nodded or grunted our understanding, for we were too tired to talk.

I lay down in the sun, a bit away from everyone else. I dreamed of cooler lakeside days. I closed my eyes to grab any Zs I could before the buzzer of the factory time clock rang to startle me back to work. Unlike many here, I wasn't used to this constant physical work, but I was determined to keep up. Silver spoon or not, I didn't want to be seen as a slacker.

Our crew took turns being in and out of the hot trailer and inside and outside of the fan-cooled factory. Sometimes our fit, balding Danny came by to join in on the work and spice up our day. He chuckled, "Hey Antonio, does your girlfriend ever get as hot like the inside of this truck?" or, "I wish I had my wife here with me in this steamy weather. She was like a bucket of ice water in bed last night." Danny winked at me.

I could only fantasize about what he was saying.

Until that time, I had had only one sexual experience, the summer earlier when I was 19. I had been determined to get into a girl's pants before I turned 20. It was a summer fling of heavy petting and more with a barely legal lass, Paula, who worked part-time in my father's office. Being the boss's son was perhaps my biggest draw.

I admit that I took advantage by borrowing my brother's Mercedes sports car to take my first girlfriend out to movies and drive-ins. I didn't dare tell my devout Catholic brother what we had done in his cramped two-seater.

Though Paula was fun to be with and touch, her gooey-gosh-golly eyes always gaped at me. When I asked her, "What would you like on our pizza, sweetie?" she responded, "Anything you want, Harvy." When I added, "Really, sweets; what would you like?" she repeated, "Anything you want."

I knew our days together would be numbered when, after a month, she continued to be deferential to me, as my mother had been to my father.

As that summer drew to its end, I wasn't sure how I should break it off with her. One evening after work, I asked my father for his advice. He told me, "Tell her that it would be hard for you to see her once you go back to college."

At the end of our next date, I said those words to her. She turned her face away and could hardly look at me. Her eyes turned teary. She exited the car quickly and ran into her home. I never saw or talked to her again.

Though I felt wretched for my callous approach, and for listening to my father, I was relieved that nothing happened regarding our unprotected fooling around. It seemed to me that she had enjoyed our time together as much as I had.

After that breakup, I continued to feel awkward around girls. Up to this day in my 21st year, I hadn't been with another. Though Danny's joke about his wife made me chuckle, it reminded me of my awkwardness and lack of experience with the opposite sex, unlike what I saw in my father.

The heavy hoisting and heaving at Montreal Phono's old warehouse built my strength and exhausted me. I lost nearly ten pounds of body weight during those few weeks. At home after work, I could hardly eat half of my supper.

Mom worried, "Why aren't you eating the good food I made for you?"

"Sorry, Mom, but I'm not hungry. I'm really tired."

"Your father should not make you do such a hard job."

"He needs me there to watch the people."

"Could you watch but not work so hard?"

"I like the work. It's good exercise. It's making me feel strong and fit."

Her eyes were on me with concern. Her wooden spoon was in her hand on her hip. "I don't like what your father is doing to you. You won't stay strong and healthy if you don't eat!"

Irrespective of my mother's worry, I kept myself focused on the lifting, loading, stacking, packing, and what surreptitious employee watching I could do for Dad. I worked to ignore the stalemate separation that lingered between my parents during these, my undergraduate college summer months and school years.

Over weekends, I tried to spend equal time with both of my parents. If Mom talked about Dad, I cut the conversation short and moved onto something else. It was easier with Dad; he rarely if ever talked about Mom.

* * *

One day, during my day of stacking pallets in the third-floor warehouse, I noticed rows of boxes with an unfamiliar label. On several side panels were printed the word "CANEX" in large black letters. Later, I said to Danny, "I haven't seen that CANEX name before. Where's it from?"

He shrugged. "It's an international trading company Montreal Phono buys through in the Caribbean." He winked. "You know, every middleman wants their pound of profit or skin off the banana." He said nothing more.

I recalled my dad had told me, "I make it or break it in this business based on how well I purchase goods overseas." Maybe a company like CANEX was his way of getting merchandise more cheaply. I gave it no further thought.

While we finished loading the last 45-footer within a day of month's end, Dad was there for the finale—complete with boss-employee fireworks.

In front of the crew, Danny said to my father, "Mr. Simkovits, we'll need one more truck for these few things we have left." He pointed to a couple of six-foot-high cooling fans, a bunch of odd-sized boxes of merchandise, and random things that he salvaged from the building—things that hadn't been bolted to a wall or floor.

Dad raised his voice. "Son of a bitch, Danny, no we don't. I'm not paying for another truck."

Danny added calmly, "I don't think we can do it, Mr. S. This truck is full and we'll need a 25-footer for the rest."

Wearing his summer uniform of a white, short-sleeved shirt, tie, and suit pants, my father turned toward the truck driver. Dad motioned to him, then the trailer, then the remaining stuff on the ground behind the truck. "Hey, driver! Open this trailer door," he said. "I want to find room for this crap."

The driver nodded and immediately complied. The rest of us stood weary, sweaty, and speechless. We offered a wide birth to both the trailer doors and my father.

With the doors open, my father spent a few seconds looking into the bowels of the truck. He ordered, "Danny, get up there with one of your guys."

Danny gestured to one guy. They jumped onto the narrow ledge in the back of the truck. They held onto odd-shaped boxes piled to the truck's ceiling.

My dad pointed to what he wanted the two men to do. "Move this box there, and that one here, and this other shit up there." Pointing to another guy and me, my father spoke brusquely. "What are you people waiting for, a special invitation? Lift these things from down here and put them into the back of the truck."

Like unquestioning privates following a captain's orders, we grabbed the things on the ground and followed instructions.

"Son of a bitch! Push that over as far as you can," Dad said to Danny. He shouted with a half-chuckle yet stern face. "*Vut?!* You screwed your old lady too much last night and now have no energy left?"

In less than ten minutes, the stuff that had been on the ground was now in the truck. Dad then looked up at Danny and joked, "Now get yourself and your guy out of there, or we'll ship you too with that baloney."

I was amazed by my father's coarse sugar. He could be very tough on people, but he was often right. Thank goodness he rarely held a grudge.

"Happy to get out of here, Mr. S.," Danny said with a half-smile. He and the other guy put a hand down on the trailer's floor and jumped to the ground.

Dad looked at the taller Danny once more. With eyes still on fire, he wagged a finger at his shipping foreman. "And don't tell me again what we can't do. Each of these truck shipments costs me $500. Fuck if I'm going to feed the trucking company." He didn't say it, but I was sure he was thinking, "And have all of you twiddling your *yaytsa* while we wait for another truck to get here."

"Yes, sir," Danny said, his back straight and his eyes looking straight front. He held himself back from making a salute.

I stood there motionless and speechless. In my mind, I had been on Danny's side, but my father proved us wrong. God forbid if I had attracted a similar outburst from my dad in front of these men.

That altercation was our biggest upset during our weeks of merchandise moving. As far as I knew, no merchandise had disappeared. Nobody had gotten into an accident with a pallet truck, moving conveyor, or dropped box. No one had slacked off or not shown up. The move had gone smoothly, just about perfectly, and I had nothing to report back to my father. In those final moments of the move, perhaps Dad needed something to yell about to make sure everyone remembered who was the boss.

Danny and one of the other crew members filled their two cars with the rest of the men. They followed the packed truck to the new factory.

Dirty, damp, and dusty, I hopped into Dad's red Mercedes 450SLC coupe, a sporty two-door with four seats. (He had traded in his 350SL for the larger model.)

My shirt felt like a wet nap towelette, and it stuck to the car's leather seat. Except for an open ashtray full of cigarette butts and ash, and the sweat stains I was leaving on the leather of the passenger seat, the car's interior was immaculate

Dad turned on the AC full blast. He put the car in gear and followed a distance behind the others. He didn't say any goodbyes to the place where he had worked the last eleven years. He focused on getting to his new factory to check on things before the day was over.

I glanced at the old factory building as we turned the corner onto an adjacent street. Before Dad sent my brother and me to boarding school, he had brought us to his office here many Saturday mornings—when Mom wanted a break so that she could do her hair and nails.

Having been ten to twelve years old, my brother and I had had a bit of fun while we waited for Dad to complete his business. We played on Helen's manual typewriter until the ribbon and keys became stuck. We rearranged pens in the staff's pen holders after playing umpteen games of hangman or tic-tac-toe on cut-up stationery. We sharpened the pencils in those holders, some of them down to nothing but nibs. We took brooms to the floors, pushing dirt around and sweeping dust into the air. We moved things around in and on people's desks, leaving those places a bit messier than before we had put our paws on them.

Dad shouted at us if we started pushing each other, but his yell kept us in line only for a few minutes before we'd be at our mischief again. He was too busy on the phone or with other people and projects to keep his eyes on us continuously.

As my father drove alongside his old place of business this final time, his eyes stayed forward. I surreptitiously waved to the old place. I was going to miss that dull, dingy building that held many memories. I smiled inside as I looked toward those ghosts of manufacturing past while Dad stayed focused on what was in front of him.

After the building had disappeared behind us, Dad said, "Let that be a lesson to you, son. People can get lazy unless you are there to make them work. You need to watch that they don't take shortcuts because it can cost you money."

"Okay, Dad," I said timidly. "I guess we were tired." I hoped he'd say that we had otherwise done a good job. He didn't.

"*Lassen* to me, son. I've been around longer than you; I know how workers can be. You have to be better than the rest and think the right way."

"Okay, Dad. But we were tired," I repeated.

Dad pointed. "There is a difference between tiredness and laziness. If you are tired, you rest. When you are lazy, you get less accomplished, and people can take advantage of you, or they can waste your time and money."

I felt quivers in my sides as cold air blasted from the air conditioner and chilled my sticky perspiration. I didn't dare change the AC's setting while Dad was in lecture mode. Weary and sweaty, I simply replied, "Okay, Dad," and turned my head away from him and looked outside.

Dad pulled out a cigarette and lit it with the car lighter. He cracked open his window to suck out the building fumes. He tilted his head toward me. "Harvy, I'm soon going to be making plans for the winter." A fatherly quietness came to his voice. "Want to come with me to Cayman when you are off from college for your Christmas holidays?" He paused then added, "Grand Cayman is a beautiful place, an up and coming tourist spot."

After he had left my mother, my father had taken several winter and spring vacations to the Cayman Islands with his accountant and other friends. I didn't know if his mistress went along.

I needed a moment to think about his invitation. "What's to do there?" I asked.

"The beach is white silky sand, and there are lots of big hotels and casinos. The capital, George Town, is very nice, with lots of shopping. There are many beautiful golf courses too."

I hoped he might speak about Cayman's nightlife, and maybe the girl situation too, but he didn't. I hesitated. "Can I think about it? Maybe I can let you know after Labour Day when I go back to school."

"Sure son. I would need to know by the end of September so that I can make reservations."

I thought about my mother. Though I hated her constant grumbling about "I'm helplessly and hopelessly here alone at home," I didn't want to cause her more angst by going off to a Caribbean paradise with my father. I needed to find out her Christmas holiday plans before I could commit to him.

On the other hand, my father was supporting me through college, and I'd possibly need him again for grad school. I didn't want to bite the hand that would eventually buy me my freedom.

This parent separation crap stinks as bad as Dad's cigarette smoke, ash, and butts. No matter how hard I tried to ignore the lingering stink in my family, the smell hung around.

Dad turned onto the highway, keeping a distance from the others. I asked, "What's Steve doing at that time? Did you ask him?"

He stabbed his cigarette into the air. "I want him to come, but he tells me he has to attend to his horse. He'll probably spend the holidays riding and being with his horse friends." I heard a little sharpness in my father's voice. "You know how your brother can be. He does what he wants when he wants."

Though I too tried to stay away from family trips since my parents' separation, Dad figured I'd be more amenable to his advances. I appreciated the invitation but wished I could say no. I needed a good excuse like the one my brother had.

"Okay, Dad; I'll think about it." It was the best answer I could provide.

* * *

In Dad's new factory's warehouse, Danny taught me how to operate a large, electric forklift the company had bought second hand—my father rarely purchased brand new equipment.

So that Danny could have more time to arrange the new stockroom, he asked me to reorganize the piles of merchandise warehoused in the building. In the rush of unloading trucks, pallets of merchandise had been stacked and scattered haphazardly in the building. They now occupied too much warehouse space.

Danny demonstrated each forklift knob and lever. He watched me drive that tall, bright yellow machine for a few minutes. He then put me in charge of it.

That 9-foot high forklift had a small platform on the back on which one stood to maneuver the machine and operate its lift controls. Instead of a horizontal steering wheel, it had a vertical flywheel to crank left or right to turn its rear wheels. I stood on that monster for nearly the whole work day, with my right foot continually on either the electrical juice peddle or the brake.

I spent the next couple of weeks rearranging every carton-filled pallet into neat, high, and tight warehouse rows. I also fed the productions lines with merchandise. I whizzed up and down aisles, took sharp and fast turns around corners, and pressed the button to engage the machine's loud horn, *BEEEEP*, whenever somebody was in my way. I offered them a big smile, and they usually smiled or laughed in return as they stepped (or jumped) aside.

As our Nick did, I commandeered the smaller manual pallet truck to move raw materials or finished goods through tighter spaces. That job provided a bit of amusement as I stood on top of the truck and pushed it like a scooter down the aisles—something I had seen Nick do.

Danny yelled at me a couple of times for driving the forklift too fast. "Whoa, slow down you Slovak-Canadian cowboy." Only once did I accidentally bump into a building support pillar—thank goodness it was at a slow speed, and I only dented but not bent the metal beam.

On another occasion, I damaged a couple of cartons of merchandise, absentmindedly penetrating my forks into a box rather than through the pallet under it. Danny shook his head and said, "Brilliant move, Simkovits."

Thankfully, he said nothing to my father about my mishaps. Dad might have bellowed at me with his signature shout: "I don't know what! I lose my shirt!"

Over the weeks, I became one with that forklift. I knew how much it could safely lift and how fast I could make turns without dropping what I was carrying. During the workday, driving that lift kept my mind off Mom and Dad.

* * *

Several days before my summer college break was over, I was sitting with my father in his newly constructed private office. He sat behind his large cherry wood desk. He asked, "Which day are you flying back to Boston?"

"I have to register for classes by Thursday next week, so I need to go back on Wednesday. I've made my plane reservation."

He looked at me. A soft expression was on his face, and he spoke calmly. "I assume you put your flight on the company credit card."

I nodded.

He pulled out his wallet. "Here's money for the cab ride to the airport." He put a ten dollar bill into my hand, nearly double what I needed.

I nodded again. "Okay. Thanks, Dad," I offered, but I felt a little empty. On the days I had flown to and from Boston during my college years, my father never once took me to or picked me up from the airport.

Dad looked into my eyes. "Harvy, I would still like you to come with me to Cayman." To my surprise, he added, "Earlier this year, I moved my offshore money there from Switzerland. I want to show you the bank where I'm now situated."

It had been three years since Dad had taken me to his bank in Zurich. Now was the first time he mentioned his overseas money since that trip. Though I had yearned for more knowledge of his hidden stash, I didn't want to irritate my father by asking him about it. I had patiently waited for him to raise the issue, if and when he wanted to, and now he had.

I tried not to show my exuberance. Raising an eyebrow slightly, I asked, "Why did you make that change, Dad?"

He thought for a moment, then responded, "The Swiss banks are too expensive. They charge too many fees. They were making money on my money, but I wasn't."

"Okay," I said as my heart beat a little faster. I was pleased that Dad confided in me about his offshore affairs, but I worked to keep my excitement in check. I looked at him and waited to see if he had any more to say.

He obliged. "I did another thing while I was there with my accountant earlier this year." From the time my father started his business in 1953, his company accountant had been a man named Mel Mozer. Dad looked at me and continued. "Mel helped me open a separate offshore corporation in Cayman. It's called CANEX."

I thought for a moment. "I saw that name written on a bunch of boxes we moved here from the old Verdun building."

"That's right, son. CANEX is now a middleman between our company and some of our Asian suppliers. With that offshore corporation, I can move a portion of the company's profit to Cayman. I pay no corporate or personal income tax there."

"How does that work?" I asked calmly.

My father explained how he routed the company's foreign merchandise purchases through that new offshore corporation. CANEX then resold those goods at a higher price to Montreal Phono in Canada. CANEX held the difference in Cayman where there would be no tax on the gain. He smiled. "The merchandise we buy overseas still gets directly shipped here to Montreal; CANEX only handles the paperwork."

"Does Steve know about this?" I asked. My brother was handling the purchasing for the company. He must have seen the CANEX name on purchase orders and shipping paperwork.

Dad responded. "Steve knows that we buy goods through CANEX, but he doesn't know that I own CANEX." He raised a hand. "I told your brother that CANEX is a good trading company that I found in Cayman and that I wanted to use them for our international purchases." He smiled. "This way, my vacation trips to Cayman are also paid for by Montreal Phono." Dad's voice was casual and calm as if he was talking about an ordinary supplier transaction.

"Is this legit?" I blurted.

It was the first time I asked Dad that question. Though I condoned my father's craving for tax-free cash, I was worried that he could get into trouble with the tax authorities.

Dad lit a cigarette and blew the smoke toward the ceiling. "CANEX has separate corporate directors in Cayman." He pulled out a business card that had been tucked away in the middle drawer of his cherry desk. "These people are handling it for me." He showed me the card of a lawyer and law firm located in George Town, Grand Cayman Island. "If you look up CANEX's corporate charter down there, you will see only their names. No one besides them can tie CANEX directly to me."

"So how do you keep control over what that law office does with CANEX?"

Dad smiled. "I signed a separate agreement with them saying they have to follow my instructions regarding CANEX. I keep that contract in my private deposit box at the bank."

I wasn't sure if I'd trust a bunch of lawyers two thousand miles away with my money. I hoped my father knew what he was doing.

My father looked directly at me, the soft expression in his eyes still there. "I'd like you to come to Cayman with me sometime and meet these people, and meet the manager at the bank where I keep my money." Dad pulled out another card from his desk's middle drawer. "This is the bank and bank manager I'm working with."

He showed me the bank manager's card but didn't place it into my hand. The bank was the Cayman branch of the Canadian Regal Bank. I wondered if the big Canadian banks were in on this hidden, offshore money game. I was concerned. "Why are you doing this offshore stuff, Dad?"

He raised his voice a tad. "It's like I told you before, son. I don't trust the Quebec government." His hand rose too. "The French separatists are getting stronger here, and they could take over the province one day, maybe even in the next election. Those socialists could nationalize the province's businesses, just like what happened to me in Czechoslovakia in '48." He made a fist. "I had nothing left in my name except for a shit piece of paper from the communist government. I don't want that to happen to me again here."

His eyes and face projected a surefire business deal. He continued. "Last year, I changed Montreal Phono's business charter from a Quebec corporation to a Canadian one. That might protect us if those bloody separatists get their way, but it still might not be enough."

I looked at my father. He had been forthcoming with me, which I took as a sign of trust. Or was he trying to cajole me into coming to Cayman with him? Either way, I stopped my inquiry there. I didn't want to appear nosy about his money.

Dad smiled again. "Let me know soon if you can come with me this winter. I'd love to show you around the island. I'm planning to invest in property there."

He didn't offer anything more. I knew not to ask him something silly like how much money he had stashed over there. I looked at him but not directly into his eyes. "Okay, Dad. I'll let you know."

Back at MIT, I serendipitously came across a *Boston Globe* article about the Cayman Islands. The article mentioned that the island was becoming a vacation paradise and a fast-growing economy. It went on to say that Cayman was developing into a new and popular tax haven for the rich. Many affluent Americans were skirting income taxes by hiding money in Cayman banks. Some wealthy people were even declaring U.S. non-residency by living there fulltime.

I wondered if my father might leave Canada and move to Cayman. Or might he be carted away in handcuffs by the RCMP (Royal Canadian Mounted Police, like the FBI in the USA) before he would have the chance?

That winter, I didn't go to Grand Cayman with my father. I didn't want to take the chance that he'd bring his girlfriend. I didn't want the third degree from my mother after I got back home. Instead of going on any southern trip with my dad, I told him I wanted to go downhill skiing in the mountains north of Montreal. He accepted my choice, but I hoped he wouldn't hold it against me.

I appreciated that my father filled me in on his offshore bank and lawyer, even though I didn't accept the opportunity to see their crooked faces and shake their slimy hands. I hoped that I knew enough by knowing where Dad kept those important Cayman business cards.

* * * *

26

Fatherly Favours

Auto Incentive

Back in the fall of 1970, during my brother's last year in high school, Dad bought a second-hand Mercedes 280SL sports coupe. That two-seater had a removable soft top for summer driving and a separate detachable hard top for winter. Dad told me, "The car cost me only $7,000, less than half the price of a new one."

I received my driver's licence the following spring and Dad permitted me to drive that spiffy green roadster. Sitting next to me in that fiery thing, he cautioned, "Be careful on the accelerator, it's very sensitive." He pointed to the gear shift. "It's also a semi-automatic. You have to start in third gear and then shift the stick to fourth when you hit 45 miles per hour."

That six-cylinder spitfire was fun to drive. Its small size, fast pickup, and quick passing led me to name the car "Dad's Little Green Machine."

My father soon revealed his true purpose for buying the car. He enticed my brother. "I'll give you the Mercedes to take with you to college if you make it into engineering school."

Though my brother put much effort into his high school work, his grades had been mostly Bs and Cs. He did manage to get his grades up enough in his junior year to get into an engineering program at Queen's University in Ontario.

It didn't hurt my brother's cause that my father handed out bottles of spirits to each of our schoolmasters at the end of each school year. Dad offered that gift privately to each master, with a bottle or two pulled out discretely from the trunk of his car at their on-campus residences. He even donated a whole radio broadcasting system, dubbed "Radio BCS," so that students could broadcast BCS news and popular music from the main school building into the lounges of the school's residential houses.

Who knows whether those gifts, along with a big Johnny Simkovits smile and a "Thank you so much for your efforts in teaching my children," might have garnished glowing college references not only for my brother but also—a year later—for me too.

Dad's "Little Green Machine" that became my brother's when he turned 18, just before entering college. Summer 1971.

When Steve received that Mercedes sports car, I was both envious and peeved that our dad was bribing my brother. I said to myself that such a fatherly enticement wouldn't be necessary for me to get into college. I wanted to show Dad that I was respectful of his money.

Dedication to my high school studies got me top grades in science, math, and geography. I received a high SAT score in math. MIT admitted me into its class of 1976. Queen's University also accepted me, but I took MIT's offer because I didn't want to disappoint my father.

I acquiesced to my dad's encouragements to see me enter what he saw as "The best engineering school in the world." I didn't demand an auto incentive from him. Instead, I said, "Dad, I'll be living in Cambridge, right next to Boston, so I really won't need a car. And there are discount student-rate tickets available through the airlines. I can fly home for the holidays for only $72 U.S. round trip, with student tickets as low as $48."

Dad said, "Okay, son," and he smiled.

* * *

Playboy Clubbing

Three-and-a-half years later, during my senior year at MIT, and six months after his factory's summer move to his St. Laurent building, I visited Dad in his new facility. It was just before his factory's Christmas shutdown. He looked at me with anticipation. "Son, please come into my back office. I want to show you something."

I followed closely behind as we walked into his private world. Next to his large cherry wood desk was an alcohol cabinet filled with his favorite libations. Dad reserved those drinks for lifting spirits after signing a big customer order or when celebrating the end of a workday with an important supplier or business friend. Dad had never asked me to share a drink with him in his private office. Having turned 21 recently, I wondered if today might be the day.

Instead of going to his alcohol cabinet, he went into the middle drawer of his desk. With a big grin on his face, he pulled out and handed me two plastic cards, one green and grey and the other black as onyx. The first was an American Express credit card. The second was a Playboy Club Keycard, embossed with that club's distinctive bunny logo. Both cards had my name stamped on them in shiny silver letters.

He offered, "Here, son, use this when you go out with your special friends. The charges will be billed automatically to the company."

My father had taken me for a couple of late evenings to Montreal's Playboy Club. There I enjoyed the sweet Yellow Bird and Bahamas Mama libations, served in tall, tapered, powder-black mugs that had a raised Playboy bunny logo on its side.

At the Bunny Club, I admired the good-looking, solo women singers dressed in long, shiny, sequined-dresses. They gyrated on a small black stage, lights flashing over their heads. A tuxedoed, three-piece band led them to musical highs.

That place was buzzing with sexy women servers. They sported tall, black, high-heeled shoes. Black nylon stockings went from their feet to their crotch and the hip bones of the outside of their legs. Jet black, tight, one-piece outfits were fitted snugly to their bodies from their crotch to the breasts. A fluffy white tail accented their buttocks. Looking at those buff and bouncy bunnies made my young body burn with excitement. I wanted to reach out and touch, but I held myself back.

Other than exposed skin from the top half of those women's breasts to their heads, these sexy women wore a wide, white collar accentuated with a black bow tie around their necks. Wrapped around the wrists of their bare, long arms were another set of white collars, attached with large cufflinks that displayed the Playboy bunny logo. Atop their heads were tall, pink and white bunny ears that stood straight up. Though those Playboy women were very stimulating, I wasn't sure I was capable of the bunny chasing in which my father seemed to revel.

"Wow! Thanks, Dad," I yelped as I stared at my father's gifts of plastic, responding the only way I knew. My mouth salivated as I stretched out my hand to receive his inducement, yet my throat felt a little dry from the enticement. I hoped to make him proud of the way I handled his perk.

My father pointed to my new American Express card. "You see that number 'Member since '76'? In twenty years, the date will mean something."

Dad had once shown me his AMX card. He had said, "You see here, I've been a member since '60. It took me seven years of working in business before my credit was good enough to get this card."

He placed the new cards into my outstretched hand. "You're lucky to get this American Express card now and have an opportunity to build a good credit history."

"Okay, Dad." I smiled. "Sounds great!"

He provided another instruction. "Be careful with these cards. Don't lose them or go crazy with them."

"I'll be very careful in how I use them," I said respectfully. I tucked the cards into my wallet. I felt a little taller.

I figured Dad's gifts were a reward to me for having been a nearly straight-A student throughout my college years. I had earned a Tau Beta Pi membership for being in the top ten percent of my MIT junior class. I was expecting a repeat performance in my senior year.

During my college days, Boston had had a bunny club near the Park Plaza Hotel. Because Dad was big on taking his business colleagues and friends out on the town, I took a few of my MIT dorm buddies out for Saturday night bunny-watching. I never saw my friends throw on jackets and ties as quickly as when I asked, "Hey, you guys want to go to The Club tonight?"

It was amusing to watch us geeks try to act like sophisticated socialites, tripping over our words and giggling like girls when we ordered drinks from a bunny. We sipped our tall libations and perused the lean ladies in their skimpy outfits. No one made any close connections—we green college guys were too intimidated.

Every classmate brought back one of those sleek, black metallic coated, sexy Playboy glass mugs as a souvenir. I happily charged our escapades to my father's company—just as he paid for his outings with his Montreal colleagues. A part of me wanted to be like him.

When I came home for a long weekend break the following spring, I visited my father again in his factory office. After saying a curt hello, Dad grabbed a document from his desk and thrust it into my hand. It was a copy of the company's monthly American Express bill.

His tone was gruff. "What are you doing in that place? I don't mind you going there from time to time, but don't go crazy!" He never before had gotten mad at me for my spending.

Circled on the statement were my "entertainment charges." My amounts were small, totaling perhaps $250, compared to the thousands I could tell that Dad had put through his card that month. Though I was shocked that he questioned me, I didn't say, "But you never gave me any limit." Instead, I said, "Okay, Dad, I'm sorry. I'll be more careful."

From then on, I kept my extracurricular college spending to less than $100 per month, a number I thought my father could accept. I never again received a credit card scolding from him.

* * *

Precious Patek

In May of 1976, at twenty-one years old, I became the only other one in my father's family lineage, besides Dad, to graduate with a university degree. (Though Dad had told me he had received a Master's in Electronics, I didn't yet know it was just a Master Electrician diploma and not a university degree.) I was also the second one in my mother's family to earn a degree. My cousin Ivan, 23 years my elder, had graduated from Charles University in Prague with a medical degree.

A big, proud smile was on my father's face when I approached him after my diploma walk. After four years of electrical engineering studies, relief was on my face for the marketable parchment in my pocket. That pass to independence, and obtaining my MIT master's degree starting in the fall, would allow me to go out into the work world and not have to endure my father's refrain, "Just *lassen* to me, son. I have more experience than you."

I decided to pursue my master's because, considering my summer studies, I had accumulated enough graduate credits to obtain my second degree within a year. I also needed to complete a master's thesis.

I felt I would be even more marketable with a graduate degree, and I wanted to reach what I had seen as my father's level of achievement. Though I had little idea of what type of electrical engineering work I wanted to do, I hoped my career strategy would pay off, especially in impressing my father.

A week after my graduation, I was again working a summer job in Montreal Phono's electronics department. I still felt bad for my brother being within hailing and shouting reach of Dad during every work day, but that was his choice.

One day, after my Montreal Phono work shift was over, I was with Dad again in his private office. I was wearing my dusty rumpled jeans and a t-shirt while he had on a summer suit and tie. He smiled, looked at me intently, and said, "Harvy, I have a *beeeg* surprise for you."

He reached into his suit pocket and retrieved a small-faced watch. It was gold with a black leather strap. He handed it to me. "Here, I'm giving you this for your graduation from MIT." My eyes opened wide as I accepted the timepiece and took in its simple elegance.

Dad grinned. "It's a Patek Philippe. I got it in Geneva, Switzerland a few years ago. I have been saving it for your graduation." He pointed to it. "Have a close look That Swiss company has been making watches for 150 years. This one is very special; it's one of the thinnest watches in the world."

The Patek's black alligator leather strap complemented its round and sleek 18kt gold body and ivory face. I later read that an extremely accurate wind-up spring movement propelled its razor-thin hands. It came in a navy blue velvet case. A certificate of authenticity showed its reference and movement numbers and attested to the watch's 18 embedded jewels.

Before Dad bestowed the watch upon me, that ultra-slim and precise timepiece had spent years tucked away in his office safe, rarely seeing the light of day and the stars at night.

"Wow! Thanks, Dad!" I chirped. I strapped the watch to my wrist and looked it over with pride. I felt as if Dad had catapulted me to the position of the chosen prince to a ruling king. As my father's youngest, it felt especially sweet.

"That watch is worth $5,000 U.S.," Dad said with gusto. "Please keep it safe. I don't want you to lose it."

Mindful of Dad's capacity for anger, I didn't want to provoke it by being careless with his gift. Three years earlier, I accidentally damaged my brother's Mercedes car door on a concrete post right outside Dad's plant. (I had foolishly backed up the car with its door wide open.) Dad later saw what I had done. His face turned red, his arm shook at me, and he repeatedly yelled, "God damn it, Harvy! How could you be so irresponsible?" It felt as if his scream could be heard around the world.

Stunned by my father's fury that day, I drove home with watery eyes and emptiness in my stomach—as if Dad had said he was going to disown me.

To my surprise, when my father arrived home that evening, he acted as if nothing serious had happened. He handed me a business card from a body shop and calmly told me to take the car there the next day for repairs. Pointing his index finger to my head, he added, *"Tink* next time son before you do something *stupeed* like *dat."*

I never forgot my father's short fuse and its lasting effects in my shuddering spine. Though Dad could calm down as quickly as he could blow up, I worked to avoid his lightning bolt anger. I kept my distance from his blast zone when anyone else incurred it.

I looked again at my new Patek. "Yes, Dad, I'll take care of it and wear it only on special occasions."

I felt as if I was binding myself with a solemn oath to a ruling sovereign. I imagined, to Dad, the Patek was an important symbol of professional and financial success. It was a unique, luxurious item, only for those who wanted to display a certain air in their social circle.

I was grateful for the timepiece. That evening at home, I again examined it and its Certificate of Authenticity. I put it on my wrist but felt a little uneasy wearing it. Though I was good with scientific concepts and formulas, I broke out in a sweat whenever I asked out a woman, and I couldn't hold my own with hard-drinking men.

Unlike my father, I shunned the limelight and didn't enjoy wearing fancy things, though I did dress in a suit and tie for Dad's birthday parties and special holiday events. Holey jeans, rumpled shirts, worn sneakers, and the occasional shower were sufficient in my MIT classroom and lab world. It was hard to trust anyone in my environs who wore a suit, showy jewellery, or flowery aftershave.

In accepting my father's gift, I felt I was acknowledging his desire for me to stand out and impress people with what I wore. A part of me aspired to be successful like him, but an inner voice said, *I don't want to be flashy*. As I took the watch off my wrist, I wondered if my father was trying to buy my love.

Dad had enticed my brother into college with the promise of a fancy Mercedes sports car. Dad later bestowed the gift on Steve when my brother became accepted into university.

Although the Patek came my way as a reward for completing college, my father's proclivity for flashy enticements dulled the watch's shine on me. This young engineer might have been more impressed with a multi-function, digital Citizens or Seiko, something that would catch the attention of my classmates.

I wore the Patek a couple of times that summer when my father took me out to a fancy supper at the Troika. A few days before I went back to MIT for grad school, I found a private moment with him in his back office. "Dad, could you possibly keep the Patek in your safe for me?"

I had to be cautious in making my request; I didn't want to disappoint him. I added, "With my going back to school, I won't get a chance to wear the watch much. And I wouldn't want to lose it."

Reading my face for its sincerity, and realizing my request made practical sense, Dad responded, "Okay, son; I'll put it away for you." He took the watch from my hands. "You can ask me for it anytime."

He returned the Patek to its resting place with his other gold watches and jewellery, where it again rarely saw daylight or starlight. Certainly, it was in good company.

Years later, Dad told me that he borrowed my Patek occasionally. He put it on once or twice for his Slovak Businessmen's Association Ball. I was okay with his doing so because I figured, from time to time, a bit of fresh air and exercise was good not only for my watch's longevity but also for my father to show off to his friends.

Every year or two or three, Dad asked me to wear the Patek for special events. I put it on when I went to his Slovak Ball or his big birthday parties. After each event, I asked him to return the Patek to his office safe for safekeeping.

As the years passed, I found that the extravagant watch suited me less and less. In 1990, fourteen years after Dad had given me the elegant timepiece, I wore it for the last time at his 70th birthday party, held at Montreal's highbrow Mt. Stephen's Club. After that, Dad no longer asked me to wear the Patek, and I never asked him again for it.

* * *

Datsun vs. Mercedes

Before I entered MIT graduate school for my master's in electrical engineering, I asked my father to buy me a car. I requested a modest Datsun F10 instead of an expensive Mercedes like my brother's. I told Dad, "Airfares have increased, and there are no more student discounts. I can drive instead of fly home for the holidays."

I spoke as confidently as I could. "The Datsun F10 is a hatchback and has plenty of space for my things when I go back and forth from school." I added the clincher. "Not being fancy, the Datsun won't be stolen off Cambridge streets."

It was now four years since Dad introduced me to his offshore bank stash. Though he knew that I knew, I never said anything about it. I didn't want to show greediness toward his money, onshore or off. I even considered that, if Dad said no to my car request, I'd offer to return the Patek he had given me for my graduation.

Dad must have been impressed with my money practicality. He soon drove me to Boston on a July weekend to buy me the car. Because of a depreciating American dollar that year, the $3600USD vehicle only cost him $3500CAD, half the price of my brother's 280SL sports coupe, and even less than my upcoming $4200USD grad school tuition.

I was proud that the timing of the purchase saved my father some Canadian dollars. He smiled and said, "Enjoy your new present, son, but be careful with it."

"Yes, Dad; I will," I said solemnly.

Some months later, my best high school friend, John, and I were in Montreal for Canadian Thanksgiving weekend (Columbus Day in the USA). Because John had worked at my father's Montreal Phono for a few summers, Dad invited both of us to come to the Troika with him on the Sunday night.

For supper, we devoured veal shanks, drank screwdrivers, and listened to lively Russian music. John told us stories of what it had been like working for Montreal Phono during our summer stints. By midnight, he came out with, "You're one tough cookie, Mr. Simkovits, but you can be a pussycat too."

Dad's eyebrows rose. "How so, John?"

My chum looked my father in the eye. "You can scream at an employee one minute, then laugh with the guy and slap him on the back five minutes later. You remind me of my father."

"Was he a businessman too?" Dad asked.

John volunteered, "When I was a kid, my father ran a Great Lakes grain shipping business out of Winnipeg." He looked directly at my father. "Guys like you can scream bloody murder when you're angry, but then be like kittens when calmed down."

My dad held onto his drink, a glitter in his eye. "My screaming—it's not that bad, is it?"

John smiled. "You can scare the shit out of a grizzly bear, Mr. Simkovits."

My father laughed. He then winked and smiled at my friend while I looked on. I admired my compadre because he wasn't afraid of my father.

Dad volunteered. "I once asked a psychiatrist what he thought about me not being able to hold back my anger."

I looked dumbfounded at my father. "You went to see a psychiatrist?"

He looked right back at me and pointed to the restaurant's bar area. "No, son; I met the guy here at the Troika." He dropped his hand. "After a couple of drinks, we got friendly. I told him that I sometimes couldn't hold myself back from exploding. I asked him what he thought."

I was awestruck that my father would share his MO with a helping professional. "What did the guy say to you?"

Dad's voice was sincere. "He told me that it's better to get the anger out of me than to hold it inside." He smirked as he raised his glass. "So that's been my policy ever since."

I don't remember how much John and I had to drink that night, but he and I certainly felt no pain as we exited the restaurant. As we walked to the parking lot, Dad said, "Boys, be careful driving home."

"Yes, Mr. Simkovits" and "Yes, Dad" came easily out of our mouths.

John and I didn't heed my father's warning. Rather than get directly on the highway, we drove through the quiet back streets of a residential section of

Montreal. My chum was in his Ford Pinto—the car model that consumer groups later accused of having an exploding gas tank in rear collisions—and I was in my Datsun.

Pretty soon, we were racing through the streets. John passed me at a red light, going right through. I chased him down the street, shifting gears as quickly as I could. We both went through other red lights, slowing down enough to determine whether a car was crossing the other way. There were virtually no vehicles on the streets that late Sunday night.

Trying to get past John at another light, I turned left suddenly to take a quicker path toward the highway. John had the same idea, turning just in front of me. He crashed his front bumper square into the passenger door of my car.

We stopped immediately and got out of our cars to assess the damage. The corner of John's front bumper was bent. Dents and scratches were surrounding his headlight. His front end had caved in my passenger door. We looked at each other. "We better stop this foolishness," I said.

"Yah, I think so." He looked again at the damage. "Let's call it even; you fix your dent, and I'll take care of my damage."

I looked at our damage again and then him. "That's acceptable."

We said goodnight and got back into our cars. We drove soberly to our respective homes.

The next afternoon, when I got back to Boston, I went straight to my car dealer and got the damage assessed. "$387 to repair the door dent," the estimator said.

I called my insurance company the next day. Not knowing the ins and outs of the Mass insurance system, I told the agent, "Somebody hit my car while I parked in Cambridge; I don't know who did it." Because people in Boston and Cambridge parked their cars in either direction on both sides of the street, I felt my fib was believable. I felt no qualms in saying what my father might say.

"Did you file a police report?" the agent asked.

"No. The accident happened over the holidays, while I was away in Canada." It was a plausible alibi for a Cambridge student.

My car got repaired, and the insurance company sent me a cheque for $137, the $387 less my $250 deductible. I paid the $250 myself and said nothing to my father. He would have given me the third degree on what had happened and an earful of shouting for racing down city streets.

A couple of months later, I received an insurance renewal letter. The invoice was for $1800 to cover the car for the next twelve months. That was three times my original policy premium. I was stunned.

I called my agent again. He looked at my file. "Two things are going on here." He spoke matter-of-factly. "First, because of your accident, they have categorized you an unsafe driver."

But my accident only cost them $137!

"Second, the insurance company has reclassified your car as a Datsun 280Z."

"But that's an expensive sports car," I blurted.

"I know," he said, "but your F10 is a new model, and it hasn't made it into their system quite yet."

My voice rose. "But last year I paid one-third the rate the insurance company wants now."

The agent stayed calm. "Last year they classified your F10 as a B210, a comparable car. Because there's no F10 in their system right now, you're at their mercy."

"What if I switch insurance companies?"

"With your accident, and being under 25, other companies won't want to touch you."

"Son-of-a-B!" I said, holding myself back from raising my voice as my father might. I took a long breath. "What can I do?"

He responded calmly. "You can write a letter to the insurance company to explain that your car is not the 280Z but more like the B210."

"Will I still be insured going forward?"

"Yes, until you get an official termination letter from the company. With your letter, they can't terminate you until they investigate and come forward with a ruling."

It took over six months of back and forth letters before my insurer came back with a decision. When I received the new bill, it said: "$1200 for the year, payable within 30 days or your policy will terminate." Though I had won my appeal, I was still dumbfounded at the premium, a third of the original cost of my car.

I called my agent once more. He repeated, "It's their prerogative. You're still considered high risk." Neither of us mentioned it, but I shouldn't have made that accident claim.

I hung up and thought about it overnight. *What would Dad do?*

The next day I called my father. "Dad, my car insurance company wants a fortune to reinsure my Datsun for the next year. I've tried to argue with them through letters, but it seems to be no use. I'd like to bring my car to Quebec and have it insured there."

The following week, I drove to Canada and reregistered and reinsured my car in Quebec for a mere $450CAD. With my new Quebec plates, I returned to Boston. I then sent a termination letter to my U.S. insurer.

In a few weeks, I received a notice of insurance termination and a bill for $1000, payable immediately, for the months my car had been insured. Wanting to be fair, I sent the insurer another letter, explaining. "If your company had rated me correctly, I would have cancelled the policy from the beginning." I offered them $600 to settle the bill, the same amount I had paid the previous year.

Some weeks later, I got another notice. They were sending my bill to a collection agency.

By now I had graduated with my master's degree. I headed back to Montreal. I figured the U.S. insurance company wouldn't chase me in Canada.

Weeks later I got another letter at home from the collection agency. *How did they get my address in Canada?* The agency threatened legal action and asset seizure if I didn't pay them the $1000 within 15 days.

Damn! The situation was getting beyond my capacity.

The next day, I sucked in my gut and took the collection letter to my father. I explained to him what happened, but I focused on my car's misclassification and left out the part about my accident the previous fall.

Dad called his lawyer, Mack, and sent me down to see him. I told Mack the whole story, including the part about my accident, and my offer to pay the insurer $600USD to settle.

"Leave this with me, Harvy," he said. "I'll send them a letter."

Mack's letter offered that the insurer had made mistakes and I shouldn't be held responsible for their errors. After that, I didn't receive any more collection letters.

I later asked Mack what he thought had happened. He said, "When the collection company saw that you had legal representation, they probably figured it wasn't worth pursuing a cross-border action against you."

I was grateful that my father had better ammunition than I had had regarding my dispute. Some time later, I went back to Dad. "It seems that Mack's letter did the trick with my insurance company. By the way, do I owe Montreal Phono anything for Mack's time?"

Dad was contrite. "We pay Mack a retainer. He doesn't charge extra for such letters; it's part of his service."

I smiled. "I appreciate what you and Mack did for me."

He winked at me. "No problem son. Glad I could be of help."

Though I felt embarrassed by the whole affair and wished I could have taken care of the situation by myself, it paid to have a businessman father and his savvy lawyer to lean on.

* * *

Hungarian Car Fixing

One morning in the office, Dad exclaimed, "That fucking 280SL is sucking money for nothing!"

It had been seven years since Dad bought the Mercedes 280SL and given it to Steve. Because of Canada's heavily road-salted winters, the car's body had rusted in several places. When Dad bought the car second hand for $7000, it had had 30,000 miles. It now had 80,000 miles, and Dad had spent $1500 on two rust-removal jobs.

He spoke gruffly, "In another year, more rust could form on the car and its value would depreciate greatly, or I'd have to spend more money on bodywork. It's time we sell the damn thing."

I had recently graduated with my MIT masters. I was working for Montreal Phono again for a short summer stint. My father hired me to be the company's "gopher." I drove across the city to "go for" this doohickey and that whatchamacallit, mostly last-minute supplies for production. It wasn't quite the job for an MIT engineering graduate, but I figured this might be my last time I could help Dad and his company.

In the fall, I was to head to an engineering position I had landed with Procter & Gamble, in their Canadian Engineering Division in Hamilton, Ontario. I would finally be at arm's length from both Dad and Mom. I couldn't wait for that distance and to earn a salary independent of my father.

Steve was currently away for a couple of months, on an Outward Bound adventure in the U.S. He was taking a breather from Montreal Phono and maybe from Dad and Mom too.

The good news for me was that I could drive my brother's spiffy wheels while he was gone, leaving my Datsun housed in Mom's garage. Because I enjoyed driving that roadster, I hoped Dad's words about selling the car were only bluster.

One afternoon, while I was hanging around Montreal Phono's front office, a boney-faced, dark-skinned man with black, slick backed, wavy hair ambled through the entryway. I had never met this tall, thin but muscular guy who dressed in work overalls. A young lad was with him. The boy, also dressed in overalls, appeared to be eleven or twelve years old.

Dad greeted them joyfully in Hungarian. I was the only other one in the office who understood what they were saying. I soon realized that the boy was the man's son.

My father looked at me. "Can you please show Mr. Farkas where the 280SL is parked, and give him your keys?"

"Sure, Dad." I looked at the man and then back at Dad. "What's with him and the car?"

"He's going to get it ready for us to sell."

Though I still hoped that Dad wouldn't sell the 280SL, I showed Mr. Farkas where the car was parked. I unlocked it and gave him the keys. He said to me in Hungarian, "Give me thirty to forty minutes and I'll give the keys back to you."

"What are you going to do?" I asked in English.

"Fix the odometer," he responded in my language. He opened the car's driver door and told his son to get in on the passenger side. I said nothing else and went back to see Dad.

I spoke quietly. "Dad, the guy told me he's going to fix the odometer. What's that about?"

Dad spoke again in Hungarian so no one else in the office would understand. "I told him to reset the odometer back to 39,000 miles from the 80,000 that's on it now. This way we can get a better price for the car when we sell it. We'll tell any prospective buyer that you and Steve only drove it during the summer and garaged it in the winter."

"Is that legit?" I asked.

"It's no big deal, son. Everybody does it with these cars."

I was a little taken aback by my father's plan, but I didn't ask more. I knew his ways.

Forty-five minutes later, Dad called me over. "Go see what's taking Mr. Farkas so long, and then come back and tell me."

I walked over to the car. Both the man and his son were lying on their backs on the front-seat floors. Their legs and butts stuck out the respective car doors. "How's it going?" I asked.

"*Kurva basza meg!* [Fuck a whore!]" Mr. Farkas blurted. "Those Mercedes engineers don't make this fixing job easy. I had to take apart the whole key ignition system to get to the odometer."

He pointed to the ignition wires hanging under the dash, and to an open hole in the dashboard where the ignition key housing should be. He continued. "I finally got the bastard odometer fixed, but now I have to put everything back together. It's going to take us a little longer. And I'll have to test every wire to see if it's put back in the right location on the ignition switch."

Seeing the wires hanging under the dash, I blurted out, "*Isten őrizz!* [God forbid!]" For the next second or two, the man and his son glared at me with expressionless faces. They then turned back to their work.

I watched for a couple more minutes while they fiddled with the wires and the ignition switch. The son looked my way a couple of times, his eyes saying, *Get the hell out of here so we can finish our work.* Though we exchanged no words, I got his message and went back to the office.

I told Dad what the guy said and what I saw. He offered, "Okay, son, wait for another 10 to 15 minutes and then go see where they are. If they haven't finished, I'll go out with you."

I went back a second and even a third time without Dad. That final time, the car fixers were finishing. My voice grew terse, "Is everything working properly?"

"Yes," he said in English. "I checked all the key functions; they're okay."

"Can I check?"

"Sure, boy; here is the key. Knock yourself out."

I sat in the car, put the key in the ignition, turned it to position 1 (where the radio turned on), then position 2 (where the dash lights turned on), then position 3 (where the engine started as it should). I looked at the odometer; it read a little over 38,000.

When I looked closely at the odometer, I could see the white lettering on one number looked smudged. "It looks like everything is working," I said cautiously, "but one of these digits looks smeared. That wasn't there before."

The man's voice was calm and confident. "It's nothing. There's a special paint on these Mercedes odometers that never fully dries and can smear if someone plays with the odometer." He waved his hand at me. "But I know how to handle these things. Nobody will ever notice."

I wasn't sure if the guy was giving me a line, but I said nothing. By the time I checked the car functions once more and then locked the vehicle, Mr. Farkas and his son were entering the factory office.

When I got there, I told Dad, "Everything seems to be working properly." My voice strained but stayed quiet. "But a middle odometer digit doesn't look right."

Dad and the man spoke again in Hungarian. Mr. Farkas casually explained what he had told me about the odometer's digit paint. He added, "That digit will simply turn into the background after you drive the car another 100 miles."

The car fixer pointed at me," "Your son seems to be a bit too anxious. He bothered us while we worked." His son glanced my way, his face crinkled into a sneer.

My father smiled and put his hand on the man's shoulder. "Don't worry about it." Dad didn't say anything about me having followed his instructions.

He pulled out his wallet and handed the man a crisp $50 bill. He took another $5 and put it into the boy's hand and added a smile and a pat on the shoulder. He offered in Hungarian, "You are a smart boy to learn the car fixing business from your father."

The boy smiled back and said, "*Köszönöm szépen* [Thank you very much]." He and his father turned and walked out without glancing my way.

After they had left, I turned to Dad. "Those people were rude."

He smiled and put his hand on my shoulder. "Don't worry about it son."

Within a month, Dad sold the 280SL for $7000, exactly what he had originally paid for it, and he pocketed the cash. Before my brother returned home from his American adventure, my father had the company buy a Mercedes 300D diesel demonstrator. He gave it to Steve as a replacement for the 280SL.

It peeved me that I got nothing for my contribution. But I knew I was working toward something bigger, so I said nothing. At least my Datsun was registered in my name. When I'd sell my car, I'd keep the proceeds.

Just *Lassen* to Me!

* * * *

27

Rich Man's Money Games

Maury Reemer was our life insurance agent. He was shorter than Dad but, like him, carried a rotund belly. Maury had a head full of black wavy hair and sported a grey business suit—his fashion not overstating his style. One day, he walked unannounced into the company's front office. He sat in the chair right next to my father's desk, as if he was sitting down at his favorite Friday night watering hole.

My father grinned and hollered, "*Hallooo* Maury!"

Maury stretched out his hand and took my father's. In his slight Yiddish twang, he offered a big "Hey there, Johnny! It's great to see you." He presented his signature Maury smile.

Maury looked around the room, and he nodded and waved to everyone else in the office. He turned back to Dad and began his joke-of-the-week. "You know, Johnny, times have changed since we were kids."

My father nodded and smiled; he knew what was coming.

Maury continued. "Back then our parents told us that we should wash our hands *after* touching our genitals. But today we tell our kids to wash their hands *before* touching themselves."

Dad laughed and lifted his coffee cup to Maury. "I have one for you too."

Knowing that Maury was an observant Jew, my father came out with his latest religious joke. "A priest, rabbi, and minister walked into a bar and sat down at a table." Dad paused for a second then blurted out, "The bartender looked at them and shouted, 'What kind of religious joke is this?'" Dad smiled and chuckled like a kid. Maury laughed too.

I sat across Dad's office and wondered if both of them were scraping the bottom of their joke barrels for those quips.

Maury offered, "You know, Johnny, you live a lot longer if you can joke and laugh." He winked and pointed his finger. "And if you can do that, I want to sell you a life insurance policy."

I liked Maury. To his credit, he was the first and just about only insurance salesman to sell my father life insurance. But those policies hadn't been consummated on Dad's life. Maury suggested that Dad cover my brother's and my lives in a whole life policy while we had been young kids.

During one of my college summer stints at Dad's company, Maury had explained to me how he got my father to agree to the insurance investment. He smiled wide. "I said to your father, 'Those policies will be a continuing source of capital for your kids. When they are out of college, they can borrow from it to buy a new car. Or, when in their thirties, they can use it as a downpayment on their first home. When they retire, it can become a part of their nest egg.'" He raised and pointed a finger. "'And when your kids die, the death benefit will go to your grandchildren as a gift from you.'"

Maury winked as he now pointed his finger at me. "Harvy, I then looked at your father and said, 'When your sons pass away many, many years from now, their wives and children can go on a nice vacation because of you, Johnny.'" Maury's face burst with delight. I laughed too as Maury showed me more of his big, toothy grin. He added, "I got a laugh out of your father on that one too."

I was impressed by how well Maury knew my dad. My father could be amenable if approached the right way.

Maury looked at me again. "When you buy life insurance at an older age, you pay for the years you never owned it. But when you buy it young, most of the money you put into it will be an investment." He raised one hand and looked at me more seriously. "And you are fortunate that you don't smoke like your father. If you did, then you are taking a risk with your life."

Maury frowned like a little kid as he wagged his finger slowly. "The insurance companies frown on risk and will charge you a bigger premium." He shook his head. "But there's no problem for you Harvy. You'll get the best insurance policy rate." Once more, his face shone with glee.

Over the ensuing years, Maury helped my father shelter the profits from the sales of his industrial and apartment buildings by putting the gains into deferred annuities.

I heard Maury explain the annuity deal to my father one day. "Johnny, rather than having your property's proceeds go directly into your hands— where you will immediately pay capital gains taxes—the gains from the sale of your buildings will go into a sheltered annuity."

Maury raised his hand as if he were conducting an orchestra. "You won't be taxed on those profits until you take payments out of the annuity after you turn 65." He eyed my father and said magic words. "Until then, your capital will grow tax-free within your policy. You'll get taxed only when you receive the income after you've retired." He raised a hand. "And the payments you receive will be guaranteed until you turn 80, or continue for as long as you live." Maury grinned. "And I'm sure you'll live a long, long time."

"What if I die sooner than eighty?" Dad asked.

Maury pointed a finger. "Then your estate or beneficiaries will get the remainder of the payments until what would have been your eightieth birthday." Maury's teeth showed through his ear-to-ear smile. He pointed to himself. "I'd be happy to be one of your beneficiaries if you need an extra one." He gazed my way and chuckled. "I don't think your sons will mind."

What Maury said made good sense. I smiled too because I knew his humour. He continued. "And if you live beyond 80 years old, the insurance company will keep paying you." He raised his hand again and pointed a finger at my father. "I know you're going to live at least until 100, so I'm sure my insurance company will lose money on you."

Dad not only returned Maury's grin but he signed on the annuity dotted line every time he disposed of another one of his industrial or apartment buildings. These annuity policies would become a major source of his income after he retired. Steve and I would probably not see anything from those assets unless Dad died before he turned 80.

I had little concern about obtaining nothing from my father's building sales and annuity investments. Dad had bought life insurance policies with growing cash values for my brother and me. I also knew that my father's offshore stash would become mine one day if Dad kept his promise to me.

Let Dad live well in his retirement. I'd be taken care of in other ways, so I thought.

* * *

At the end of another summer day in the late 1970s, Maury again walked into Montreal Phono unannounced. He knew my father was less busy after five o'clock—a good time for an impromptu visit. Or he might have called Helen earlier in the day to find out if Johnny would be there.

Maury once more sat down as if he owned the place. My father was speaking to a supplier on the phone. He motioned to me to take Maury into his private office and keep him company until he finished the call.

Over coffee, Maury started our conversation. "Hey, *bubala*! How are things going for you at school? Are you the big Canadian man on the MIT campus?"

I chuckled. "Not too many of us Canadians there but I guess I'm representing our country well. I'm just about a straight-A student. Both Tau Beta Pi and Sigma Xi have invited me into their honorary societies."

"That's great, Harvy. I see you're learning Greek too," he quipped. "I bet the college girls like that kind of talk."

He leaned toward me and patted my shoulder. "Sometime, you should meet my son. He recently graduated from law school in Ottawa. He speaks Greek as you do." Maury chuckled like a little kid.

Maury didn't let another breath pass. "Harvy, I know you like to ski. In the winter, you should come over to my estate at Avila, right next to St. Sauveur. It's not quite like your father's chalet in Val Morin, but you're welcome to drop in for a little après ski."

He looked at me with big eyes. "I've been on the ski patrol at St. Sauveur for years now." He grinned again. "I can get you a free ride down the mountain if you slip and break an arm or leg."

Once, during a future weekend ski trip, I visited Maury's "estate." His place was a compact *roulette* (mobile home) in a trailer park that was a short walk from the ski lift. As I stepped into his cramped quarters, he said, "Welcome to my humble chalet. Let me give you the nickel tour."

He showed me around, turning what might have been a two-minute outing into a ten-minute presentation. "I had it professionally decorated, you know," he offered. "It's got small bedrooms at each end, and a compact kitchen and living area in the middle. I even have a TV." He pointed to a small television with a rabbit-ear antenna. "My place is not as big and fancy as your father's chalet. But because I'm near the ski hill, for me this is The Taj."

Maury had impressed me with his modest ways and fun attitude. His wealth was small compared to the rich people he served. I trusted him.

Maury and I finished our coffee and still waited for Dad to join us after his phone call. Maury took me through his latest insurance products. Fancy words like "fully-participating," "single-premium," and "whole life" filled our conversation. And, of course, every insurance permutation was topped with maraschino cherry benefits, like "lifetime borrowing rights" or "continually growing cash value" or "tax-free return of premiums." Maury stressed, "The policy is flexible. You stay in control of how you want to use it."

I listened and looked over Maury's documents and spreadsheets. I asked many questions. This money stuff interested me. If I was going to inherit Dad's wealth one day, I might as well learn as much as I could about such things. It seemed as if Dad wanted me to get a free life insurance education while killing time with Maury.

Maury showed me sample printouts of how a single-premium whole life product could grow over my lifetime. He explained, "Harvy, you better get this now while you can." The government knows it's too good. They'll set limits on such things in the future. If you buy it now, you'll be 'grandfathered in.'"

Maury continued confidently. "When you retire at 60," he winked, "that policy's death benefit will be twenty to twenty-five times what you paid for it, and it will continue to grow." He pointed to his printouts. "And, when you reach 100," he smiled, "which I know you'll do because of the way you keep yourself in shape, we'll pay the whole death benefit out to you, no questions asked."

He chuckled again as if he was jolly Santa Claus with me on his knee. "If you would like me as a beneficiary, instead of your future wife and kids, you can add my name to the beneficiary line right here."

I decided to invest two year's salary into Maury's product. I had saved money from the many years of end-of-year bonuses I had received from Montreal Phono. Dad had saved a bundle in corporate income taxes by giving his sons company bonuses rather than college allowances. Dad's accountant at the time, Roger Delliard, had told him, "Corporate cash distributions to your children make sense because your kids are in low tax brackets. Why give money to the government when you can give it to your kids?" I appreciated Roger's advice and Dad's generosity.

My brother had used his bonuses to take multi-month Outward Bound and other trekking trips every couple of years. He had traveled to the western U.S.A., East Africa, and the Middle East. I had kept my bonuses in savings.

I wanted to demonstrate to my father that I was a wise saver and prudent investor of the money he bestowed on me. I didn't want to "piss it away" as my father said of Steve's faraway adventures. My brother may have had more fun in his young adulthood, but I was working toward a bigger benefit: to carry on my father's estate, especially the one offshore.

Throughout my young adulthood, frugality and patience became my mantra with money. I figured time was on my side as I kept one eye on Dad's offshore legacy now situated in blue Caribbean waters. I wasn't going to spend my money indiscriminately to travel the world the way my brother did.

Placing my money into a whole life insurance policy with a safe insurance company was for the benefit of my future. I wanted to impress my father with the way I invested.

Maury's hunch turned out right. Some years later, the Canadian government regulated the use of single-premium policies like the one I had bought. They limited how much cash one could put into them, and they curtailed their benefits.

As Maury had said, I stayed "grandfathered in." Twelve years later, I would borrow from that policy to make a down payment on my first condo, and the policy's cash value and death benefit would continue to grow.

I appreciated that my father allowed me to obtain a useful life insurance education from Maury. I especially thank my father for the bonus money his company gave me as a financial cushion.

Maybe that was Dad's plan all along—both to secure my financial future and to test me as to how I was going to handle his money. I played right along, making the prudent investments I thought my father wanted me to make, and what I thought made sense.

* * * *

28

Founding Fathers & Business Brothers

"That Mic was a real SOB!" my father declared after he had drained his second scotch-on-the-rocks of the evening.

It was a Thursday night in the summer of 1977. I was twenty-two years old. Dad and I sat at his regular table at the Troika. In the background, Polish minstrels Sasha and Vladjec roamed the restaurant playing lively Eastern European melodies. The portly Sasha strummed his acoustic guitar of red and gold while the svelte Vladjec squeezed his hefty piano accordion.

My father chuckled at a song Sasha had just sung. He explained it to me and the others at his table. "The lyrics are about potent Russian eggs—the kind you find between a Cossack's legs." He laughed.

My father slipped Sasha a $20 bill as payment for this round of musical services. The musicians moved on to serenade other patrons, seeking more big tippers in the smoky restaurant haze. They were sure to return to keep my father and his guests singing, smiling, and money slipping.

A high, black metal railing separated the Troika's bar from the dining area. Tonight, customers jammed the bar area waiting for tables in the restaurant. But Dad never had to wait for a table on a Thursday night. Years earlier, he had earned that perk.

On a previous Thursday night at his Troika table, Dad had told me the story of how he had gotten his preferred restaurant seating. Lifting his chest and speaking with bravado, he offered, "I was here at the bar having a good time with some friends."

He took a big breath. "The bartender thought it was too late at night." Dad pointed to himself. "The guy thought I was too drunk to notice what he was doing."

He looked at the palm of his hand on the table. "When I got the bill from him, I asked myself how the tab could have been so high." He pointed to his head with his other hand. "I did a quick mental calculation and realized that my group could never have drunk as many drinks as the bartender was reporting on the bill."

His eyes turned narrow and angry. "I went up to the guy and blasted him for trying to screw me. I screamed at him, 'You think I was born yesterday?'"

Dad took another long breath. His lips became tight and his eyes fiery. "The bartender denied what he had done. He pretended the bill was legit."

My father raised his arm and hand to show me what he was about to tell me. "I picked up a shot glass that was sitting on the bar. I yelled at the guy, 'Don't you ever treat me that way!' Then I threw the glass at the big mirror behind the bar."

My father waved his arms. "The mirror smashed into pieces. I screamed at the bartender that I would never come back to this fucking shyster restaurant. I left the goddamn bill on the table and walked out with my friends."

I sat stunned. *What had my father done?!* Would there be retribution from the restaurant owner for Dad's display? Would the cops be summoned or a lawyer's letter dispatched?

Dad's voice dropped. "The Troika's owner, Ted, called me the next day."

I wondered if Ted was going to have it out with my father for damaging his premises. Dad surprised me again. He offered, "Ted apologized for what

136

the waiter had done and told me he fired the guy. He told me to forget about the bill."

Dad looked at me with a glint in his eye as he took a sip of his vodka. "I give this place a lot of business. I told Ted I was mad at him for allowing that kind of bullshit to happen in his restaurant. I didn't go back there for months."

Dad once showed me a cancelled Montreal Phono cheque from January 1976, after his company had paid for a Christmas party at the Troika. He told me, "I kept the cheque as a souvenir, in case I have to remind Ted of the business I've given him." I nearly gagged as I looked at the amount written on the slip. It had been more than half my MIT tuition that year.

My father took a deep breath as he continued the story. "Three months after that incident with the bartender, Ted called me again. He told me that the Troika wasn't the same without me. He said I should come down with my usual gang for a night on the house."

His voice rose again as he pointed away from himself. "I told him, 'Ted, I'll do it but only on one condition." He took a long breath. "Every Thursday night, I want that big table in the back to be mine. If I'm not there by seven o'clock, then you could give it away.'"

My father grinned and then knocked back a swig of his drink. "Ted agreed, and I've been back here with my friends ever since."

I smiled too as I took in my father's moxie. His prized Troika spot was located in the back of the restaurant, on a pedestal one step up from the main floor level. From there Dad could be seated above the rest, get a great view of the whole place, and see who was walking in the front door.

I continued to chew on a tasty rib from my rack of lamb as Sasha played in the background. Dad offered, "The best meat is around the bone."

His statement permitted me to eat each delicate rib with my fingers. I relished every sweet and succulent bite. My father's osso buco sat half devoured in front of him. He loved digging out the bone marrow and spreading it like sweet butter on French bread. With a sprinkle of salt, that marrow became his Russian caviar.

I had accompanied my father to his beloved hangout only a handful of times. Now home from completing my Masters in Electrical Engineering and

Computer Science at MIT, I was again invited to join Dad's Thursday night revelry. Maybe he wanted to show off his recent college graduate and have me once more experience his manly world of good food, libations, and fun.

Within weeks, I was to leave Montreal for an entry-level engineering job with Procter & Gamble in Hamilton, Ontario. I was proud of my starting annual salary of $17,000—comparable to the five years of undergraduate college tuition Dad had paid for me.

Maybe my father wanted me with him this night to experience what I would miss when I left lively Montreal for lackluster Hamilton. In Hamilton, the bars and restaurants closed at 1:00 in the morning. "Here at the Troika," my father winked, "if enough people are having a good time past 2:30 a.m., the manager pulls the front curtains, locks the big main doors, and pretends the place has closed for the night."

My father sat at the head of the table, which offered him the best view of the restaurant. Behind him, on the burgundy velvet wallpapered wall, hung an oil painting. It captured a Russian troika—a sleigh drawn by a set of three handsome horses—plowing through the snow. Sasha had painted it. The jovial faces of the people sitting in the sleigh matched the revelry in the restaurant.

I sat to my father's immediate right, the rest of the dining room to my back. A strategically placed floor-to-ceiling mirror on the wall in front of me let me watch Sasha and Vladjec walk and sing between tables of smiling and laughing gourmands.

Across from me, to my father's left, were Dad's business colleagues, Aras and Hans. Aras usually had the coveted spot right next to my father. Past him sat Hans. At the far end of the table sat Mack, both my father's and Hans' corporate attorney. Hans and Mack rarely said no to a Johnny Simkovits's invitation for drinks, supper, song, and to celebrate the near end of another business week with their good friend.

Earlier, Aras had mentioned, "The party doesn't get started until Johnny Simkovits arrives." Looking my way, Hans added, "Yep! Some evenings your father not only opens the place but also closes it."

"The crowd here is the liveliest on Thursdays," Dad offered. "Many fellows come here to be with their friends or to find new ones," he added with a wink. "Some down the booze and shoot the shit until they can't stand anymore. Others come to fish for a new catch." He smiled and winked again.

Few men permitted their wives to enter into this late-night world.

Speaking of wives, Dad had returned home to my mother during my senior year of college. Mom was happy to have Dad back, though I was amazed that they had reconciled. Both Dad and Mom had told me their versions of what had happened the previous summer.

* * *

In a quiet moment in my father's private office soon after he had come back to Mom, he told me, "I declined a marriage proposal from the woman I had seen these last few years."

He took in a long breath and shook his head. "That woman turned out to be one screwy broad. Early one Saturday morning, up north at my chalet, the bitch barged in on me. We had already broken up, but I had not gotten my key back from her."

The muscles in my father's face strained. "She soon realized that your uncle Edo and I had been sleeping in the king bed in the master bedroom."

Dad explained. "When we were kids, Edo and I had occasionally slept in the same bed. Now we sometimes sleep in that big bed in my place when we have no other guest; that way, we don't dirty the other bedrooms."

I understood. As kids, Steve and I had occasionally slept in the same motel bed when our family stopped overnight during our holiday car trips to Florida. It never felt odd or out of place.

My father shook his head again. "I had told her that I wasn't interested in getting married. But when she saw that your uncle and I were together in the same room, she started screaming." His voice rose. "She called us 'filthy homosexuals.' She said that's the real reason why I didn't want to get hitched to her."

Dad's voice became edgy. "Then she took whatever few things she had left at my chalet and ran out of the house, still screaming bloody murder at us like a goddamn crazy whore." Dad paused for a second, looked away and then returned his gaze to me. "What a screwy bitch! I'm glad I said no to her."

I listened and nodded, showing little reaction. I wondered why my father was telling me about his dramas with other women. Had his mistress's tirade been Dad's way to justify his return to Mom?

Mom later told me her version of Dad's reentry into her life.

"After he finished with that other woman," she offered, "out of the blue your father started calling me." She sighed. "He said he wanted to come back home."

She took a long breath and added, "Your father sent me roses and talked to me nicely for the first time in years. He promised me that he would stay faithful to me and not fool around again."

The thought of Mom and Dad getting back together made a vein pulse in my head. Why my father would go back to a wife he had left twice was a mystery to me. And why my mother would take her husband back after his infidelities was an even bigger puzzle.

Mom looked at me, "Your father always comes back to me after he gets the other woman out of his system. He knows that no one else would take care of him the way I do."

On the other hand, while Dad had still been with that other woman, Mom started divorce proceedings—or maybe it was divorce noises—against her husband. In Quebec, marriage was common law, which gave my mother leverage. Her verbal threats to freeze and seize Dad's personal properties may have caused him to nudge himself back into her life.

Mom added, "Before he stepped back into the house, I signed an agreement your father wrote. It said he wanted the freedom to entertain his business colleagues without my nagging him about getting home late at night." She looked relieved. "I signed that paper so that your father would come back to me."

I prayed that Mom would be right about taking Dad back. I hoped everything would become okay between them. I suspected that no other woman would cook, clean, and iron for him, and serve him hand and foot the way she did. She even brewed hot tea for him whenever he came home tired— or loaded—after a late night. I prayed he no longer wanted other women and was ready to settle down completely with my mother.

I was glad I had been away in college when my father had had his altercation with his mistress and then reconciliation with my mother. At MIT, I had worked to keep my nose on my engineering lectures, problem sets, and my bachelor and master's theses. If Dad decided to leave Mom again, perhaps I'd be long gone from home by then.

* * *

Sitting with my father and his colleagues this Thursday night at the Troika, I tried to ignore my discomfort about Mom sitting home alone while we men were out on the town. Had Dad not been away on business so often during their marriage, Mom might have welcomed a free night without him, but I knew that she yearned to see more of her husband.

Because Dad had paid for my five years at college, thus making it possible for me to earn two engineering degrees, I felt I owed him my time this evening. I also found the great fare, stimulating stories, and lively melodies at the Troika as intoxicating as the strong rum and Coke in my hand.

My brother didn't participate in such fatherly amusements. Though he worked for our father's company by day, his notion of evening fun was to ride and tend to his horse in Hudson, Montreal's off-island horse community. There he could muck out the horse stable and meet with his horsey friends.

I felt distinguished to be dressed in a suit, out on the town with Dad and his gang, and wearing my Patek timepiece. (Dad had retrieved the watch from his safe for me.) My only regret was that I would have to prepare myself for Mom's interrogation at breakfast tomorrow morning. She'd want to know who had been at tonight's gathering and what we discussed.

I glanced over at Mack who sat to my right. The tall, good-looking Jewish Canadian dressed in a three-piece, pinstriped suit. He had been a newly-minted lawyer when he started to work for my father in the 1960s. What hair he sported was combed neatly over his balding head. Though the evening was young, he was into his third vodka.

Mack was the one who started the conversation about Dad's first Montreal employer, Mic. Mack had said, "Your father has come a long way since he started in business 24 years ago. If it weren't for Mic, he might not have become as successful."

"Yes, it takes one schmuck to know another," the loud East German, Hans, chimed in, comparing Mic to Mack. He chuckled as he raised his third scotch of the evening and pointed it Mack's way.

Hans was an entrepreneur and an immigrant like Dad and Aras, though the German had landed in Canada decades after them. Hans' company rented and sold earth moving equipment. His brawny and tough machines matched his tall and muscular physique and gruff personality.

Mack replied "Yah, what do you know, Hans, you big German oaf?" His half-serious voice turned into a guffaw.

Hans' "schmuck" comment made me wonder why my dad invited Mack to the Troika. The attorney appeared a bit too flashy in his gold monogrammed cufflinks, expensive wingtip shoes, and imported silk ties. Mack bragged about the politicians and Jewish business people he knew.

Dad had once told me, "Mack is a smart corporate lawyer; he helped me a lot in business. He separated my business into various companies so that I could take advantage of lower small-business tax rates. He also helped me restructure the entities so there will be less tax to pay when I die. It will be a big benefit to you and your brother."

It seemed to me that Dad repaid Mack a bit too much for the man's smarts. I sensed that Mack mooched free suppers and drinks from my generous father who wanted everyone at his table to have their fill. Dad and his cohorts may have tolerated Mack because he could put down shots of lemon, pepper, and honey vodkas, and still walk and talk straight at the end of an evening.

In contrast, Hans could lose his civility after a few. To Mack's "oaf" comment, Hans expelled a big laugh and poked at the lawyer's shoulder. "At least I know what I'm talking about." He was referring to, as my father sometimes did, how lawyers might complicate their advice so that it would yield larger legal bills.

Mack looked annoyed and moved his torso a couple of inches away from his boisterous client. The prim and proper attorney didn't like being jabbed by this engineer entrepreneur in a rumpled suit.

The short, svelte, and small-mustached Aras cleared his throat to interrupt the juvenile exchange. Aras was ten years my father's elder and had a similar deep, Eastern-European voice. He was well dressed in a two-piece business suit, but not flashy like Mack.

Of those at our table, Aras had been the only one around when my father started his business in 1953. He knew Dad's escapades firsthand. "Johnny," Aras said, "Tell your son the whole story about Mic and his company. I'm sure he'd want to know how you started the record player manufacturing business in Canada."

Both Hans and Mack nodded, though they seemed to know more about my father's business beginnings than I did.

"That Mic was a real SOB!" Dad repeated as he finished his drink. "And if you two phony baloneys over there stop farting around, I can tell the story again." He glared at Mack and Hans.

Both of the men, Dad's junior by a decade or more, nodded and added nothing more. Dad turned to me and calmly asked, "Would you like to hear the story, son?"

"Sure Dad," I replied. Hearing about my father's business ventures and adventures made me feel closer to him. "I've heard you mention Mic before, but I never got the whole picture. Wasn't he your first boss when you came to Montreal?"

Dad turned slightly away from the table and motioned to our black-suited waiter. He caught the server's eye with a single wave of his hand. He lifted his empty glass and, at the same time, pointed to my nearly finished drink. The waiter nodded. He'd soon have fresh ones on the table.

My father turned back to the table. "Yes, son; after your mother and I arrived in Montreal in 1950—after a year working as domestics in Pembroke, Ontario—I found my first job with Mic. He was running his family's home entertainment distributorship."

Dad pointed his fork at me. "Mic was looking for electronic technicians to work in his company's product repair shop. There they performed warranty repairs for the radios and record players the company imported from the U.S. and sold across Canada."

Dad stabbed and took a bite of his veal, and then he used his fork to push aside the boiled potatoes. He chewed slowly, talking between swallows. "Mic and I hit it off right away." He took a long breath. "I admired the guy."

He gestured in my direction again with his fork. "Mic was a business school graduate. Because he was a few years older than me, I respected him as I would a big brother."

My father looked up from his supper. "Mic liked me too. I was a fast worker and a good technician. I knew how to fix anything he put in front of me—not only repairing burned-out electronics but also replacing broken mechanical parts and patching busted cabinets."

He raised his arm again. "My father had been a cabinet maker, so I was good at handling particleboard, wood glue, and the special vinyl paper that covered the wooden record-player boxes in those days."

Our waiter placed our fresh drinks on Troika's logo-embossed coasters on our red-on-white tablecloth. Dad nodded his thanks to the server but didn't lose a beat in his story. "I helped Mic's company save lots of money. I taught our other technicians how to make repairs quickly. And I showed them how to salvage good parts from broken radios and record players, which helped the company save money on spare parts."

My father looked at me again. "After a while, Mic asked me to manage our whole parts inventory." He smiled. "Within a year I was in charge of the whole shop, watching and training my techs during the day and spending evenings organizing the parts department."

Dad kept chewing on his dinner. "I wasn't shy either about asking Mic for money. When I started with him, I was making 50 cents an hour, but within a year I was making over a $100 a week. That was a lot of money back then. Your mother and I were able to live well on less than half of it. We could get groceries for a week for about five dollars. I put the rest into the bank, saving for a rainy day."

Aras leaned forward. "Johnny, didn't you and Anne live around here on Crescent Street back then?"

Dad nodded and pointed. "Yes, we did! In the early '50s, this part of Crescent Street was all three-story apartment buildings. We lived only a few doors down from here." He turned to me, "After we leave here tonight, I can show you where we lived until your brother was born."

"Sure Dad. I'd love to see that."

My father paused, put down his fork and knife, pulled out a pack of cigarettes, and offered them around the table. Aras came forward with matches, but my father beat him to the light with his Dunhill. Dad passed around his lighter, but he didn't offer me a smoke.

"You don't smoke," Hans asked?

From the time I had been in my mid-teens, my father had told me, "Son, you can drink as much as you like as long as you stay in control." But he kept cigarettes away from me, saying curtly, "If I ever catch you smoking, I'll punch your nose." He usually said that with a cigarette burning between the fingers of his left hand while his right hand gestured at me with a closed fist. All I did was nod and smile at his quip.

I winked at Hans and kidded, "No thanks; I'm trying to quit."

"Terrible habit these things," Hans responded. "It's better that you don't smoke. It will get you in the end."

I grinned and spoke matter-of-factly. "My father told me many times that he'd punch me in the nose if he ever caught me smoking." I smiled. "I still believe he would!"

Everyone chuckled, including Dad.

After everyone had taken in another drag of their smokes, my father continued. "Every week or so, I made parts lists for Mic. I came in as early as he did. We sat in his office while he showed me how to call our vendors and get the best prices.

"Mic could be nice to the supplier's agent to get what he wanted, and he could scream when he had to. He knew the bigger bosses at those companies, and he would go over the purchasing agent's head if he needed to. Mic knew who to press for answers and who to feed with gifts. He got good prices and fast service. I learned a lot from him."

Dad took a sip of his fresh drink. "The guy was smart and knew what he was doing. Instead of buying replacement parts from the U.S. manufacturers that made our products, we developed Canadian and offshore sources where we got parts cheaper. We built a network of suppliers."

Aras leaned forward and put his forearms on the table. "Mic was at the right place at the right time," he proclaimed. "Radios and record players were taking off in the 1950s."

The elder gentleman waved one arm. "People were going crazy for rock-'n'-roll. Record players sold like hot cakes. We were selling them too at my appliance distributorship. After people had heard songs they liked, they wanted a vinyl record and a player to play it over and over again in their home. Because those devices came in from the U.S., and Canada was a small market for the big American companies, we couldn't get our hands on them fast enough."

Aras leaned back, and Dad resumed. "One day, near the end of my first year with Mic, I came to him with a proposal. I remember going to his office at seven o'clock that morning when I could catch him before anybody else arrived."

My father put his hands on the table. "Mic was behind his desk." He gestured forward with one hand. "He asked me to sit down and have a coffee and cigarette with him." He pointed a finger forward. "That's when I told him my idea."

Dad took in a big breath. "I said, 'Mic, we have the electronic parts suppliers we need so that we could build radios and record players right here. All we need are the cabinets.'" He looked at me as if he were talking to Mic. "I told him, 'We could save a lot of money if we found a woodshop operation in Montreal to build the boxes for us. We could build the electronic components and do the electrical assembly ourselves.'"

He raised his fork into the air. "'I know how to construct cabinets,' I said to Mic. 'We just have to show the woodshop how to build what we need. We can easily copy the U.S. designs we see at the consumer electronic shows, changing them a little to make them our own."

Dad pointed his fork my way as he made his point. "'Saving on transportation costs by not having to ship completed cabinets from the U.S., and not having the big overhead costs of the major American manufacturers, we could easily undercut RCA, Emerson, and the other big guys.'"

My eyes opened wide to my father's idea.

Dad's deep blue eyes were on me. "Mic didn't have to think long before he said, 'Great idea, Johnny!' Then he thought for a few more seconds, took a sip of his coffee, and said, 'Johnny, I want you to go ahead and do it. Handle this project for us. You run it and report directly to me. Tell me what people and space you need, and we'll set up an electronic assembly right here.' Mic was almost jumping out of his chair. 'We'll be the first ones in Canada to manufacture record players. We can also make bigger units and put a radio into them.'"

I could see a proud look on my father's face. Today, his Montreal Phono Company employed nearly a hundred people. His manufacturing company built tens of thousands of kids' record players as well as console stereos up to sixty inches in width. His biggest units were pieces of furniture that could be a showpiece in peoples' living rooms, dens, and bedrooms.

I took a sip of my fresh drink. "But how did you get from Mic's company to your Montreal Phono?" I asked.

He looked at me. "There's a lot more to this story. Be patient," he said.

"Your father was at the beginning of a wave," Aras said. "I only wished I had had the idea first."

"Yes; he was at the right place at the right time," Mack added." And he had the know-how to gain an advantage in the market."

"But that's only part of it," Aras proclaimed.

"Go ahead, Johnny. Tell your son what happened next," Hans insisted. He eyed my father intensely as if he wanted to catch additional nuances in the story that he had heard before.

Dad continued. "So I told Mic that I would handle it for him under one condition. I said I wanted 1% of the production turnover as a bonus at the end of the year."

Aras explained. "So if Mic's company sold $500,000 of products that year, then your father would get a $5,000 bonus. In those days, five grand was the cost of that three-bedroom suburban home your family now lives in."

"Wow!" I said. "That was a lot of money back then."

Dad continued. "Mic tried to dicker with me about the percentage, but I was firm about it. He finally agreed to the 1%. We shook hands on the deal, and I immediately went to work on the project."

The waiter came by to retrieve our empty plates and ask if we wanted dessert. "What about cherries for everyone?" Dad declared, referring to the Troika's cherries jubilee specialty.

Everybody but Aras agreed. "I'm good with my cigarette," the older man said. "You guys are younger and can afford the sweets."

"Come on, Aras, you're not an old man yet," my father asserted. "You're hardly older than I am," he winked, "and so thin that you'll live to one hundred."

"I'll take Aras's portion," Hans blurted out, his hand raised.

"Go ahead," said Aras as he waved his cigarette in the air. "Not eating too many sweets is why I'll live to 100."

"Okay, cherries for five," my father declared to the waiter. "Split the extra portion between my son and that growing German bear over there."

When entertaining, Dad was generous with his friends and with me. He was very different behind his office desk. There, he could raise hell at a supplier for raising the price of pressed wood by a penny per board foot.

The waiter nodded then departed. Dad resumed. "The next year with Mic went quickly. I worked like a dog and was never home before 9 or 10 o'clock at night. I hired, trained, and supervised the production people during the day. In the evening, I managed the inventory and set up the production line for the next day." He raised a hand and brought it down in a fist on the table. "It was as if I worked two jobs."

Though I couldn't imagine working as hard as my father, I could see the satisfaction on his face for what he had been achieving. On the other hand, in our younger years, Steve and I had missed him for not having been home much; Dad's business and evening meetings had taken priority. I was glad I was now old enough to be with him at the Troika. In a couple of months, I'd be off to start work at P&G and to make my mark in the world.

Dad continued. "By the end of our first year, we had achieved three-quarters-of-a-million dollars in record-player turnover at our manufacturing price. It was a great start to what we were doing, and we were going to shoot for $1,000,000 the following year. The 1% I expected as a bonus would have more than doubled my income.

"No one works harder than your father," Aras said as he looked at me. "He deserved that money for what he did for Mic's company."

Dad continued. "A week before Christmas, Mic called me into his office. He was feeling good about the year we had had, and he appreciated my work and dedication. He usually liked to give out bottles of booze to his best employees." My father smiled. "Instead, he put five hundred dollars into my hand and said, 'Here, have yourself a great holiday, Johnny. Buy your wife a nice gift for Christmas. We'll settle the rest after the New Year, once we finalize our sales and profit numbers.'"

Dad was giddy. "I was so happy with that money that I bought presents for everyone in my production crew and planned a big New Year's Eve party at our home. I invited my best employees and their wives, our friends and apartment house neighbours, as well as Mic and his wife."

Aras spoke again. "Your father gives back to the people who help him. That's another reason why he is so successful and has many good friends."

I grew up seeing my father's generosity. At his Montreal Phono Christmas parties, his secretary, Helen, put out huge spreads of deli meats, cheeses, bread, and all kinds of salads. In the early years as boss, he enlisted his rotund Polish electronics-department foreman, Walter, to dress as Santa Claus.

Walter handed out company-purchased cartons of cigarettes and bottles of liquor to the company's best employees. For the women, there were good nylon stockings and sweet perfumes that he had bought during business trips to Europe. Though my father knew how to scream at his people for making mistakes, he also knew how to celebrate with them and to thank them for their loyalty and dedication.

"But that Mic was a conniving character," Aras added. "Tell Harvy about what happened regarding him and his son."

"Sure," my father replied. "I heard this from Mic himself." He looked at me. "One day at home, Mic was playing with his youngest boy. The youngster wanted to jump off a couch and into his father's arms. Mic said, 'Go ahead and jump,' and his son did." Dad put out his arms as if he were going to catch the kid, but his head turned downward. "Mic missed catching his child on purpose. The boy fell to the ground and scraped his knee."

Dad's eyes looked peeved. "The kid then started to cry and said, 'Why didn't you catch me, Daddy?' Mic looked down at his boy and wagged his finger. 'Let that teach you a lesson, son,' he said. 'You shouldn't trust anyone, not even your father!'"

"Wow!" I exclaimed. "What a jerk he could be." My father had never done anything like that to my brother or me. He could be callous to my mother in going golfing with his buddies on weekends while leaving her alone with us kids, or about having roaming eyes and hands for other women. But Dad was never mean to his boys in the way Mic had been to his son. Though Dad's angry shouts could stir my stomach and send shivers through my still young spine, I knew he'd never lay a hand on me or allow me to get hurt on purpose.

"That's not everything Mic did," Aras said. "Go on, Johnny, finish the story."

"Yes, yes, Aras." Dad took a last drag from his cigarette, blew the smoke high into the air, and stubbed the butt out in the ashtray. "At our New Year's Eve party, we were all having a good time. Our apartment became crowded with guests, and Mic dropped in with his wife. I ran around most of the evening serving drinks to everybody, and your mother made sure that people ate the food from the big spread she had prepared."

He took a long breath. "As the party quieted down toward the end of the night, I had a chance to spend time with Mic. We had a drink together, and I said that I was looking forward to getting my big bonus in January."

Dad's voice turned to shock. "To my surprise, Mic looked at me and said, 'What do you mean, Johnny? I owe you only a few hundred dollars.'"

Dad's voice rose. "'What?' I said to him. 'Didn't we have a deal that you would give me 1% of the turnover?'"

"Mic said, 'No, Johnny. You're mistaken. It was 1% of the profit we agreed to.'"

"'How could that be?' I asked him. 'I have no control over your profit numbers, only you do. We agreed on 1% of production turnover.'"

"'I'm sorry you think that way Johnny, but you're mistaken.' Mic told me.

"Because it was New Year's Eve, I didn't want to make trouble, but I was angry at the guy. I had expected over $7500, and he was talking about giving me maybe $800 in total."

"Yep, he was a real schmuck," Mack repeated. "But you showed him, didn't you Johnny?"

"So what happened, Dad?" I asked. "Tell us before the waiter arrives with the cherries. I want to hear your story and to see the dessert show too." The way the Troika waiters made jubilee was a delight to watch.

"Okay, okay," my father said, pawing his hand at me as he continued. "For the next couple of days, I thought about what to do. I came in early on the first day of work after New Year's and confronted Mic in his office.

"I told him again what we had agreed to, but Mic insisted that I had gotten it wrong. I argued with him, but he ended the conversation by saying, 'I'll pay you what I said, end of discussion!'"

Dad's face snarled. "I was pissed off at the guy and was prepared for his bullshit. I took $500 out of my pocket, threw it down on the table, and said, 'Here's your money back, Mic, I don't want a penny of it. Use it for medicine when you get old and sick.' I then walked out of Mic's office and out of his company. I never went back. And he and I have not spoken to each other since."

Everyone at the table was quiet as if we had just heard that a close friend had died.

"That's amazing, Dad," I said to break the silence.

Aras leaned back in his chair and grinned; he had known what had been coming.

"Bravo, Johnny," Hans piped in with a big clap, his cigarette burning between his smiling lips.

"Your father has his ways," Mack added.

The waiter wheeled forward his dessert cart, which included a flame burner. He spooned pitted cherries into a copper fry pan and lit the burner's fuel. He added sugar, some water, and many ounces of brandy to accompany the fruit. He let the mixture simmer on the burner, carefully tilting the pan so he could delicately spoon the sweet concoction over the perfectly ripe cherries.

At the right moment, the waiter tilted the pan a little more. The boiling liquid touched the fire and burst into flames. The restaurant filled with the strong smell of sweet fruit and brandy. It was exciting to watch, and my mouth watered.

Five dishes of vanilla bean ice cream sat in a big bowl of ice cubes on the cart. When the liquid in the pan simmered down to a sauce, the waiter spooned the hot cherries and sauce on the ice cream. He put each bowl on a plate and added a wafer biscuit on the side. "Ah! A sweet dessert to go with your sweet story, Dad," I said.

"Yes, son; I'll drink to that." My father downed the last sip of his scotch.

"Here, here," Aras chimed in, saluting with his glass and then taking a swig of his drink.

The cherries ritual ended with the waiter placing the jubilees before us. He put the extra serving between Hans and me. Everyone *oohed* and *aahed* at the rich sight and fragrance. *"Bon appetit,"* Dad said.

Everyone, except for Aras, dug in. The elder lit another cigarette and enjoyed it with the last of his drink. I tasted the cherries, relishing the warm, digestif-infused concoction mixed with the cool ice cream.

After a moment I said, "So Dad, how did you get from working for Mic to starting Montreal Phono?"

My father finished a spoonful of dessert then pointed his spoon at me. "When I left Mic, I didn't have enough money to start a company. But I did know a Russian Jewish financier, a guy named Shimshi. I also had a Czech friend, Dvorak, who was a good salesman. We three got together and started a business to compete with Mic. We called it SDS."

His voice lowered. "Because Shimshi invested the money in getting us started, we gave him 51% ownership. Dvorak and I got the rest as sweat equity."

Hans jumped in. "That means they worked like dogs to build their business as I do with my heavy equipment company."

"In your case, Hans, it's sweating like a horse," Mack offered with a grin.

The proud East German glared at his lawyer. "What do you know about it, Mack, with your fancy suits and a law degree that your parents paid for?"

"Okay you two," Dad shouted. "Who is supposed to do the talking right now, you or me?"

"Sorry, Johnny," Hans offered. "I can't help myself with this guy who doesn't know what it's like to get his hands dirty."

"Hey, Hans. I was a part of building my legal practice with my partners," Mack insisted, pointing at himself.

Aras leaned forward. "I hate to tell you, Mack, but it's not the same." He pointed to Dad and Hans. "We build products and have showrooms and factories. You only sell your knowledge and ideas."

Dad chimed in too. "Because of all the laws and regulations that you lawyers and our dear politicians have created, we business people can't live without you. And we can make or lose money in business, but the professionals get paid no matter what."

"Yes, that's what I meant," Hans added with a smirk.

Mack leaned back in his chair, looked to one side, and said nothing more. I again wondered why Dad permitted the attorney to be a part of his Thursday night crowd. Maybe they needed somebody at their table to mock.

I looked at my father. "Dad, tell me what happened to SDS."

"Okay, if everyone else can stay quiet." My father looked across the table to see that Mack and Hans were paying attention. They were, so he continued. "Dvorak and I ran the operation together. He was the outside salesman while I was the inside purchasing and production guy. We made and sold our radios and record players to small home furniture retail stores and home appliance distributors."

He looked at his friend. "That's how I met Aras. His home appliance company, Spectrum Distributors, was one of our first customers."

"Your father and I hit it off the minute we met," Aras offered with gusto. Dad gave the elder businessman room to speak. "Back then, I was a junior partner in my uncle's business, working as a showroom salesman in our distributorship. Spectrum's showroom was in Old Montreal, near SDS's factory."

He raised his cigarette. "Here and there, your dad and I enjoyed going out for suppers and drinks. We went to the Tokay on Stanley Street and the Hungarian Club on St. Lawrence." He grinned. "Both of those places had great food and lively gypsy music."

I spoke. "I remember the Tokay from when I was a kid." I pointed to my father. "Dad used to take us there for dinner after church on Sundays. They had great Wiener schnitzel and cucumber salad."

Dad grinned. "And their Hungarian violinist, accordion, and cymbals [cimbalom] players could make you shout to the ceiling or cry into your soup with their lively and sad gypsy music."

"That place was packed every Thursday too, like here," Aras added." It's too bad the owners let it go, and the place went out of business." He raised his glass to Dad. "We had good times there."

"The Tokay going out of business was good news for the Troika," Mack proclaimed with a soft chuckle. He was referring to the business that Dad now brought to this establishment.

I looked at my father. "Dad, I remember you saying that SDS went out of business. How did that happen?"

My father obliged. "Unfortunately, Dvorak and I were inexperienced, like newborn babies on the street. Unlike Mic's company, few people knew us. It was hard to get record player orders."

Dad raised a hand off the table. "And the three of us didn't get along as partners. Friends warned me about our financier, Shimshi, but I had no other place to get capital." He put his hands flat on the table. "Before our first year was over, we needed more money." He shook his head. "But Shimshi was a skinflint; he wouldn't invest more cash."

My father's face turned somber. "One night, I was working late into the evening to plan the next day's purchasing and production." He looked up from his cherries and pointed his spoon forward. "Before I left for the evening, I saw Shimshi rummaging around in the back of our factory. He didn't realize I was still there, and I didn't pay too much attention to him because I wanted to finish my work and go home."

My father took a deep breath and pointed with his spoon into the distance. "All of a sudden, as I was ready to leave, I saw a fire in the back."

He arms rose. "I right away ran toward it. I didn't see Shimshi anywhere. I did see that the blaze had started in a pile of oily rags we used for cleaning the record-player cabinets." His eyes were darting back and forth. "I had to move quickly, or the whole place would have burned down. I ran around to find a couple of extinguishers. I put out the fire before it got out of control."

Mack couldn't help himself. "Your father can get himself mixed up in such messes," he blurted. "Good thing he's got a good lawyer to watch his back."

"Just listen to the story, Mack," Hans snapped. "You might learn something."

My father raised his voice once more. "You guys keep your mouths on your desserts unless you have something good to say. Otherwise, this is the last time I'm buying you supper."

"Okay, Johnny," Hans replied shyly. He looked at my father. "I apologize to you and Mack too." He glanced Mack's way and then looked at me. He offered a smile. "Go ahead and finish your story for your son."

Mack said nothing and took another spoonful of his dessert.

My father took a long breath and continued. "I put out the fire and decided not to call the fire department. I went home that night and thought about what I should do."

His face turned somber. "I figured Shimshi started the blaze to burn the place down for the insurance money. He also may have wanted the fire department to blame me for letting our production people leave the oily rags laying in a big pile."

I was aghast, but neither I nor anyone else at our table dared say a word.

Dad continued, his voice rising in anger. "Early the next morning I confronted Shimshi. I told him, 'You bastard! I know you started that fire last night. I saw you in the back.' I then said, 'I want out of our partnership right now. If you make it difficult, I will report you to the police.'"

Dad's voice calmed. "The guy knew I had him. He had his lawyer immediately prepare the papers to dissolve our partnership. I said to myself that I would never again associate myself with a crook like him." His tone turned somber. "But Dvorak and I were now out on the street."

"Okay, Dad," I said. "It's good you got out of that mess with that Shimshi character. So how did you get your company started from there?"

He pointed his spoon my way again. "I'm coming to that. Finish your cherries and listen."

"Okay," I replied sheepishly.

My father continued. "The day after we closed SDS, I went to RCA's office and filled out a job application." He shook his head. "Without the money to start my own business, there was nothing else I could do. I needed a job."

He raised his hand. "RCA Canada was a big and growing company. I got to know people there during the consumer electronics trade shows I went to when I was with Mic's company and then with SDS." Dad showed a boyish smirk. "Those big-company guys liked to drink, so I got to know a few of the fellows well."

My father pointed. "Down the hallway from RCA's employment office was the RCA buying department. The longtime head buyer there was Mr. Dumouchel."

"I remember him," I said. "He was an old guy, a nice fellow. He came to your Montreal Phono Christmas parties and our summer barbeques at home. He always spoke nicely to you. He had a very raspy voice, didn't he?"

"Yes, son; his friends called him Doumie; he was a real gentleman. Everybody respected him, and I looked up to him as if he were my second father."

Dad gestured forward with his hand. "Doumie was a straight shooter. When he promised you something, he shook your hand on it and kept his word."

Dad took another long breath. "Just by chance that morning, while I was filling out an application in the RCA hallway, Doumie saw me. He came up to me and asked, 'Johnny, what are you doing here?'"

"I told him, 'I'm looking for work.'"

"Right away he said, 'Come into my office.'"

"After we sat down, Doumie asked me, 'What happened to you and SDS?'"

"I told him about the fire and how we dissolved the company."

Mack interjected. "Did you tell him what Shimshi did?"

My father looked at Mack and responded, "No, I figured I should keep that under my hat."

"That was good, Johnny," the lawyer said. "It was better that way."

Aras now raised his voice. "You lawyers have a legal opinion about everything, huh Mack?"

"I guess we can't help it," Mack confessed. He leaned back in his chair and added nothing more.

With his eyes sternly on his lawyer, Dad continued. "I asked Doumie if he could help me get a job."

My father took in another long breath. "Doumie's face turned serious, and he stepped behind his desk. He pulled out a piece of RCA letterhead from his drawer and began to write. He told me, 'Johnny, I can't help you get a job at RCA, but what I can do is give you a purchase order for 500 record players.

Take this order, set up your operation, then come back to me and let me know when you can deliver.'"

Dad pointed to his face. "Doumie looked straight into my eyes and said, 'Consider this purchase order not only as my investment in you but also as my confidence in your ability to make products for RCA.'

"I was flabbergasted!" Dad cried out, hitting his palm on the table. "Yet Doumie was not only a good man but a smart one too. He recognized I would never be happy to work for anybody but myself. And he knew I would never let him down."

I sat straighter in my chair. "Wow, Dad; I'm impressed."

"That's still not everything, son." He took another spoonful of his cherries. "I said to him, 'Doumie, I have no factory, no employees, and no capital. How am I going to make products for RCA?'

"Doumie said, 'Start a new company! Use this purchase order as good faith collateral with your bank. You have demonstrated to us at RCA that we need a subcontracting manufacturer in Canada rather than our having to import our products from our U.S. factories. You can be that manufacturer for us.'

"I couldn't believe it!" Dad laid his spoon down and then looked at his hands now placed along the edge of the table on either side of his dessert plate. "I then asked Doumie, 'What do you think I should call my company?'

"Doumie thought for a moment and said, 'You're in Montreal, and you are going to make phonographs. Why not call it Montreal Phono?'

"I said 'Okay!' and that's how the Montreal Phono name was born." My father was grinning ear to ear.

Aras smiled too, looked at me, pointed to himself, and said, "Your father then came to me because his bank wouldn't lend him money."

"Yes!" my dad exclaimed. "My bank manager had looked at my RCA PO and said, 'That's a beautiful piece of paper, Mr. Simkovits, but how will we know you'll deliver on your commitment to RCA?'"

Aras came back. "Johnny then came to see me, and I took him to see my Uncle Chasen. Your dad showed my uncle the RCA order, and I vouched for your father's honesty. Chasen looked at the paper, looked at your father, and then asked him how much money he needed to be able to build those record players.

"Your father responded, 'Five thousand dollars.'"

The elder smiled. "Chasen then went to his office safe and brought back $5000 in cash. He had your father count it in front of us, and they agreed on an interest rate."

Dad added, "I was flabbergasted again by Chasen's trust in me. I wanted to sign a promissory note to him, but he said, 'Johnny, your word is more important to me than your signature on a piece of paper. I trust you to pay me the money back as soon as you can.'"

Hans jumped in. "That's the way your father helped me out too when I came to Canada ten years ago. But Johnny lent me $50,000 to help me get started." He grinned. "I guess that's inflation for you."

"Yes," Dad said. "You were a good investment, my dear Hans. I knew you were a hard worker like me, and you had good references."

Dad was referring to Hans' father-in-law who was the general manager of a major European supplier to Montreal Phono. My father knew that Hans would never renege on the loan, even if his company would go belly up. Dad may have regularly invited Hans to the Troika because, in addition to the German liking to party, my father could be sharing with his good friend some of the loan interest payments he had received from him.

"With Chasen's money," my father added, "I rented a space in Old Montreal where I could be close to both RCA and Spectrum."

Aras jumped back in. "Montreal Phono built record players for us too. My uncle made that part of the deal with your father."

"I was able to rent a three-bedroom flat above Joe Beef Tavern in Old Montreal," Dad smiled. "It was small, had a few rats, but it was good enough with which to start. I converted the space into a production facility."

He gestured forward as he was giving a tour of his facility. "The biggest bedroom became the electronics department where we built the amplifiers and soldered together the components. A second bedroom became the stockroom and shipping area. In the living room, I set up our assembly line. The smallest bedroom became the office. The kitchen was our lunch room." He smiled.

"Later, I hired a good, young Slovak secretary—you know, Helen, who still works for us."

"Yes," I said. "When I was a kid, Helen let me play with her typewriter whenever I visited your next factory, the one on Nazareth Street. That was before you moved to the even bigger place on St. Patrick's Boulevard in Verdun." I smiled too. "I'm amazed she never got mad at me for messing with her ribbons."

"You don't know the half of it, son." Dad chuckled. "She was afraid you were going to break her machine. After the third time you had messed up her ribbon, she asked me not to bring you and your brother to the office until you were grown up."

Dad dug back into his cherries and his story. "When I started Montreal Phono, we bought record-player cabinets from a woodshop nearby that delivered what we needed when we needed it. We shipped the finished product immediately to RCA and Spectrum's warehouses so that we didn't need to hold finished goods at our place."

He smirked with self-satisfaction. "As quickly as I got paid from Doumie, I paid my suppliers. I worked so hard the next couple of years that I didn't go home many nights. Instead, I grabbed a few hours' sleep on the couch in my small office."

Dad took a big breath. "With RCA as my best customer, I was able to pay back Chasen within two years."

Aras smiled. "Your father couldn't pay my uncle fast enough. He didn't want to lose Chasen's trust in him."

Dad continued. "I eventually got a line of credit from the bank that had initially refused me. I've been with that same bank now for twenty-five years. RCA has been my best customer that entire time, though, as you know, we sell products also to Admiral, Philco-Ford, Fleetwood, and others."

Aras looked at his friend. "You have come a long way, Johnny." He looked at me as he turned his thumb toward Dad. "The only mistake I made was not becoming Johnny's partner instead of only helping him with that loan." The older man chuckled.

My father and everybody smiled, including me. I had heard Aras's line many times before. But he didn't have anything about which to complain. Aras

160

received a continual return on his uncle's investment by hanging around his business buddy for half a lifetime, obtaining complimentary dinners and drinks for all those years.

Dad paused, his eyes looking into the past, and he offered, "Until he retired, Doumie did a lot for me. I owe him my freedom and much of my success."

He looked at his friend. "And, if it hadn't been for Mic being such an SOB, I would have never started my business so quickly. And Aras and Chasen were there for me when I needed them, like a good older brother and a second father."

Dad's voice turned solemn. "Too bad Chasen died young, in his early 60s."

Aras nodded and pointed to himself. "I owe my life to that man. He was like a father to me too. He had taken care of me from the time my mother and I escaped Lithuania with him and his wife before World War Two broke out. He was a good provider and a good man."

My father turned to me. "Son, it's not only what you know that gets you ahead in life, but also who you know that can make a big difference. And it's important that you work hard to become somebody, and not waste your life and become nobody."

"And you've got to pursue opportunities until you hit a winning combination," added Aras.

"*Skol* to that, my good friend," Dad said, raising his now empty glass.

Hans smiled and lifted his glass. "Something good always happens when Johnny's around."

Mack and I followed suit. "*Skol!*" he and I said, and we raised our drinks to my father.

I could see in the mirror that the Troika musicians were returning. They sauntered back to the table with Sasha strumming his guitar and Vladjec playing softly on his accordion. I saw myself too in the mirror, a smile on my face. I felt included in Dad's gang and appreciated that I had arrived in his manly world.

That evening at Dad's table, I learned that my father's luck and success came not only from good schooling and hard work but also from his unflinching desire to succeed. Dad built trusted friendships and gave back to the people who helped him. He stood up for himself when he needed to, and he didn't take crap from unscrupulous people, even if they were friends.

Though a part of me wanted to run away from my father's life and the pain he had caused my mother, another part of me was deeply awed by and drawn to him. His ways were enticing. The ambiance he created was tantalizing. Like the minstrels, Sasha and Vladjec, he serenaded his colleagues and me with his stories, charm, generosity, and savvy.

I wondered if I could I equal my father's example and be worthy of his respect and legacy. I wasn't sure I could hold my songs, liquor, and Russian eggs as he did, or if I even wanted to.

Though his world was enthralling and intoxicating, my father's live-for-today, late-night partying lacked something important. It was as if these men singlehandedly made the world go round. The woman's part was to stay at home, have babies, raise the kids while they were young, and to keep supper hot and the bed warm for their husbands. Something was not right about that marriage contract. Thoughts about my mother's longing, aching heart kept on reminding me of the inequity.

As they neared Dad's table, Sasha and Vladjec bowed and spoke to my father in a Slavic tongue—together they knew many. The musicians engaged their fingers to start a soft melody. They played as if their instruments were whispering only to us at my father's table.

Dad nodded and seemed to recognize the tune. He tapped the table with his hand and hummed to the music. Sasha moved close to my father, bent down a little, and spoke a few words in their Slavic dialect. Dad nodded again, and Sasha turned and nodded to Vladjec. They changed their pace and started to play Kalinka, an uplifting Russian song.

Aras had a trained voice and sang along with Sasha. His exuberance told me that the song reminded him of his Lithuanian homeland. Sasha made room for the older man to sing a verse before Dad and I jumped in with the refrain. Hans and Mack joined in too, their drinks in hand, enjoying the near end to another successful Thursday night at the Troika.

Johnny and Sasha at the Troika. C.1982

* * * *

Part VI:

Patriarchal Disenchantments

29

Costly Convictions

It was a summer Sunday afternoon during Steve's and my childhood. After our family attended church at St. Patrick's Church and had a filling dinner in Montreal's Chinatown, Dad walked us down to the Old Montreal wharves. We entered the Notre-Dame-de-Bon-Secours (Fisherman's) Chapel. There, Dad, Steve, and I peeled up the narrow, circular staircase of the steeple while Mom lumbered up the steps behind us.

Mom once told us that the church reminded her of a place called the *Halaszbastya* (Fisherman's Bastion) that overlooked the Danube River in Budapest. Though the latter was more like a castle than a church, Mom's memories helped her to get—huffing and puffing—up those many chapel steps.

From the outside landing at the top of Fisherman's Chapel, we could get a good view of the St. Lawrence River. Dad propped his foot on the metal railing. He lit and puffed a cigarette—perhaps his reward to himself for having done the climb.

He pointed to the gigantic Five Roses grain silos standing near the docks in front of us and then gestured to his right. "You boys see the Lachine Canal over there?" he asked. Before we could answer, he said, "Big grain barges go through those locks. They come to Montreal all the way from Thunder Bay, Ontario, and Duluth, Minnesota on Lake Superior, a thousand miles away."

Old Montreal's Fisherman's Chapel. Present day.

He pointed to the big ships below us, then to the fast-moving river as it split and curled around St. Helen's Island, famed for its old French fort that never saw battle. "The grain gets stored here at the wharves and reloaded onto these big ships to be taken all over the world."

Dad stood for a moment taking in the laden ships, the silos that reached into the sky, and the river rushing in the distance. I could see his eyes widen, his shoulders square, the look on his face confident. He was determined to make a mark and leave his legacy in his adopted country

* * *

In 1953, Dad had started his first Montreal Phono production operation in an apartment above Joe Beef Tavern. The building was located right across Common Street (later renamed Rue de la Commune) from those harbour wharves in Old Montreal.

Joe Beef Tavern in Old Montreal.

Dad's secretary, Helen, had once told me, "I was named after St. Helen Island in the middle of the St. Lawrence." She pointed into the distance. "I could almost see St. Helen's from your father's first factory on Common St."

She raised a hand and spoke proudly. "Your father knew my Slovak parents through our church. He came to our home and asked for their permission to hire me part-time to be his first Montreal Phono secretary." She looked away and then back at me. "I was only a teenager when I started working for him."

She smiled as she recounted that past. "That apartment above Joe Beef came with a few big rats. In 1955 or '56, on the day we finished our move out of there to your dad's next factory on Nazareth St, I saw one of those ugly things scurrying around the office." She put her hand on her chest. "I got so scared that I stood on my chair and screamed, 'Somebody, get me out of here!'" Her voice gave a shrill.

She looked at me, slapped her side, and smirked. "Your father picked me up and carried me out over his shoulder." She laughed. "I couldn't calm down until he got me completely out of the building."

I smiled and laughed at her story. Dad was certainly a hands-on guy.

* * *

Dad's three-floor Nazareth Street facility was the first industrial building he owned outright. Less than a decade later, in 1964, Montreal Phono had to evacuate the premises because the city annexed the street to make way for the new Bonaventure Expressway for Montreal's Expo 67.

My father was forced to move his factory again, which he did to St. Patrick Street by the Lachine Canal, then a five-minute drive to RCA's head office. (That was years before RCA moved its head office out of the city to Montreal's West Island.)

Dad once told me he appreciated the names of those city streets (Nazareth and St. Patrick), which fit in with his Catholic faith. He offered, "I feel as if God is with me every day."

One Sunday afternoon, days before the city demolished our father's Nazareth Street factory, Dad, Steve, and I visited the abandoned building. Some windows had been cracked or broken by rock-throwing kids. The three of us got in the act, chucking stones as high as we could at the remaining window panes.

In front of that derelict building, my brother and I competed to see who could get closer to hitting a particular window on each floor. When one of us hit it, Dad told us a little about what had taken place behind that opening.

Clang! A big stone cracked a second-floor window pane. "That was the amplifier department," Dad said. "That's where your Uncle Edo worked when he came the first time from Czechoslovakia to visit us in Canada."

Ping! A stone skimmed a third-floor pane. "That's the stock room where we stored record players from England and radio chassis from Japan."

Smash! A piece of broken brick put a gaping hole in a ground floor window. "Down here on the first floor was the shipping area where big trucks would pick up finished goods and take them to warehouses across Canada."

Crack! went another second-floor pane. Dad added, "Behind that window, your uncles Geza and Viktor worked for me when they came to visit us from Czechoslovakia."

Dad had given our Czechoslovak uncles temporary jobs. He paid them in cash so that they could earn hard Canadian currency during their usual six-month visits.

My father heaved a stone at a third-floor window, seeing if he could do more than skim it. When he did, the whole glass smashed. "With some dollars," he said, "your relatives could make a better life for themselves when they went back to their poor communist country."

I threw one more stone at a second-floor pane and cracked it. Dad didn't need to fill me in on this one. I recalled the loud clinking of machines and the smell of sizzling solder flux when Dad showed Steve and me around his factory on a Saturday morning, a day of the week when most employees worked a half-day. I had received happy smiles and friendly pats on the head and cheek from Helen, and from my uncles when they had worked there.

* * *

Soon after his Common Street factory had started up in '53, Dad was having dinner at Joe Beef. He spotted the restaurant owner behind the counter. "Joe," he said, "I need a good accountant; do you know one?"

As the story goes, in a booth nearby was Mel Mozer, a young, short and svelte, dark-haired CPA with an independent accounting practice. Overhearing the question, Mel stood, approached my father, pointed to himself, and said in his baritone voice, "Hello there. I'm a good accountant."

Dad shook Mel's hand. After they had spoken for a few minutes, he took Mel upstairs to show him Montreal Phono's operation. Mel started as the company's accountant that very day. Over the next twenty years, he remained my father's business advisor as Dad moved to his successively larger facilities.

Mel and my father grew close. Dad took him on frequent business trips to Europe to help make purchasing deals with electronic component suppliers. While they travelled, they visited England, Switzerland, Monaco, and the French Riviera.

I once saw them in a super-8 film that they took during one of those trips. Dad and Mel were on a hotel rooftop overlooking a Mediterranean beach. When not conducting business, I imagined Mel and Dad getting around town, enjoying late-night casino gambling, drinking Cognac and smoking French cigarettes at beach bars and cafes. I could imagine them shopping for duty-free Swiss watches and gold baubles, and looking at the pretty French coquettes.

In the film, they looked out onto the beach and sea, big smiles on their faces. They pointed here and there while their hair blew all over in the Mediterranean breeze.

For years after Dad came home from his first overseas trip with Mr. Mozer, he recounted a funny travel story to his Eastern European friends and colleagues. I once overheard him repeat it.

He smiled and offered, "During the first night we were in France, Mel asked me, 'What's that odd device in the bathroom next to the toilet?'" Dad raised a hand. "I told him, 'It's a bidet.' Mel then asked me, 'What's it used for?'" Dad's grin widened. "I kept my face straight and told him, 'You use it to brush your teeth.'" Dad started to chuckle, and so did his friends at the table.

He went on. "The next morning, Mel told me he tried to use it. He said, 'Isn't it a little low to the ground for teeth brushing?'" My father guffawed. "I then told him what it really was for." Dad howled with laughter, and so did his cohorts. "The colour went completely out of Mel's face," he said. "The guy couldn't believe it."

The Simkovits and Mozer families came together many times for holiday celebrations and family vacations. Mel's wife was tall, slender, and pretty. She wore her black hair up in a poof. The Mozers had two boys close in age to my brother and me.

Our family had occasional dinners at the Mozers' house in Hampstead (a suburb Dad called "Montreal's Golden Ghetto"). The Mozers came to our house in the West Island for Saturday back-yard barbeques. At Mel's prodding, our families vacationed several times together at the Attaché in Hollywood, Florida from Christmas until after New Year.

Mel introduced my father to pipe smoking. He owned several straight- and curly-stemmed pipes on which he could puff for hours. Mel's sweet burning pipe tobacco smelled much better than Dad's cigarette smoke. Because of Mel, my father went through several pipe smoking phases, sucking on those things during long car rides.

I liked Mel and his family. He and his wife spoke calmly and caringly to each other and their kids. They were unlike my parents (or relatives) who screamed at us kids if we bugged each other one time too many.

* * *

Twenty-one years after they met at Joe Beef Tavern, and soon after I returned for my senior year at MIT in the fall of '75, my father and Mel had trouble with the RCMP and Revenue Canada.

Over one Sunday dinner, while I was home from college for Canadian Thanksgiving, Dad told Steve and me what had happened. He fumed like one of his cigarettes. "Last week, the goddamn RCMP walked into Montreal Phono and seized everything. They gave me no warning. They had a court order in their hands from Revenue Canada's tax department."

Our father's eyes were glaring. "Those bastards opened every fucking company filing cabinet. They filled boxes with stacks of our papers and carted everything away in a van. They even told me to open my private office safe, and they removed my files from there too."

Steve and I stayed quiet as Dad puffed furiously on a cigarette. "I then got a call from my bank's branch manager. He told me that the RCMP raided my safety deposit box in the bank. They took away all my private papers."

Dad raised his voice. "It was a fucking disaster." He raised his hand, his cigarette burning between his fingers. "Mozer's accounting office was raided too, on the same day."

He looked down at our table. "At Montreal Phono, we had to call all our customers and suppliers. We had to recreate our documents from scratch until we could get our papers back from the government. It's going to take me months to put everything back in order!"

I was stunned. My brother looked at our father. "Why did they do that, Dad?"

He huffed. "Some son-of-a-bitch squealed on me." His voice lowered. "When we did our last year's corporate income taxes, Mel told me that it would be okay to write off obsolete business inventory from our books."

Dad shrugged as he puffed away. "Instead of depreciating that aging inventory, or even showing it at no value on our ledgers, we thought it would be okay not to show any of that useless garbage in our books."

"What's the benefit of doing that?" I asked.

Dad looked at me as if I was a naïve kid. "Son, it allows Montreal Phono to show a smaller business profit, and thus pay less corporate tax. That inventory was worthless anyway. There was no real harm in doing what the company did."

I asked or said nothing more, though I figured the government didn't see it Dad's way. As I had learned from my summers of working at Montreal Phono, Dad's rules for running his business didn't always coincide with government regulations and tax obligations. I wondered if his tricky money-making ways, and his casualness about skirting the taxman, were now catching up to him.

* * *

Decades later, after my father's death, I located Mel at his retirement condo in Florida. I had found him via the Internet, and he agreed to see me. I felt apprehensive about meeting him, knowing how his and Dad's friendship changed radically after the RCMP raided their respective offices.

Mel looked as svelte and fit as he was on the day I last saw him in my father's office before the summer of 1975. His face seemed longer and had lines, but he held a grounded sureness. His voice was as deep and calm as I had remembered. Perhaps he agreed to see me because he wanted to set the record straight about his former client.

After small talk about our families, I got to my line of inquiry. I asked Mel about the RCMP raid. He raised his hand and motioned as if he was signing a document. "Your father asked me to sign an incomplete inventory ledger and company financial statements based on written-off inventory." He took a long breath. "He claimed that the excluded merchandise was obsolete, and not accounting for it in the company records wouldn't hurt anybody."

He looked away and then back at me. "I didn't feel right about it, but your father asked me to sign those erroneous statements." His eyes looked down. "I did sign, and I very much regretted it."

Mel paused to take in a breath. He looked past me. "Johnny made such egregious things seem as if they were no big deal. He was a good friend, so I closed my eyes and signed. That was certainly a mistake. Your father liked to play such accounting tricks. That time, both he and I got into serious trouble for it."

"I see," I said, shaking off my surprise at his statements. I wondered if Mel might have been a tad gullible to my father's assertions and too compliant with his requests. Then again, I could have said similar things about myself.

By this time in my life, there was little about my dad that shocked me. I looked at my father's ex-friend and came forth with my toughest question. "Speaking about my father's money shenanigans, might you know how he funded his offshore account in Switzerland?"

The 85-year-old Mel studied my face for a moment. I gazed at his chin and not directly into his eyes. He offered, "In those days, people conducted a lot of business in cash. Your father sold some record-players to smaller stores and distributors that way. He may have deposited the proceeds directly into his personal bank account and not his corporate account, thus not showing the cash in his company books."

The elder blinked a few times. "Later, on business trips to Europe, I guess your father transferred that money into his offshore account. The government had fewer rules and regulations back then to prevent or monitor such activities."

Mel's use of "He may" and "I guess" told me he might be protecting himself. I didn't ask if he collaborated with my father in his offshore tax deception. I figured Mel wouldn't give me a self-incriminating answer.

I moved to an easier subject. I didn't want to hit all the tough notes in this conversation all at once. "Mel, might you remember how Montreal Phono became successful in the record player and console stereo business?"

Mel thought for another moment and then looked at me. "There were several factors, Harvy." He raised a finger. "First, Montreal Phono could offer a fixed price and predictable delivery to the big home entertainment companies. When companies like RCA bought from their U.S. factories, sometimes those factories were plagued by delays and price overruns. The American parent put Canadian deliveries second to their own bigger U.S. retailers. RCA Canada could never be sure of what final price and delivery dates they'd get from their own U.S. plants."

Mel laid a hand on his lap. "But with Montreal Phono, there was a certainty, especially on the higher-volume, lower-end products you father could build. That stuff sold quickly, so RCA Canada gave your father its business. And, being local, he could deliver faster on product reorders."

Mel raised two fingers, his face staying accountant blank. "Second, your father participated in the Canadian manufacturers' lobby. He went to Ottawa with other subcontracting manufacturers to get the federal government to apply Canada's then manufacturing sales tax to the lower subcontractor's price rather than to RCA's marked-up price to the retailers."

I jumped in. "I remember my father mentioning that, but I never completely understood how it worked."

Mel placed his hand horizontally, shoulder high. "Back then, when RCA sold its manufactured product to its dealer network, it needed to pay the government a 14% manufacturing tax on its sales price." He lowered his hand so that it was waist high. "But your dad and other Canadian manufacturers got Ottawa to apply that manufacturing tax on the subcontractor's lower price to its customers like RCA, rather than on RCA's fully-loaded price to its dealers."

Mel's voice remained steady as he put his hand back on his lap. "When the government made that tax ruling, it suddenly became cheaper for Canada's big distributors to buy direct from Canadian subcontractors like your father. Your father pretty much captured their lower-end record player and stereo business, products that were retail priced below $200 in those early days of his company."

Mel raised his hand again with three fingers showing. "Third, your father knew how to run a tight ship. He wasn't a union shop. Twice the unions tried to get in, but your father outfoxed them."

"Yes, I know." I wanted to show Mel that I wasn't naïve to my father's ways. I looked at him. "Dad told me that when the union was trying to get into Montreal Phono, he took his longer-time employees off the punch-card system. That way, the union rep miscounted how many hourly employees the factory had. They subsequently thought they had a larger percentage of employees signed up for their union than they actually had."

Mel grinned slightly. "That's right. And your father also knew how to save every penny on costs."

He showed a fourth finger. "Johnny called Quebec Manpower [the employment office] and got every Asian, Indian, and Eastern-European immigrant that had recently come off the boat, and he paid minimum wage."

He took a long breath. "Most of those labourers were just happy to get a job. After weeks or months working for Montreal Phono, many of them parted ways for better positions and wages. Johnny then got back on the phone with Manpower and took in the next crew."

Mel stopped for a moment and then continued. "There was a fifth reason too. Johnny entertained his big suppliers as much as he did his customers. On the one hand, he'd take them out drinking and dining all over Montreal. He would even find them lady friends with whom to spend the evening."

Mel didn't elaborate, and I didn't ask.

He smiled. "On the other hand, with every order, your father would negotiate his suppliers down with a wink and a smile, all the way to the ruddy nails, screws, and glue that held together the record player and stereo boxes."

Mel chuckled. "And he knew how to scream at them when they didn't meet their deliveries. When Johnny got angry during a call, his voice could make his staff cower under their desks. Anybody sitting near the salesman at the other end of the phone line would hear this shouting coming out of the receiver. It was quite a display."

"Yes, I knew well my father's screaming. It sent shivers into my back even when I wasn't the one he was yelling at."

Mel showed a half-grin. "I know it too. Even though we were good friends, I sometimes got an earful from Johnny for my accounting bills. It was hard to say no to your father; he wore you down."

Dad's former accountant stopped talking; his eyes shifted as if he were looking for words. "Lastly, your father was a wheeler-dealer, Harvy. He and his salesman friend—I forgot his name—worked up a creative incentive plan for the buyers at RCA."

I was nervous, for I wanted to ask Mel more about his and my father's Revenue Canada court case. I blurted out, "I believe that was Ned Meyer. He and his family came to Florida with us for many Christmas holiday vacations."

Mel pointed at me. "That's the guy! That Meyer stuck with your father through thick and thin."

"Yes, I know. Like my father, Ned escaped the communists after the Soviet Socialists took over his homeland of Romania. He and Dad met soon after they both arrived in Canada. They were close friends until they died fifty years later, within months of each other."

Mel interrupted. "Meyer worked as a salesman for Aras of Spectrum Distributors. Both of them were 'hanger-on fellows' with your father. Anyway, Meyer and Johnny met many Saturday mornings, either at Aras or at Johnny's office, to think up ideas to help both of their businesses."

I leaned forward in my chair but didn't respond to Mel's comments about Aras and Ned. What Mel may have considered "hanger-on fellows" made up many of my father's long-time friendships.

Mel kept his eyes on me and continued. "Meyer and your father cooked up a scheme to give cash gifts to the RCA buyers for the purchase orders Montreal Phono received before the end of each calendar year."

My ears perked up. "Do you mean kickbacks?" I asked. "My father told me he had great relationships and business arrangements with the people at RCA Canada. The way he grinned about it, I suspected there had been more to it."

"Those RCA guys considered it a gift," Mel responded. "It was a percentage of the dollar amount of the orders Montreal Phono received before the end of each year. That way, Johnny could better plan his production the following year, thus keep his costs down. And RCA would get guaranteed deliveries from Montreal Phono rather than just promises from their American factories."

Mel pointed at me again. "Other than himself, your father didn't have a sales force. He could afford to give something back to the customer." He took a long breath. "I don't know exactly how Johnny pulled it off or in what way he gave those money gifts, but his strategy worked. It was a win-win for him and the people at RCA."

"You're very right," I said with a smile. "My father's initials could be MWD for 'Mother of a Wheeler-Dealer.'"

The reserved Mel chuckled as if he held no grudges against his former customer and friend.

* * *

Montreal Phono's tax case with Revenue Canada meandered through the Quebec federal court for the better part of a year. While home from college for winter vacation, I was out for dinner again with my father.

He took me to one of his favorite Italian restaurants, Carlos, situated in the old and upscale Windsor Hotel. The hotel lobby's marble staircase, and the dining room's high ceiling and pillars, made the place seem as if it were a French chateau.

A recent meeting with his lawyers seemed to rile Dad. His frustration rose with his second scotch. "Son of a bitch! The police and the federal government have no right to invade my privacy." He jabbed his index finger hard into the pristine white tablecloth. What bastards they are for screwing up my business."

"How did this come about, Dad?" I was more careful with my question so my father wouldn't think me naïve.

Dad calmed a bit. "A business colleague gave me the idea of having two company inventories. The reduced inventory list, which I kept in the office, I declared to the government." He lowered his voice. "I kept the complete inventory in my bank's safety deposit box."

He took a swig of his drink, and his voice hardened. "The merchandise I wrote off the shorter list was worthless. Why should Revenue Canada care if the garbage we carry is written down on a piece of shit paper?"

Though my father's incessant cursing made me cringe, I didn't say anything that would stop him from recounting his story. "Who might have squealed on you, Dad; and why?"

His voice softened. "I have no idea, son." His tone rose again as he perused the room to see that no one was listening. "Somebody I trusted screwed me good." He pointed to a wall. "If I catch the bastard, I'll crucify him."

Count on Dad to turn his anger into a religious crusade.

He took a long breath and pointed his index finger. "That's what I get for trusting people. You have to be very careful in business as to whom you say things."

I wasn't sure if my father was following his own advice.

One night at his Troika table, after a few stiff drinks with his business buddies, I had once heard Dad recount, "I wrote off most of our family's last vacation as a company expense." A big grin filled his face. "I put the hotel bill on a gas credit card so that the auditors wouldn't find it."

I became distraught when I heard my father brag like that. Why would he stupidly divulge to his compadres about the blatant tax-skirting he was doing? Were all those guys going to keep their mouths shut?

During one college summer break when I worked at Montreal Phono, Dad told me, "Please stay quiet about my upcoming trip to the Cayman Islands. I don't want our people here to know where I'm going."

When his staff later asked me where my father had gone for the week, I shrugged my shoulders. I said, "I don't know; perhaps an overseas trip?"

After Dad had come back from Cayman sporting a well-tanned body, he boasted to everyone in the office how wonderful Grand Cayman had been, and how he had bought beach property. His open brag made me wonder if he or I were the bigger bozo.

Someone to whom Dad had bragged about his inventory scheme might have spilled the beans to Revenue Canada. I considered my father might have been the one who screwed himself.

Those incriminating inventory lists from Dad's office safe and bank deposit box certainly gave Revenue Canada ammunition against both my father and Mr. Mozer. Over our meal at Carlos, I felt a lump in my throat for both Dad and his accountant.

Well into his spaghetti a la carbonara, Dad added, "I'm at risk not only for company fines but also criminal charges. I should have never trusted Mozer to have signed and submitted those false inventory papers." (I didn't know at the time that Dad was not telling me the truth about Mozer's role.)

"What will happen to Mr. Mozer?" I asked.

He took in another forkful of his spaghetti and talked out of the side of his mouth. "Mozer could lose his licence to practise accounting for signing false financial statements. Revenue Canada filed a complaint against him with the Canadian Order of Chartered Accountants. He's at risk of fines in addition to losing his accounting practice."

Dad added that he and Mel now only spoke by phone or through their lawyers. He added, "I have the best lawyer working for me, Wardberg from Davis & Wardberg." He paused then said. "Mel had to find a separate lawyer for himself."

He put down his fork, leaned toward me, and raised his voice once more. "The goddamned lawyers can suck you dry." His eyes were piercing, his face stern. He lowered his hand under the table and seemed to grab his crotch. "When your life depends on them, they got you by your *yaytsa*."

* * *

In the spring of '76, over six months after the RCMP raid, my father and I were again at Carlos Restaurant. He twirled large portions of his fettuccini Alfredo and gulped it down. He was smiling again.

"My lawyers did their job," he chirped. "The government dropped its criminal charges against me for falsifying Montreal Phono's annual statements. At most, they will convict Montreal Phono for submitting a false inventory, and levy a fine against the company. Soon I will get back my company files and personal papers."

Dad pointed his fork toward his seat. "I've been sitting on pins and needles for months. All I can say is *hallelujah!*"

Dad lowered his voice. "Don't tell anybody, Harvy, not even your brother about what I'm now going to tell you. Steve would put such things on the drum for everyone to hear."

I nodded my understanding, though I knew that Dad had his own beating drums. But I liked being in the know regarding his money shenanigans. It made me feel closer to him, even if it was about dishonest dealings. He knew that I would keep his illegitimate money musings hush-hush.

My father continued. "Only my lawyer knows this." He looked directly at me. "When the RCMP raided my bank safety deposit box, they discovered the statements from my Cayman accounts. Those statements revealed that I had cash over there." He pointed south.

I looked around the restaurant to see if anyone was in earshot. Fortunately, there were few others in the restaurant, and no one was close to us. "Gee, Dad; that's serious." I sat frozen. "How did you deal with that?"

Dad chewed his pasta as he talked. "When the prosecutors asked questions about those offshore accounts, my lawyer, Wardberg, had a good idea. He told them, 'Those funds came with Mr. Simkovits from Czechoslovakia in 1949 when he escaped from behind the Iron Curtain.'"

My father grinned and chuckled. "After the government thought about it, they bought my lawyer's story about that money. They decided to focus only on Montreal Phono's tax-evasion charges and to leave my personal finances alone."

He took a swig of his drink. "The only thing the government now expects regarding that Cayman money is for me to declare the annual earnings on my tax returns." Dad smiled, winked, and flicked his hand that held his fork. "I agreed to do that."

Though Dad's Cayman strategy had backfired, I was relieved that his offshore money slipped through the government's claws. But it sounded as if he couldn't hide that money any longer; he'd have to pay annual taxes on the income from those funds. I wondered if he'd keep that money clean or pull off another scheme. I didn't ask, deciding to wait and see.

I wasn't quite sure of how to feel about Dad's misfortune and good luck at the same time. I could have easily adopted my father's approach of blaming the government and Mel Mozer for my father's troubles.

But Dad was the one with the tax-dodging hands. I'd never want to test my *yaytsa* with the RCMP as he had done. If and when I gained control of my father's hidden money, I'd certainly be more careful than he had been; I'd keep my frigging mouth shut about it.

I held firmly to the end of the table and held my breath too. I wanted to point my finger at Dad and shout at him for bragging like an idiot to his friends about his tax-avoidance games, but I was still my father's loyal son. "I guess you were lucky, Dad," I said. "What about your Cayman shell company, CANEX? Did the government find that agreement in your bank deposit box?"

Dad twirled his pasta. "They did, but they said nothing about it. They decided to focus only on Montreal Phono's inventory issue." He was almost giddy. "Those bureaucrats have a one-track mind. Heck if I'm going to open their eyes about my personal affairs."

I was glad there wasn't going to be time behind high walls and metal bars for my father. I was terrified about Revenue Canada's claws but relieved that they had left most of them retracted. I let go of my breath. Dad hadn't lost much blood in this taxman skirmish.

I was curious—or maybe worried—about my father's accountant and friend. "Dad, what about Mr. Mozer? Doesn't he know about your Cayman dealings?"

He took another sip of his drink. "Mel promised me that he'd say nothing about what he knows about CANEX, and so far he's kept his mouth shut. There is no reason for him to talk to the government. It doesn't help his case with the Order of Chartered Accountants, which the Order will hear after my case is over."

"Why would he keep quiet?"

Dad smiled. "Revealing such information to Revenue Canada gives Mel no benefit. The government doesn't give anything to whistleblowers." He pointed his fork at me. "Also, it would make him look bad if he discloses confidential client dealings—he could then lose his other clients even if his accounting licence gets reinstated."

Dad's smile faded as he looked down at the table. "I guess he could try to blackmail me with what he knows about CANEX, but he's not given me any indication."

He continued to devour his meal. After a moment, he abruptly stopped eating and pushed his plate away. "Without my lawyer's help, I would have been personally prosecuted. Wardberg convinced the government to drop their criminal charges against me and focus only on the corporate charges on Montreal Phono."

He grinned again. "Luckily, I had the best lawyer in Montreal. A good lawyer is like a good wife; you can't live with them, and you can't live without them." He pointed at me. "They can charge like crazy, but they can save your ass too." He chuckled.

Because Dad was upbeat, I hazarded another question. "So who was the guy who gave you the idea to have two company inventories?"

Dad looked around the room and then confided quietly, "It was Jiri Varga—you know, my friend with whom we sometimes play golf?"

My eyes opened wide, but I kept my mouth shut.

My father continued. "Jiri steered me in a bad direction. He gave me the idea to carry the two different inventories for Montreal Phono and to keep the full inventory hidden in my bank's safety deposit box. Somehow it led to Revenue Canada's raid on the company."

He glared at me from across the table. "I asked Jiri if he had anything to do with the raid, but he assured me that he wasn't the one that squealed on me."

No matter where the inventory write-off idea had come from, Dad had chosen to implement it.

By now, I knew my father well enough. His practice was to ask three professional or business people for advice on a problem he was having. He'd then act on the answer he liked most. If anybody else subsequently asked him about a bad decision, he'd say, "Oh, so-and-so told me I should do it that way."

A year after Revenue Canada's 1975 raid on Montreal Phono, Dad agreed to the government's charges and penalties for corporate tax evasion. The company paid an $80,000 fine, in addition to thousands of dollars in legal bills.

Soon after the court case was behind him, my father told my brother and me, "I had to let Mel go. He lost his licence to practise."

There ended Dad and Mel's twenty-one-year business relationship and friendship.

Some years later, a Canadian lawyer I knew (who also knew about my father) told me that Montreal Phono case had made history in the Canadian tax case law journals about how to "write down" (effectively reduce) the value of aging inventory in a small business.

My brother told me that Montreal Phono also earned the dubious distinction of "Winning top position in Quebec for corporate tax fraud," reported that year by a major Montreal newspaper. Though I knew Steve wouldn't lie about such things, I later searched the Montreal newspaper microfiche archives for that news clipping, but I couldn't locate it.

At the time, I said to my brother, "It's not the way I'd like to see our Simkovits family become famous."

He replied, "I know what you mean, Harvy."

But he didn't know what I meant. Damned if I would be as careless as my father had been about his hidden offshore assets. When my day came, I'd do everything I could to avoid such attention and prosecution.

Decades after Dad's Montreal Phono court case, another tax lawyer clued me in on government tax prosecutions. "The tax authorities usually go after what's easiest to prove," he offered. "Though tax evasion is a criminal offense in Canada, such charges require a large burden of proof for the government. There's a lot of work in generating subpoenas to gather

187

transactional information from banks and the like. In your father's day, government prosecutors often went with what was easiest to prove."

I guessed that my father had been damned lucky. In my case, I was going to work to be damned smart.

A year after his court case, in 1977, my father changed his company's name to JHS Electronex, JHS standing for "John Harvy Stephen." With disdain, he told Steve and me, "The Quebec separatists and their French language police are forcing me to get a new name for the business. That bloody *L'office Québécois de la Langue Française* is making us comply with Bill 101, Quebec's bloody French language charter."

Dad smirked. "I didn't want to rename Montreal Phono to *Montréal Tourne-Disque* [Montreal Record Player]. 'JHS Electronics' wasn't French enough, so I renamed our company JHS Electronex, with an *e-x* at the end, which is universal."

He looked at Steve. "And 'JHS' sounds and looks better than 'JSH,' that's why Harvy's initial comes between yours and mine."

It was pretty obvious to me the message my father was communicating with his new company name, other than not wanting the Montreal Phono tax-fraud branding. I appreciated the position of my first initial right after Dad's, but hell if I wanted to feel squeezed between him and my brother.

* * *

Thirty years later, when I asked the 85-year-old Mel about his side of the Revenue Canada suit, he was matter-of-fact. "When your father knew that he was out of the woods with the Canadian authorities back in '76, he called me."

Mel raised both of his hands. "We had no conversation; he just told me point-blankly, 'Mel, you're fired!' and then hung up."

A frown came to the retired accountant's face. "I couldn't believe it," he said. He pointed to himself. "I had been the one who proposed the explanation that your father's offshore money had come from Czechoslovakia. Your father's lawyer said my idea was worth a shot." Mel pointed right at me, "And the government bought it."

Though I was taken aback by Mel's declaration, I kept moving forward with my questions. "I heard from my dad that you lost your accountant licence."

Mel looked perplexed. "Not at all! The Order only suspended my licence until my case was heard and decided. I got off with a slap on the wrist. My licence was reinstated right after the Order's ruling."

His voice didn't waver. "I kept my nose clean after that, to the day I retired. I even got through my ex-partner trying to take clients away from me during the year they suspended my licence."

Mel shook his head. "It didn't matter what I did to help your father through his court case; he still let me go. We never saw or talked to each other again."

I said nothing as my eyes gazed down at the floor. I wondered if Dad needed a scapegoat, or perhaps he suspected Mel would no longer let him get away with any corporate monkey business. Though Dad had been the one to cause his own trouble, he had cast off his trusted confidant as if Mel had suddenly become a disloyal employee. A shiver went through my spine for my father's callousness.

Mel hesitated for a moment. His shifted in his seat as if he wondered whether he should say more. He offered, "Your mother came to me once, privately, without your father knowing. She asked me if I could talk to Johnny about going to see a doctor about his medical problem."

Surprised, I looked directly at Mel. "What problem was that?"

"That's what I said to your mother. I told her, 'I don't understand, Anna. What are you specifically saying or asking?'

"Your mother then told me, 'Johnny says he can't sleep with me because he has an impotence problem. Can you ask him to see a doctor about it? You're a good friend; he'll listen to you.'"

"What! My father was impotent?" I blurted out.

"That's what I thought, Harvy. I knew your father well enough to know that it wasn't true. I turned to your mother and said, 'I'm sorry Anna, but Johnny's my customer. I really can't ask him that.'" He took a breath. "Your mother looked disappointed but never raised the subject again."

Why did Mel tell me this? I felt ashamed, not only that my father had summarily dismissed Mel, but that Mel revealed to me such an intimate detail about my parents. He certainly had cared about my father. Maybe he wanted me to know my father's true character, or perhaps he wanted to stick a knife in me to get back at my father in absentia.

In all the ways my father had manipulated my mother, I found this to be the most egregious. After I had said goodbye to Mel, I wondered how Mom had felt about her husband losing interest in her.

It must have been devastating when it finally dawned on her that she was unwanted and unloved by the person to whom she had given her whole life. If Dad were still alive today, I'd slap him in his face for his cruelty. *Shit! I should have slapped him decades ago.*

My father's relationship with Mel seemed to be one of convenience rather than true friendship. It reminded me of an expression I overheard my mother tell a friend after my father had left her a second time: "If you have Johnny Simkovits as a friend, you don't need an enemy."

Now, years after his passing, I considered, *If you have Johnny Simkovits as a father, you don't need a...... what?*

* * *

Dad never found out how Revenue Canada discovered his dual company inventory scheme. After my father had dismissed Mel, he engaged a new accountant, a senior partner in a larger and reputable Montreal accounting firm.

Roger Delliard was a seasoned CPA, a top executive in his big firm. He had been brought in by Wardberg as an expert witness to testify on Montreal Phono's behalf. Dad later told me, "When Roger was on the stand, he impressed me with his sophisticated knowledge and his calm manner when he talked to the judge."

Years after my father's death, I sought out Roger through his old accounting firm. I wanted to know his side of the Revenue Canada court case. He was long retired, but his firm contacted him on my behalf. Within a day, he called me, and we arranged a time to meet for dinner the next time I was in Montreal.

During our meal, I asked the short, stout former accountant about his testimony during the Montreal Phono court hearings. He remembered the proceedings as if they had been conducted the previous week. He offered, "I had said to the judge, 'It's clear that the company's accountant, Mozer, was at fault for not claiming all the company's inventory. Mozer made the mistake of pulling sheets of listed merchandise out of the inventory ledger.'"

Roger motioned his hands outward as if he were pulling pages from a binder. "Had Mr. Mozer kept those sheets in the ledger," he said, "then there wouldn't have been any question about your father's guilt or innocence."

He raised a finger. "There only might have been a debate about the value of that merchandise, which, in itself, isn't a criminal or tax offense, only a matter of opinion between Revenue Canada and Montreal Phono." He spoke matter-of-factly. "The inventory assessment matter would have been handled out of court between the two parties."

I told Roger what the elder Mozer had told me about the pressure he felt from my father to sign incomplete (even false) inventory statements.

Roger stared at me for a few seconds, his eyes looking earnest. He offered, "Oh, I didn't know that."

* * *

One day after work in the summer of '77, during my last JHS employment stint before heading to a job with Procter & Gamble, I sat with Dad in his private office. His Revenue Canada court case was now history and things were back to normal at his company. He spoke in a low tone. "Roger thinks I shouldn't trust Mel to stay quiet about CANEX in Cayman."

He looked at me with intense, serious eyes. "Roger and I decided that I will declare CANEX as my personal corporation. I will then close it down in a year or two."

He leaned toward me. "Now that the government discovered those CANEX papers in my bank safety deposit box, I have no way to hide my association with that company. I can't use CANEX anymore to siphon the company's profits offshore."

His eyes were piercing. "Son, *lassen* to me. Keep what I told you just among us." He pointed to me, then himself, then the wall. "I don't want your brother to know what you, Roger, and I know."

"Okay, Dad," I said as I nodded my understanding. I was relieved that he, with Roger's counsel, was going to curb his offshore shenanigans.

I was thankful that a dark money chapter was behind my father—especially the sleepless nights, protracted legal proceedings, and the continual grouchiness that he displayed that difficult year. I hoped that Roger Delliard and his big accounting firm were going to hold Dad back from conducting more clandestine money mischief. I wouldn't want to see Revenue Canada raid his company once again, confiscate a pile of papers, scrutinize his money-making methods, and perhaps put him behind bars the next time.

I wondered if there would be more for me to survive concerning my father.

* * * *

30

Czechoslovak Miscalculations

One early evening during my college summer break, my mother had our hard-cased suitcases lined up and opened in the guest bedroom. After my favorite supper of sweet Hungarian stuffed cabbage and potato gnocchi that she had simmered on her stove all afternoon, she called me into that bedroom. She wanted to go over the things I should pack for our trip.

After we had sorted my clothes and packed my bag, she said, "Harvy, I need a special favor from you." In her hand were a couple of small packages wrapped in brown paper that she had retrieved from a handbag. "I want your help to hide these in our coffers [her term for 'luggage']."

It was 1976, days before my fifth overseas trip to my parents' homeland. I was twenty-one years old, in between having finished my engineering bachelor's degree and starting my master's.

In the months before our journey abroad, Mom's hometown relatives, anticipating our visit, had written to her. They had made their special requests for Western goods.

In past trips, my mother had brought them the basics—peanut butter, inexpensive perfume and aftershave, and nylon stockings—all of which were difficult, if not impossible, to obtain behind the Iron Curtain. This time she wanted to surprise them with something special.

"What are those things?" I asked. I stared at the neatly wrapped and taped packages in my mother's hand. They were about the size of a cigarette pack, but thinner.

She pulled out an unwrapped silver-grey item from a dresser drawer. In her hand was a simple calculator. She offered, "I want to bring ten of these as gifts for my relatives."

Electronic calculators were becoming a hot consumer item. Inexpensive models, performing straightforward arithmetic, could now be bought at any department store. Mom saw an opportunity to do something nice for her Czechoslovak family. Such devices were expensive or unobtainable in her homeland.

I was uncertain about Mom's plan. "Aren't you worried that Czechoslovak customs agents will find them and take them away from us?"

Her voice was undeterred. "That's why I want you to help me hide them in the suitcases." She took a quick breath. "And I want you to say nothing about it to your father."

For the last number of months, for better or worse, Dad was living at home after he and Mom had reconciled after their second separation. She was pleased to have her husband back. She once again cooked his favorite Hungarian-Slovak meals, washed his underwear, and ironed his dress shirts as if he had never left. Their habitual fighting had subsided for the time being.

My time at college had given me some distance from my parents' sporadic troubles. I hoped I could tolerate two weeks in Eastern Europe with them—they probably wouldn't have gone there without me also going. My older brother, who lived at home, said he couldn't come on this vacation because he had to attend to his new horse. Maybe he knew something I didn't.

I braced myself for the worst. If my parents argued during our travels, I was old enough to walk away and head to a café or bar until tempers cooled. They usually put on their best smiles and behavior when visiting relatives back home. I obliged them and agreed to tag along.

Mom's calculator request made me uneasy, not only because of my parents' history but also because we'd be crossing a communist border. When Steve and I had traveled to Czechoslovakia with my mother when we had been kids, I remembered the stern-faced border guards having asked myriad questions. They searched luggage and checked handbags. They had no qualms about detaining visitors, charging high import duties, or taking away Western goods from those who tried to bring in merchandise above legal limits. I remembered seeing the exasperated faces of foreign travellers as border officials rummaged through coffers and removed contraband. I wondered why Mom would take such a chance with these calculators.

Dad too had warned us about not attracting excessive attention at the Iron Curtain frontier. It might cause him to be detained or denied entry into Czechoslovakia, especially since he hadn't escaped his homeland legally in 1949.

I looked at the calculator in my mother's outstretched hand. "What would happen if the border guards catch you with these?" My tone was serious. "What would Dad say if he found out?"

She trumpeted out her case. "These cheap things cost only $10 each. If I declare them, Czechoslovak customs will charge us more duty than what they are worth." She swept her calculator-filled hand toward the floor. "If the border guards find them, I'll just leave them there or throw them away."

To avoid an argument, I complied with my mother's request. I helped her spread the ten wrapped calculators among our three big suitcases. I didn't feel right, but I said nothing about it to my father. If any trouble happened, I felt it would be my mother's responsibility.

A few days later, we flew into Munich, Germany. Dad preferred to fly into a Western European city where he could rent a reliable sedan with which to travel into his poorer homeland. He offered, "You never know what kind of car you'll get in Czechoslovakia. They'll say they have what you want but then give you something else. That's just the way it is there."

Dad rented a good-sized, automatic Mercedes for our trip into his country of pint-sized Czech Skodas and unreliable Russian Ladas. We masked any association with rich and showy Americans by attaching a small Canadian flag to the car's antenna. In Slovakia, this gesture turned heads and attracted smiles. Friendly waves and broken-English *hallos* would come from toothless villagers and unkempt gypsy children as we rolled over potholed village streets.

A child's open palm might receive a Canadian dollar coin or fifty-cent piece passed by me through an open car window.

After we had arrived in Munich, Dad drove us the whole afternoon toward the Czechoslovak border. When we were close, he asked me to look at the map and locate a sizable town on the route. "I want to spend the night in Germany," he said, "before we tackle the border crossing tomorrow morning."

He knew that the entry gauntlet could take hours and involve standing in long lines at the border station. The border crowd might be smaller if we crossed early in the day, and we'd have fuller stomachs, fresher faces, and be better rested.

The three of us had a leisurely supper at a *penzion* (guesthouse) we found in a village a few kilometers before the Bohemian frontier. During our meal, Dad repeated his instructions. "I want us to get up early tomorrow and make it quickly to the border."

"Let's avoid turning things upside down in our luggage," Mom offered. "Leave your travel clothes out and put them back on tomorrow. We'll unpack everything and change our clothes when we reach our hotel in Prague."

Morning came. After a filling breakfast of fruit, fresh-baked bread, bratwurst, and eggs, Dad repacked the car's trunk, and we headed east. It was a clear and calm summer morning.

Approaching the border station, I could see the barbed wire fences and tall tower outposts that overlooked the treeless no-man's-land between a free West Germany and a communist Czechoslovakia. We then saw a long lineup of cars.

Crap! Dad wasn't the only one with the early morning border crossing idea.

After waiting in a car line for nearly thirty minutes, we were permitted to drive up to a station booth. Dad opened his window and talked to a uniformed Czech border guard.

The officer was a tall, good-looking, thirty-something guy with strong jawlines. He wore the Czechoslovakia star on his khaki-green shirt pocket and the shirt's two epaulettes. He asked for and examined our passports and entry visas. He pointed to where he wanted us to park and where we needed to walk into the building to get through the entry process.

The few pictures on the walls of this non-air-conditioned and dull florescent-lit border station were of blank-faced Czechoslovak presidents and stern-looking Russian officials. The only interesting decoration was a wall map of Czechoslovakia. Dad and I perused it briefly to trace our anticipated multi-day journey from the Bohemian border to Prague and then onto my parents' hometown of Košice at the east end of the country.

Though the few windows in the station were wide open, the place reeked of the musty odors of communist cigarette smoke mixed in with Slavic body odor. The cigarettes here smelled fouler than the Canadian brands my father smoked. The body odor fragrance was like cooking oil gone rancid.

Along a side wall were high desks where we found and filled out entry forms. Dad asked me to write our names and home address on the documents while he filled in the rest.

While Mom grew hot and sweaty in our car, Dad and I shuffled through three slow-moving queues in designated order. First was the Passport and Immigration line where another uniformed man—sitting behind a counter and glass window that had a small opening—took and eyed our passports and visas. He asked my father questions in Czech, a language I didn't understand because I had grown up with my parent's Hungarian.

As the officer examined my father's Canadian passport, he saw that my father was born in Czechoslovakia, which my dad openly acknowledged. Then the immigration official abruptly excused himself and disappeared into a back room.

"Where is the guy going?" I asked Dad.

He shrugged. "I don't know."

After what seemed a long ten or fifteen minutes, the officer returned. He proceeded to have an animated discussion with my father, giving Dad the third degree.

My dad stayed calm and spoke confidently. He looked the officer in the eyes, opened his arms and motioned with his opened hands as if he was saying, *So what do you want from me?* They talked more, and Dad threw out the word "Tesla" within his Czech sentences.

A blank expression on his face, the officer abruptly stamped our visas and passports, and then he returned them to us. When we walked away from the man to head for the next line, I looked at my father. "What was that about?"

He kept his voice low. "It's always something different whenever I come here. I've never before entered through this particular border crossing. It says in my passport that I was born in Czechoslovakia, but they have no record here of me having left the country legally in '49."

Dad took another breath. "The officer didn't want to let me enter the country, but only allow you and your mother to do so."

Turning his face away from the immigration official, Dad grinned a bit. "I told him about my connection with Tesla's company president here in Czechoslovakia. I then said, 'Okay! If you don't let me in, then I can't do any business with Tesla.' The guy then stamped my passport with no more of his border baloney."

Dad's console stereo company imported speakers from Czechoslovakia. This arrangement not only allowed my father to combine business with pleasure when returning to his homeland, but it also gave him the border-crossing leverage he needed. I revered my father for his shrewdness.

The second line in the border station was for the Currency Exchange Bank. Each entering visitor was required to buy 100 Czechoslovak Koruna for each day they were in the country. It amounted to 1800 Koruna for the three of us for the six days we would be there.

After Dad had given the woman teller $180 in U.S. cash, she counted out the Koruna bills with excruciating slowness. The bills varied in colour, like Canadian currency, but the shades were extremely muted. The denominations were of varied sizes; the smallest bill—worth maybe a quarter in Canada—was the size of an over-sized business card.

As the teller reached half-way through her money counting, Dad's face was glum. He quipped quietly to me in English, "These communist workers are slow like pokes."

The total value of these Czechoslovakian bills, 38 Koruna, was worth nearly $4USD at the official government rate. But they could be obtained for just a little over $1USD on the local black market. C. 1970.

After collecting our cash and walking away from the teller window, he added, "The Czechoslovak government makes a killing on its legal currency black market at the border. They require the tourists to change money at ten Koruna per dollar." He closed his fist. "I can get over three times more from the moneychangers who work on the streets of Prague or Košice."

Though I knew that such black-market money-changing enterprises were illegal, I didn't say anything. I still very much admired my father's moxie for putting one over on the communist rulers of his homeland, right on the streets of his hometown.

The last document hurdle was the Customs and Duty line. Waiting there, switching his weight back and forth on fatigued legs, Dad confessed, "Things were much better here before the Communists Party took over. There's no fire in these people anymore."

My back too was sore from standing so long. I nodded my understanding as I glanced at the blank-faced officers and clerks behind glass windows and grey metal desks. Their faces looked as if Soviet communism had sucked the life out of them.

When we came to the front of the customs line, Dad divulged to the attending officer that we had gifts to declare. He named them one by one, counting them off on his fingers.

I felt uncomfortable keeping my mouth shut regarding Mom's brown-paper wrapped items, but I had given her my word. I stood behind my father's shoulder so he wouldn't notice my uneasiness. I was glad that nobody asked me anything, so I wouldn't have to lie.

Dad answered more questions about a carton of cigarettes he was bringing into the country. He had brought Canadian cigarettes with him both for his personal use and to share with his relatives over a shot glass or three of strong Czechoslovak plum brandy.

There was no telling expression on the customs man's face as he rubber-stamped our customs declaration. He motioned us to go back outside and see the border guard with whom we had started.

Dad and I returned to our car to complete the last hurdle. Prepared for this moment, my father opened the automobile's rear door, poked his head into the vehicle, and grabbed our bag of declared gifts lying on the floor next to Mom. He said to her, "We're almost done here."

Mom's hair, usually teased high on her head, was now sagging from the humidity. She looked at him. "What took so long?"

He replied, "I'll tell you later." He hardly looked at her.

Head raised, Dad's stride was confident. He carried the bag of gifts to the border official who stood at his guard post a few paces in front of our car.

The guard motioned with his hand and spoke in an inexpressive voice. He put out his palm for our stamped papers. He laid our documents on his counter and checked things off in his mind. He gazed down at the bag of items in Dad's hand and put his long fingers into the sack to move things around. After a moment, he raised his head. He spoke to my father and motioned to our car.

Dad's face was blank. He nodded, turned to me, and said, "The guard wants us to open some of our luggage."

I tried not to show any tension on my face. I hoped that Mom's and my calculator packing job was going to work. I followed Dad and the guard to our car where my father opened the trunk to reveal our three big suitcases and a couple of bulky handbags.

The guard gazed across the stuffed compartment. He pointed to one of the suitcases, indicating he wanted that one opened.

Mom remained silent in the back seat.

Hands sure, my father complied with the guard's request. He put the designated valise on top of the other cases and opened it wide.

My heart beat harder as the guard put his hands into the suitcase and started to move clothes around.

A moment later, the officer's hand stalled. He pulled out an item. It was one of the small brown-paper wrapped packages.

My heart jumped into my throat. Beads of sweat formed on my forehead.

The officer stared into my father's eyes, showing him the small package held between his long thumb and index finger. He spoke in a hard but inquisitive tone in his native tongue.

Confused, my father shrugged his shoulders and displayed his open arms and palms. He shook his head and said something in their common language. He turned around, looked directly into my eyes, and asked acidly, "Do you know anything about this?"

I didn't return Dad's glare but confessed then and there. "Mom wanted to bring cheap calculators as gifts for her relatives. I'm sorry, but she asked me not to tell you about them."

"How many are there?" he demanded.

"I think ten," I said sheepishly.

"You *think*, or you *know*?" he replied.

"We packed ten," I stuttered.

His face flushed, Dad turned back to the guard. He talked fast but in a conciliatory way. He explained what he now knew, pointing to Mom in the car and then to me. His arms and hands rose in a gesture of disgust and resignation as the guard unwrapped the package to expose the simple calculator. My father stopped talking abruptly and watched the guard consider his next move.

Through the car's open windows, Mom had overheard what had been going on outside. From her backseat perch, she poked her head out and started to talk loudly in Slovak (close enough to the guard's Czech for him to understand).

The guard walked to her window and listened for a moment to her animated monologue. Soon it became clear that the officer preferred to deal with the man of the family. He turned back toward Dad and talked with him again.

My father's face was glum and anxious. He turned to me. "Your mother now says she brought only six calculators and she is willing to declare them." He took a deep breath and continued, "The guard wants to go through our bags and find all of them."

I was surprised by Mom's new assertion but went along. Dad and I pulled out our suitcases from the car's trunk and placed them side-by-side on a large metal rack on the sidewalk. Dad's face looked grim, but he said nothing. He opened the cases while the guard silently looked on.

The officer used his long arms and hands to rummage through the clothes in each bag, counting the calculators as he uncovered more of the wrapped devices.

"Two…, three…," he counted in Czech as he completed his inspection of the first bag. "Four…five…, six…," he continued as he searched the second bag, wrapped calculators falling out from among the clothes.

My heart beat so hard that I thought the guard might hear it. I held my breath. *Is that all Mom brought?* We still had one more suitcase in which to look.

The guy whipped his hands in and out of the third and final case. *Maybe Mom took the calculators out of this last bag and didn't tell me.*

After a few more seconds of rummaging, the guard stopped. He retracted his hand, and in it was another brown package. "Seven!" he said loudly in his language. My heart sank.

The young guard looked sternly at my father and said harsh words. But his voice was calm, very much unlike my father when he became angry. The seven calculators in hand, the guard retired to his booth to do paperwork.

Dad turned to me. Fire rose in his face and eyes, but he held back his ire. "We need to go through the rest of the luggage and show him the ten calculators."

Dad approached Mom's window. Using an angrier tone—yet still holding back his full fury—he told her the bad news in Hungarian, a language no guard here would understand.

For the next minute, both of them talked past each other, having their typical hard-headed verbal tussle. But Mom and Dad talked quietly enough that I couldn't make out the words. In the way he grabbed the car firmly with both hands and leaned in toward her, I could imagine his heat and edginess. I wondered if he was putting on this display so the border guard would gather it hadn't been him who had lied.

I stayed fastened to the spot next to the open luggage. I didn't dare move. I tried to tune out my parents' bickering but bemoaned my complicity in this abysmal affair. Why had I gone along with my mother's foolishness in hiding those calculators from Dad? Why did she get me involved as her accomplice in the first place?

I felt as if I had failed my father and hoped he wouldn't have hard feelings. I wondered if he and she would fight about this for the rest of our two-week vacation. What could I say to him to put this border fiasco behind us?

After rounds of spousal parlays and thrusts, Dad came back to me as I stood behind our car. Redness was still on his face. He motioned to our bags. "Let's get this over with."

We first made sure no calculators lingered in the first two coffers. I then put my hands into the remaining suitcase. I continued the count, "Eight…, nine…, ten…," putting each discovered package into Dad's hands.

While I repacked our clothes into the last suitcases, I unexpectedly felt another hard object at my fingertips. I pulled it out from its hiding place. My father and I looked at it, and then stared at each other for the next few seconds. In my hand was another calculator, the eleventh!

I kept the wrapped device out of view within the suitcase. "Jesus, Dad!" I whispered. "I didn't know about this one."

My father shook off his stare and whispered, "Quick! Put it back where you found it. We'll pretend it wasn't there."

Dad took the three additional calculators to the guard's booth. He walked past Mom's window without saying anything to her. I felt the irritation oozing out from his every pore.

When he reached the guard booth in front of the car, Dad showed the officer the "remaining" calculators. The guard took them and put them on his small desk. Dad put on as congenial a look as he could muster. He spoke again to the guy—perhaps an apology—while he motioned once more toward Mom in the car.

I couldn't tell if Mom had overheard Dad or not, but she opened her door and nearly leaped out of the vehicle. She walked swiftly to the guard and talked to him vigorously.

Dad stayed with them for a moment. He then walked back to me, his head shaking, his face showing a sick-to-his-stomach look. His hands and forearms were flying around. He clenched his teeth and tried to stay calm and quiet. "Your mother thinks these people are stupid. She's arguing with the guy about the calculators. I can't understand how she thinks he will believe anything she says."

Dad turned around and stood next to me and said nothing more. We watched as Mom dug herself deeper. My guilt kept me from asking my father more about what she was saying.

Though the officer towered a full head and shoulders over Mom, my mother waved her partially-closed hand at him. She had done similar hand-waving with me as a child when she became peeved at me for contradicting her in front of others. She had done the same with her youngest brother, Viktor, when he came to our house for supper and ate with a spoon instead of a fork.

Even though I was shivering from the drama unfolding in front of me, I was relieved that I wasn't standing in the direct path of my mother's vehemence as she tried to explain away her transgression. Maybe she felt she was defending her right.

Head lowered and stone-faced, the guard listened to her for another moment. His unresponsive air told me he remained unmoved by her explanations. After having enough, he looked her straight in the eyes, like a judge who glowered into the eyes of the guilty. He offered strong words while pointing his long index finger at her. He gestured toward the car and seemed to order her to move.

In a huff, my mother returned to her backseat spot as she muttered unintelligible words under her breath.

Having waited for this moment, my father turned to me. "Son, please put the luggage back together slowly into the trunk." He tilted his head toward the guard. "I'm going back to finish with the guy."

I nodded my understanding. I figured Dad didn't want me to rush and thus attract more attention to our car's trunk.

Dad ambled over to the guard. He talked to the officer in an apologetic tone, his hands forward, open, and at waist level. He shrugged and once more gestured with both hands toward the ground in front of the car, possibly attempting to explain the behavior of his foolish wife.

Then it was the guard's turn. He spoke forcefully. Dad listened to him like a shamed child caught with his hand in his father's wallet or mother's purse.

Soon the officer stopped talking. He looked again at everything on his desk and put attention on his paperwork.

Dad waited patiently to see what Iron Curtain verdict awaited us. He pulled out a pack of cigarettes and grabbed and lit one for himself. He offered another to the officer.

The guard raised his flat hand to say no to the appeasement. Dad stood there and smoked alone.

While he waited for the guard, I finished repacking the luggage. I left the truck's hood open to indicate that Dad and I were not trying to hide anything. I ambled toward the front of the car on the opposite side of the vehicle from the guard booth.

Mom stuck her head out the open window and started to talk to me harshly, in the way she had talked to the guard.

I didn't listen to what she had to say but quietly and firmly told her in English, "You didn't tell me about the eleventh calculator. Dad and I found it and hid it back in the suitcase." I was angry at her for bringing me into her mess.

Mom immediately stopped talking. She sat back in her seat and crossed her arms.

I sauntered past her window and hung out next to the car's front hood. While my mother stewed, I watched my father and the guard perform the last of their dance of animated hands and Czech words.

The border official didn't return to the car's trunk. He did return to Mom's window to say a few things and to ask her a question or two. No longer in a fighting mood, she calmly answered.

After a final round of remarks between the officer and my father, my dad pulled out his wallet. He slowly counted out American cash and handed it to the guy.

Our punishment?

The guard handed Dad our papers and stamped a greyish receipt for the money. All documents in hand, Dad turned and came toward me. When he was a yard away, he asked, "Is everything back in the trunk?"

I nodded. "Yes," and asked in a low tone, "So what happened with the guard?"

Dad explained calmly. "He charged me a $100US penalty for the undeclared calculators, then another $100 for your mother lying to him, and $10 more for each calculator she wanted to bring into the country."

He was matter-of-fact. "Mom told him she now wants to bring in only four calculators as gifts. We'll need to take the rest with us when we leave Czechoslovakia."

He took a long breath. "The guard put a note on my entry visa saying that we will be taking the other calculators out of the country. We'll have to show them to the Czechoslovak customs people when we cross the border again."

I knew Dad was fuming inside, only acting calm so as not to make a scene in front of the border official. Once we left the premises, it could become World War III between my parents, verbal barbs thrown like grenades. I wanted no part of that.

I had been thinking about what I could say to put this abysmal situation behind us. I looked at my father, raised an open hand, and said peacefully, "Dad, I know you are angry at Mom and probably me too." I avoided his incensed eyes. "I know what she did was stupid and I'm sorry I didn't tell you anything earlier."

I paused to gather my courage. "And if you and Mom are going to have a big fight about this then please take me to the Prague airport today. I'll arrange to fly back to Montreal by myself."

Dad shot a look of surprise at me and then took a second or two to gather himself. There was a resignation on his face, and his voice was tranquil. "Okay, son; close the trunk, get in the car, and we can go."

Dad took out another cigarette, lit it, opened his driver's door, and climbed in behind the wheel. In English and Hungarian, he matter-of-factly explained to Mom what he had told me.

After he had finished, Mom sat back in her rear seat, and no one said another word about it. We pulled out of the border station and merged onto the highway to Prague.

I worked to change the subject. I asked about what we were going to do in the capital city, but neither of my parents was in a talking mood.

Dad drove with his eyes straight forward. Mom looked out a side window. Feeling alone in our crowded car, I pulled out a map of Czechoslovakia and occupied myself by studying our anticipated route.

Thirty minutes later, Mom asked in an upbeat tone. "Hey! We are very close to Mariánské Lázně [a Bohemian resort town]. It's a beautiful spa village, and we have never been there together. How about we stop there for dinner?"

Dad didn't respond, as if he hadn't heard her request. I briefly looked up from my map yet offered no response.

A few minutes later, Mom leaned further forward, put her hand on the back of Dad's seat, and asked in an upbeat tone, "Johnny, how about we go there?"

I could see the fire rise again in my father's face. His hands stiffened on the steering wheel. Shivers started up my back. Dad loudly grumbled, "I'm not going there!" He didn't glance back at her.

Mom fell back into her seat and said nothing more. I sat still. Dad had carved out his pound of spousal flesh.

Later, I provided map directions to guide Dad into downtown Plzeň, a Czech town known for its famous Pilsner Urquell beer. We stopped there for a late mid-day dinner at an outdoor restaurant downtown.

We ordered a few Pilsners to wash down our meal and wash away our long border ordeal. I steered us to the safe topic of what we planned to do in Prague over the next couple of days.

Our Czechoslovakia vacation continued without further incident. Being among our Prague and Košice relatives seemed to cut any lingering tension between my parents.

Dad shared our border woes with Mom's brother in Prague and with a couple of his uncles in Košice. At the end of his narration, he tacked on a Hungarian "*Asszony* [Women] *Yech!*" His laugh was harsh as he knocked back a shot of Czechoslovak plum brandy. After recounting Mom's fruitless conversation with the border guard, he reprised one of his favorite Hungarian expressions. "There's nothing in your hand. Hold on to it tightly."

Mom gave her four declared calculators, and the eleventh undeclared one, as gifts to her closest kin. It was nice to see their eyes sparkle as they unwrapped the little brown paper packages and started to fiddle with the buttons.

I smiled, knowing that most of them had no idea of the price that Dad had paid to import those items into their country.

Playing it by the communist border-crossing book, we took the six other calculators out of Czechoslovakia, but the border guard at our exit point never asked to see them.

* * * *

31

Sibling Wedge

A few months after Dad had returned to Mom, my brother and I were having supper with her. Dad was out that evening for a business meeting. As usual, he didn't call Mom to tell her when he'd be home. Our mother spoke harshly, "Your father is once more with who knows who doing who knows what."

Steve retorted, "Mom, why did you even want to have him back?"

I froze in my chair. I never considered being as direct with my mother as my brother was being.

She answered without hesitation. "Your father is a good provider, and I love him deeply. And what would I do without him?"

She thought for a second and then said tersely, "I want him to be with us more instead of with his whore friends."

That weekend, Mom laid out supper for Dad on the coffee table in front of the TV. Afterward, he casually—perhaps even unconsciously—said, "*Nagyon szépen köszönöm, cica.* [Thank you so much, kitten.]"

Mom put a hand on her chest and became overwhelmed with emotion. "Kitten" had been Dad's term of endearment for her before he had left her. She turned toward her kitchen and wiped a tear from her eye. She worked to keep her reaction hidden from us, though I saw it.

Mom lived for such moments. It remained a mystery to me as to how little it took for Dad to make her happy.

* * *

My mother had many times told my brother and me, "I am a good and loyal wife to your father. I'd do anything for him."

Privately, Dad might counter to us, "Your mother puts more attention on her Tatransky family than she does on me."

Within a year of Dad's second return home to Mom, trouble surfaced again in our extended family. It once again had to do with Mom's brother, Lali.

In the spring of 1977, I was home from grad school for a week's vacation. Mom got a call from Dad late one afternoon—a rare occurrence during a workday.

I could hear Dad's voice blaring over the phone. After listening for a moment, Mom's voice became agitated. Dad had said something about her brother. I could tell from her groans, sighs, and *Oys!* that she was beside herself with worry.

After hanging up with Dad, Mom made a call to Lali. They exchanged harsh words. After screaming at each other in both Slovak and Hungarian, Mom banged down the receiver and stormed into the kitchen.

I stayed in my room and didn't approach her. I stuck to my policy of staying out of our family's mishigas.

That evening over supper, Mom told me what Dad had told her. "Your father says that Lali is trying to steal what is in your father's safety deposit box at the bank! Lali is telling the bank that he's the owner of that box. Both your father and Lali are saying the box is rightfully theirs and not the other's property."

Her eyes were wet from crying. "Your father said that his lawyer now froze the box and neither he nor Lali can get into it. He told me it holds his private papers, gold coins, and some jewellery, and that Lali has no right to them."

I spoke as calmly as I could. "Did Lali say anything more when you called him?"

Her voice became loud. "You father wanted me to tell Lali that he has no right to what's in the box." She wiped away a tear and repeated, "But Lali said that what's in the box is his." She cried. "I don't know what to do."

That night, Dad came home late and angry. He went at it again in Slovak with Mom. Lali's name bounced off the kitchen walls as I stayed in bed upstairs, trying to get to sleep. I couldn't understand their conversation, but there were more groans, sighs, and *Oys!* that emanated from Mom. She seemed to be at a loss for what to do about her bull-headed brother and livid husband.

I gnashed my teeth as I thought about my mother now stuck between the two men she loved the most.

A couple of days later, I had a chance to talk to Dad privately. He told me his version of what was going on.

"It was stupid of me!" he bellowed. "After the RCMP raided my bank safety deposit box two years ago, I asked Lali if I could use his name for one particular box I had. I didn't want to be exposed once more if Revenue Canada was going to prosecute me again."

Dad talked to me as if he was confiding in a close friend. "I didn't want the government to see my private papers, even the ones having to do with CANEX and my offshore money." He took a deep breath. "I told Lali I wanted to protect my personal papers, so he agreed for me to use his name and address for that one deposit box."

I was confused. "I thought you were going to close CANEX, Dad."

His voice was edgy. "Yes, but I haven't done it yet, son. These things take time. I already declared CANEX to the Canadian government in my most recent tax returns. I need another year or so to close it for good."

He took another long breath. "There are statements in that bank deposit box from my offshore accounts that I don't want anybody else to know about besides us." He pointed to himself and me. "Lali could cause trouble, even blackmail me, if he knew how much money I have in Cayman. Revenue Canada closed their eyes on those papers when they confiscated them in '75. Lali could open their eyes again if he gets his hands on them."

"What makes Lali think the box is his?"

My father shook his fist. I could sense that he was holding himself back from reacting. He continued. "Initially, Lali went along with our arrangement of allowing his name to be attached to that box. I had it worked out with the girl at the bank, the one who handles safety deposit box renewals, to mail the bill each year to Montreal Phono and not to Lali."

His tone turned terse. "But this year, the regular person was on vacation, and a new girl was doing the renewals." He put out an open palm. "She saw Lali's name and address at the top of the deposit box application, as the primary owner of the box. Instead of her sending the bill to my office, as the regular woman usually did, the new girl stupidly mailed it to Lali's home."

Dad's voice grew intense. "Maybe Lali had forgotten about lending his name to my box. And I forgot that his name was there too. The bank's renewal request opened Lali's eyes." He took a long breath. "Lali went straight to the bank with the paper. He told them he lost his key and demanded that they open the box."

I felt my blood pressure rise. Sweat was coming off my brow. "Oh! My God! How did you find out, Dad?"

"Luckily, the regular girl at the bank was back when Lali showed up. She realized what had happened and then talked to the branch manager."

His tone rose even more. "The manager didn't know Lali outside of his name on the deposit box application, but he did know that the box was mine. Only my signature was on the card the bank had me sign every time I went into the box." His hand rose too. "The manager right away called me and told me Lali was there. He asked me if he can allow Lali to get into the box."

Only such things could happen to my conniving father. I didn't say it, but for as clever as he was, he could be as stupid as shit. Why did he ever trust his brother-in-law? Hadn't they had enough murky water under their in-law bridge?

"So what did you do, Dad?" I asked.

He pointed away from himself. "I told the bank manager to stall Lali until I could get there, and he agreed to do that."

He took a long breath. "But before I left the office, I called Mack and told him what was going on. He told me not to go to the bank. Instead, he immediately wrote a legal paper to put an injunction on the box, claiming my exclusive rights to its contents. He couriered the document to the bank right away."

"So what happened with Lali?"

"The bank manager told him that the box was frozen until its rightful owner could be determined. Lali left the bank unsatisfied."

Dad looked away and then back at me. "Lali went right away to find a lawyer to sue both the bank and me for access to the box. The next day, Mack countersued Lali and the bank, claiming I was the rightful owner."

"I can't believe it, Dad!"

"Me neither!" He paused, looked into my eyes, and added, "Just keep this knowledge between us; okay son?"

"Okay, Dad; okay."

Oy! What an f'ing mess of a family! After what Dad and Lali had been through in Vienna and then Montreal, how the hell could Dad have trusted his brother-in-law in this way?

During the next months, whenever I was home from college for a long weekend, I got glimpses from my parents of their Lali mess. Mom and Dad continued to argue about him, and foul Lali air continued to hang around our home.

I could feel my uncle as a wedge inextricably lodged between Mom and Dad. I didn't ask my parents more about what was going on. I hoped the lawsuits would go away or Dad would win his case in court. I thanked my stars that I was in graduate school and not at home for much of those months. I didn't even talk to my brother about Lali. I didn't want to let on that I knew what was in my father's deposit box.

It took nearly a year for the civil suit between Dad and Lali to be settled by a judge. Dad was declared the box's rightful owner. The bank manager had vouched for Dad, and my father proved that his company had been the one paying the box rental fees. Afterward, Dad recited his signature Hungarian expression, "There was nothing in Lali's hand that he was holding onto tightly."

Mom had stood with Dad throughout the lawsuits and court ordeal. She saw Lali's intrusion as the last straw between her and her brother.

After the incident was behind them, neither Dad nor Mom ever saw or called Lali, his wife, or daughter again. Whenever Mom or Dad mentioned Lali's name, somewhere in their sentence was the Hungarian *bolond ember* (crazy person) or the Yiddish equivalent, *meshugener*.

Twenty-five years earlier, Lali had been kicked out of my parents' Vienna apartment when he wielded a knife at Dad. He was now out of our family for good, but my uncle hadn't finished his knife-wielding.

Less than a year after losing his suit to Dad, a car accident caused my uncle's resentment to rise again. Lali had been driving to the Montreal airport to greet his and Mom's brother-in-law who was flying in from Czechoslovakia for another six-month visit. As Lali drove around a busy traffic circle near our house, another vehicle rear-ended his car.

Lali was in the hospital for weeks with a serious case of whiplash. His subsequent recovery at home took many months. He could no longer work. His wife had to go back into a nursing job to support their family.

To pass the time and exercise his bitterness, Lali dialed his sister every week. In one call, I overheard Mom angrily blurt out, "You ruined my marriage and destroyed my life!" She banged down the receiver. She then let the phone ring until it stopped.

Lali took another tack. He sent letters. After Mom cried over the first ones, the subsequent ones she "returned to sender" unopened. She never told my brother or me what Lali had said in the letters she had opened. I could imagine his words pitted her love of Dad against her devotion to her brother. Mom's choice was to follow her heart and her husband; she cast Lali's approaches asunder.

Lali changed his methods once more and sent postcards to his sister. He wrote in Hungarian so the postman couldn't make out the meaning.

One afternoon while I was again home from college, the postman arrived as I passed by our front entryway. He had pushed a bundle of mail through the front-door slot, and it dropped onto the ground a few feet from me. A postcard caught my eye as it landed script-side-up on the floor. I could tell from the handwriting that it was from Lali.

I couldn't make out most of the writing (I knew Hungarian only by ear). I could decipher a few words written in big, bold, black, block letters with many exclamation points attached to them. The writing on the postcard was in every direction, covering every square inch of the card.

215

Mom rushed out of the kitchen to gather the mail. She put herself in front of me to obstruct my view. She reached down to pick up the postcard along with the rest of the mail.

But she was too late; I had deciphered the words *"DISZNO!!!* [PIG!!!]" and *"CSAVARGO!! [TRAMP* or BUM!!]" among the scattered writing on the card. I could tell from Mom's tight face that she was agitated, but she said nothing as she gathered up everything. She scurried back to her kitchen.

For the next few minutes, moans, whimpers, and whispers emanated from her. I didn't dare ask her about it. It seemed as if she didn't want me (or my brother) involved, and I was afraid to ask. I was angry and confused by the written wounds Lali was inflicting on my mother. I wondered why my uncle's wife and child weren't stopping his hurtful slashes. Did they not know?

There were certainly two sides to this in-law conflict, and I was only seeing glimpses of my parents' position. I imagined Aunt Martha and Cousin Janet going through turmoil over these bickering brothers-in-law.

I asked or said nothing, and I never contacted my cousin. I didn't speak to the rest of my extended family about these unsettling events. Feeling as if I never had a normal family life in Montreal, I kept myself in Boston as much as I could for the remainder of my MIT days.

It would be years before I got a glimpse of what had happened on the other side of Mom's sibling fence. One day, my Uncle Viktor's Canadian wife (he had been married before in Czechoslovakia) and I were traveling by bus to meet my uncle in the city. While we sat side by side, she turned to me and said unexpectedly, "You know, Harvy, no matter what happened between your father and Lali, I try to stay as close to Lali's family as I do to yours."

My ears perked up. I nodded and waited for more. My aunt continued. "I love Lali, Martha, and Janet as much as I love your family." She stopped for a moment and then added, "Not long ago, Janet asked me why Uncle Johnny had sued her father."

What?! Wasn't it the other way around? I kept quiet.

My aunt continued to speak calmly and caringly. "I told Janet, 'I'm sorry to tell you, sweetheart, but it was Lali who had sued Johnny. Your Uncle Johnny only countersued him to protect what he rightfully owned."

What craziness! Had Lali lied to his daughter? What damage had our family's strife done to her? I could feel my heart beat fast and my stomach tighten. I looked away and stared out the bus window. I stayed silent. I wanted the harsh memories to go away. I wanted to bury any pain of my extended family's actions as if they had never happened.

Perhaps sensing my uneasiness, my aunt said nothing more as we together stared out the bus window.

My and Janet's families never hugged or kissed each other again during the remainder of Lali and Mom's lives. Their sibling love had survived a brutal World War, an escape across Soviet-controlled borders, and even the loss of not having gone to Israel. But it couldn't survive the spouse in Mom's life.

Mom never again spoke Lali's name to my brother or me. She never again called or visited him or his family after he had his car accident, or when he was diagnosed with cancer a year afterward, or when he became hospitalized another year later while he was in the last stages of that disease. It was only Lali's early death, near the end of 1978 at the age of 66—twenty-eight years after the two families set foot on Canadian soil—that punctuated Mom's silent suffering and tattered trust.

Years later, Mom shared with me her recollections regarding Lali's final days. Her eyes were moist as she started to speak. "One afternoon, during Lali's last days on this earth, Janet unexpectedly arrived at our front door to tell me about his dying soon."

She raised her hand and pointed. "Through the glass of our front door, Janet spoke to me. She said, 'My father wants to see his kid sister one last time. He wants to apologize for his bad behavior such that he could die in peace.'"

Mom's whole body welled up; she could hardly look at me. She blurted, "I didn't open the door for Janet but talked only through the glass. When I saw her show up unexpectedly, I got upset and angry and said, 'Lali ruined my life! Go away and call me when he's dead. I'll have a party to celebrate.'" Mom burst into tears and wiped her wet eyes with the back of her hands.

I later heard from my brother that Lali's oldest sister, Ilonka, had been at Mom's home when Janet had arrived unannounced. Ilonka was visiting Mom for an extended stay. When my aunt saw Janet through the front door glass, after years of not talking to her or Lali, she too went a little crazy. She rushed back and forth across Mom's living room and shook her arms over her head. She invoked the name of their long-dead grandmother, crying out, "Matelaye!... Matelaye!... Matelaye!"

As I had done for years, I kept my distance from our extended family madness. I said nothing to what Mom had shared and to what my brother told me. I pretended I was not a part of our family's craziness. But that distance neither brought tranquility to my mind nor peace to my heart.

* * * *

32

Shameful Evening

It was a minute past noon on a windy, rainy, day in March of 1978. As my father might say, "It was a good day for the ducks."

I was sitting behind my grey metal desk at P&G's Canadian Engineering Division in Hamilton, Ontario. I faced a blank wall, my back toward a bank of permanently-sealed office windows. My engineering mate, Jim, was sitting behind me too, with a bag lunch at his desk that stood next to the window. I was having hot soup and a cold sandwich as I flipped through an engineering and construction magazine.

My phone rang. It was Dad from Montreal.

"Hi, son." His tone was upbeat. "How are you doing?"

"Fine," I said. I didn't want to give long answers during my short break, especially with my office colleague within earshot.

"What are you doing tonight?" he continued.

"Not much." I wondered where he was taking this conversation.

"Then come and meet me for supper at the Blue Sky Hotel." His tone was upbeat. "You know where it is, on Airport Road near the Toronto airport. I'm driving there this afternoon from Montreal on business." In his enthusiasm, he barely took a breath. "I'd like to see you if you have time for me. I should be at the hotel by six-thirty."

The Blue Sky was where Dad stayed when on business in Toronto. It was close to the city's consumer electronic exhibition hall, and near JHS's

219

customers, Sears and Woolco. During my college years working for Montreal Phono, I had stayed there a few times with my father when I came with him to see a customer or go to the annual Canadian electronics show.

"Hmm," I hesitated for a moment as I glanced out the office window at the gusting wind and streaking rain. The Blue Sky was over an hour away from Hamilton, longer in rush-hour traffic on the busy Queen's Way to Toronto. It would take even longer in today's spitting rain. Dad would have to race his car down Highway 401—doing 160 kilometers per hour in his Mercedes coupe—if he was to do any business in Toronto before getting to his hotel by six-thirty.

I offered, "I'm seeing a friend of mine in Toronto mid-day tomorrow for a squash game. What if I come in the morning for a late breakfast? The weather should be better then."

Dad's voice was firm. "I'm only going to be there tonight, son. I have to drive back to Montreal early in the morning. You can come to my hotel after work and bring your things. There will be an extra bed in my room. You can sleep there and go meet your friend after breakfast."

I was never good at declining my father's requests to see me, especially because I hadn't seen him since the Christmas and New Year's holidays. Because he had paid for my college education, I felt I owed him my time when he called. Not having a better excuse to avoid the commute to Toronto, I said, "Okay; I have to go home first to get my things. I can probably get to you by seven, depending on traffic."

"Good boy!" Dad said enthusiastically. "I'll see you tonight. Look for me at the hotel bar next to the dining room."

I put down the receiver. From across our small office, my colleague asked, "A hot date in T.O., Harvy?"

I turned around to look at him. "No, Jim; it was my father. He's driving down from Montreal today on business. I guess I'm going to Toronto after work today to see him, during the evening commute in this God awful weather."

"Better you than me, my friend," he said with a smirk. He turned his head back toward his desk and took a bite of his sandwich.

Hanging on the side wall of Jim's and my office was a large aerial photo of Procter & Gamble's turn-of-the-century, Hamilton manufacturing plant. It was a hodgepodge of brick buildings, steel towers, concrete smokestacks, painted outdoor metal pipes, and stainless steel ductwork. In the photo, the plant looked as if it were squeezed between Canada's biggest steel mills, Stelco and Dofasco. Through our engineering office window, Jim and I could see the P&G manufacturing complex across the street.

During the last eight months as a novice engineer, I had become familiar with every major manufacturing process in that factory. I now knew more than most would ever want to know about how to make Ivory and Zest soap, Tide and Cheer detergent, Head and Shoulders Shampoo, Crest toothpaste, and Crisco shortening and oil.

My family had used Ivory soap from the time I was a kid. As a P&G employee, I learned that an operator error had invented that soap. When the employee accidentally mixed too much air into the pure soap paste, he discovered that the dried, hardened bars could float. Thus, a new brand was born.

Inside those factory buildings ran a plethora of electrical conduits and chemical-, steam- and brine-infused pipes. Product-making and product-carrying conveyors went in multiple directions in every room on every floor. To install a new manufacturing process, one had to rip out part of the old.

Over the decades inside that aged plant, engineers had redesigned and upgraded those installations repeatedly. The inside of every building now looked like a jumble of pipe and conveyor pathways going every which way. The walls and ceilings of some production rooms looked like tangled giant pasta shapes in an up-side-down spaghetti bowl.

My P&G job wasn't glamorous. I designed and installed electrical systems and process control instrumentation for the company's soap, detergent, edible oil, and other product-making processes. I had to wear ugly safety glasses that made me look even nerdier than I was.

I had proven myself at college. In addition to being named a member of two honor societies; I had completed two IEEE research papers and conference presentations based on my bachelor's and master's theses. I had earned the credentials I needed to work outside my father's company. I told my father, "Let me get a couple of years of engineering experience before I apply to business school."

Though he responded, "I still want you to go to Harvard Business one day," he accepted my decision.

As I finished my sandwich on this wet, chilly March day, I thought about my parents. It had been two years since Dad returned to Mom after their second separation. From the time I started my P&G job the previous fall, I tried to keep my distance from those two.

Every Sunday evening, over the phone, both Mom and Dad asked, "So when are we going to see you back home?" I told them, "I don't know. I'm pretty busy at work. I'll try to come back over the next holidays."

Hamilton was a six-hour drive from my family. Though Dad was living with Mom, he continued to stay out half the night with his business buddies. Mom stayed home alone wondering where he was and with whom.

Dad was up to his old tricks. One Sunday afternoon, Mom cried to me over the phone. "He gets home at all hours from his meetings and outings. Some nights, he doesn't come home at all, and he never calls me to tell me where he is." She was weeping and on edge. "And he disappears on weekends to play golf or do who-knows-what with his so-called friends."

She calmed down. "Harvy, when are you coming home? I hardly see your daddy. He never takes me anywhere or is hardly at home to be with me. I'm alone with no place to go and no one to be with." Though she had a driver's licence, Mom had no car and wasn't a confident driver. "Can you talk to your father and tell him to be more at home with me?"

I knew that talking to Dad wouldn't help my mother. She once told me she had asked him to see a marriage counselor. He had replied harshly, "You go if you want. I don't need to."

Even when Mom didn't cry to me, I could hear the sadness in her voice. I wondered why she stuck with that man. Did she expect this live-for-today tiger to alter his wife-abandoning stripes?

I felt sorry for her, but I had to keep my focus on my work and life in Hamilton. I had to keep my distance for the sake of my sanity. She had made her marriage bed with a two-timing husband. I told her, "I'm sorry Mom, but Dad won't listen to me." There was nothing else I could do.

What could I say to my father? Could I curse him for his abandonment of my mother? Could I disown him for what he was doing to her? It was easier to tell Mom, "Good night; I'll talk to you next week."

My brother was closer to my parents' situation than I was. Now in his fifth year of working at Montreal Phono, he spent workdays listening to our father shouting at employees and screaming at suppliers. After work, Steve went off to ride his stallion that never nagged him. Afterward, he went home to shower off the horse smell, have a late supper that Mom had prepared for him, listen to what ailed her that day, and then retire for the night. That scenario repeated daily.

How Steve managed to keep himself sane is a mystery to me. He must have grown a horsehide skin or acquired a mule's stubbornness, or maybe both. When he and I talked, we spoke either about his horse or about the multi-month sojourns he unashamedly took to Outward Bound programs in the Canadian or American west. Dad told me, "Your brother picks up and goes for months at a time, leaving the company high and dry. I have to train someone temporarily to do his job and then let that person go when Steve returns."

My brother never confided to me what it was like for him to work for Dad and live with Mom. Frankly, the less we spoke about what was going on with our parents, the less angst I felt about it. Living in the noxious air of Hamilton was better than being with my toxic family in Montreal, where my mother cried, my brother denied, and my father connived.

I never felt quite far enough away or stayed away quite long enough.

* * *

I cleaned off and closed up my desk at precisely five o'clock. I scurried out of the building along with the rest of my P&G colleagues to gallop home on this dreary day. The rain poured, and the wind blew near-gale speed as we headed for the outdoor parking lot that held over 500 cars.

Jim was by my side as we bolted into the weather. He winked. "Have a safe trip to T.O. and a good date with your father." Little did he know about my parents; I shared little about my family with my P&G colleagues.

I drove to my apartment in the Friday traffic. I thought about the evening to come. Dad liked having me with him while he was doing business or entertaining customers. Maybe he wanted to show off his MIT son to his Toronto cohorts and friends, or maybe he thought he was educating me about his "real world of business."

I sensed he wanted me to become an extension of himself, to meet everyone he knew, to watch and learn from his every business move. I sometimes felt like a prized show horse in training rather than a loved son.

On the road home, I impatiently waited at a stoplight, my eyes looking around to see where I could dart my little Datsun when the light turned green.

I wondered why I was rushing. Did I fear my father would abandon me as he had done to my mother, now twice? I didn't want him to stop making me privy to his private dealings, like the offshore assets that he was building for us. Was it my father's money or acceptance I deeply desired? I wasn't sure.

The light turned green. I stepped hard on the gas and jockeyed past other cars. My throat dried and my chest hurt to think about my mother living pretty much alone, having a husband only in name. I didn't want to lose my father's good graces the way she had.

I felt drawn to Dad's world of prime steak suppers, stiff-drinking colleagues, and lively business chit-chat. As I turned onto the street where I lived, I kept my mind focused on what might be the more interesting part of the evening to come—spending time with the fun side of my dad.

I arrived at my apartment to pack my racketball gear and fill an overnight bag. I wondered who my father had to meet on a Friday afternoon in Toronto. Will I be alone with him at the Blue Sky, or might JHS's Toronto sales rep, Jeff Peters, be in the mix? I wished I had asked Dad more questions before agreeing to go out with him.

Jeff Peters lived in a modern, middle-class, Toronto suburban house, complete with backyard patio. He had an Anglo-Canadian wife, Wendy, who had a round face complete with cute dimples and a wide smile. Jeff and Wendy had a young teen son and two black Labrador dogs.

Dad and I sometimes met at Jeff's home when my father was in Toronto. There we gnawed on Jeff's spiced T-bone steaks and Wendy's giant mixed salads and homemade blueberry pie, my favourites in those food categories.

Unlike my childhood with my parents, the only complaint I ever heard the paunchy Jeff say about his short, smiling, slightly pudgy wife was, "Wendy drives less than 5000 kilometers a year in that brand new Buick I bought her." He winked. "Instead, I should have gotten her a bicycle with a carriage attached—the way geisha wives do it in Japan."

Wendy didn't take offence because Jeff smiled caringly at her. He patted his gourmand stomach with his big hands as a testament to his appreciation of her great cooking.

I continued the conversation in my head as I headed for the highway to Toronto. I wondered what Dad and I would talk about. *I hope he's not going to mention Harvard Business School again.*

I was getting tired of him asking me when I was going to apply once more to Harvard. I had applied to both Harvard and Stanford, among a half-dozen top U.S. business schools, during my graduate year at MIT. I was pleased when rejection letters came back from most of those institutions.

Though the University of Chicago and UC Berkeley's MBA programs had accepted me, my MIT friends told me, "Harvy, go out and work a couple of years before entering business school. You'll then have work experience to bring to the table." What they said made sense to me but not to my father.

Initially, Dad seemed to accept my taking a job at P&G. Months later he started to drop the "H" word again. "Harvard's the best business school in the world," he said every time we met at Jeff Peter's home. "You'll not only get a good education there but also make connections that will help you succeed for the rest of your life."

He could go on and on: "I wish I had that opportunity when I was your age." . . . "Take as much schooling as you can, son. Do your MBA before it's too late for you to go back to school." . . . "Now's the time in your life to take advantage of the best business education out there." . . . "You are lucky I can afford to support you through it." I was weary of hearing his dripping B-school faucet.

When my father wasn't pushing the MBA degree, Jeff jumped in for him. One time, with an innocent smile on his face, Jeff dropped a hint as he poured me a second rum and Coke. "So what are you considering for continuing your education, Harvy? I hear that Harvard is the best for business."

I avoided my dad's eyes, looked at Jeff, and said, "I want to finish a couple of years of working before considering going back to school. I have a good job at P&G in their Canadian Engineering Division, and I want to see how that goes. I still have lots of time for business school, and those schools usually prefer students with at least a couple of years of work experience." *In other words, guys, leave me the fuck alone for at least two years.*

Wendy came to my rescue. "Harvy's right; leave him be about this business school stuff. He's a bright boy; he'll make up his own mind. Let him live a little in the real world before he decides about more schooling."

I imagined the exasperation gathering in my father's face. He turned to Wendy. "I want Harvy to have the benefit of schooling that I never had when I was his age. I had to go into the military when I was eighteen and fight in a bloody war. I then escaped Czechoslovakia, immigrated to Canada, and started from nothing. Harvy should take the advantages I never got."

Jeff turned to my father and smiled. "It's so much easier with dogs, Johnny. My two Labs have been trained to obey my every command."

I sped down Queen's Way for the one-hour drive to the big city. I darted in and out of traffic, trying to gain an advantage by zipping into faster lanes. I had promised to be there by seven o'clock, and Dad appreciated punctuality. But was that why I tailgated the car ahead of me and abruptly changed lanes on wet pavement when I eyed an opening into a faster track?

I wondered again what Dad and I would say to each other. *Should I bring up the topic of Mom?*

I could hear him respond. "Don't worry about your mother and me, son. Focus on your future and get ahead in your education and career."

Will he show any interest in me and my life?

My father rarely asked about my work at P&G, preferring to talk about what was going on in his business or his travels to Europe and the Caribbean. His words reverberated in my head, "It's better to work for yourself and be your own boss. You shouldn't have to go through your whole life with others telling you what to do. If I had done that, I'd still be an electro technician in a factory."

Might there be another reason he wanted to see me?

Dad had many business colleagues in Toronto. One, a long-time graduate of Harvard Business School, was the president of a company that supplied JHS with electronic parts. A part of my father's Harvard campaign had been to corral his colleague to invite us to Toronto's Harvard Club for a lecture by a B-school professor.

All during that supper, Dad's cohort laid it on thick about his great years at Harvard and the business connections he had made there. He said how his Harvard MBA had propelled him to become president of the Canadian subsidiary of a large U.S. company.

But that accomplished B-school graduate didn't know my father the way I did. Whether my dad would admit it or not, I suspected he wanted me to get a business education so that he could entice me back to JHS.

Today, Dad hadn't asked me to put on a proper suit for supper, so I knew we weren't going to do anything fancy. My foot still couldn't back off my car's accelerator.

* * *

Toronto's Blue Sky Hotel was a long, rectangular, brick and glass obelisk that jutted out over a dozen stories above Toronto's Airport Road. It was a popular, businessman's establishment that offered a large well-stocked barroom, thick steaks and juicy roast beef entrees in its lobby restaurant, and the reasonable room prices that my dad preferred.

Though the place was not shabby, the building's interior had too many long, straight lines for my taste. There was no lobby fountain or colourful artwork as was found in Montreal hotels. Though clean and modern, the Blue Sky's interior was dull beige and brown. A Montreal joke of those days was: "CJAD radio is having a contest. First prize is an all-expense-paid week in Toronto; second prize is *two* all-expense paid weeks." I understood why.

Since the early 1970s, Dad visited Toronto more often than before. Many of JHS's customers had moved their head offices from Montreal to Toronto in the wake of Quebec's multiple French-language bills. New laws required Quebec companies to use French as their main language.

That provincial legislation generated a wave of corporate head-office defections during that decade. It eclipsed any other business migration in Canadian history.

One summer while I had been working at JHS, Dad had made noises about moving his money and company to Toronto. He once again said, "Those bloody Separatists are trying to ruin *notre belle province de Quebec*. One day, they are going to nationalize everything, as the communists did to me in Czechoslovakia."

Dad never did make good on his threats to move his money or his business to Toronto. Maybe he couldn't uproot himself from what he had in Montreal and at the Troika. If he had moved, I might have had to find a job in Vancouver.

Tonight at the Blue Sky, I hoped it would be only him and me for supper. I didn't want to put on a happy face for anybody else.

I arrived at the Blue Sky a few minutes past 7:00 and walked in through the parking lot entrance at the back of the hotel. In the seemingly football-field-wide hallway, a high screen and hanging plants obscured the lobby bar.

The place wasn't busy this Friday evening. It wasn't hard to spot my dad sitting at a table in the middle of the barroom area. Perhaps he was expecting the room to fill with people around him as it did at his beloved Montreal night spots. He was wearing his usual three-piece, dark business suit. There were drinks on the table and cigarettes smoldering in the ashtray. And there was more.

He's not alone! A woman sat with him. She had reddish-brown hair and wore large, tinted glasses. She appeared to be ten or more years younger than he. *Perhaps they're finishing a business meeting while he's waiting for me.* Dad didn't like to drink by himself. Maybe this was a Toronto colleague who was sticking around to keep him company.

As I approached their table, I looked more carefully at her. *Where have I seen this woman before?* I came closer, and both my father and she looked up at me and smiled.

Oh my! I had met her last summer at my father's Troika table. *What the heck is her name?*

When I had met her at the Troika, she sat between my father and his long-time friend, Aras. She was good looking: big hazel eyes, long black eyelashes, and a coif that was sculpted nicely above her shoulders. She had an attractive figure. Though her burgundy eye shadow and red lipstick had been applied a bit too thickly for my taste, she tempered her makeup with a dark-grey conservative business suit, the skirt going down to her knees. Her colourful scarf and large handbag had well matched the Troika's rich red décor.

During that Troika evening, I couldn't tell if this woman was closer to Dad or Aras. She laughed with and talked to both of them equally. She gently touched Dad's shoulder or Aras's arm whenever they lit her cigarette. Her big yet not overpowering voice didn't shy away from conversation. Her laugh was full and infectious. She matched Dad and Aras's smoking and drinking, which made her seem as if she were a regular in my father's crowd. It was hard to tell whether or not there was anything more than a business friendship going on between her and either man.

Though I had been curious, I never asked my father about the woman's status with him or Aras. A part of me hadn't wanted to know. But here at the

Blue Sky, I silently cursed myself. I wished I had asked Dad more questions before accepting his supper invitation.

I smiled as I approached them and offered hellos. Dad stood to greet me. He grabbed my shoulders with both hands and kissed both of my cheeks. He gave me a wide grin and a big *"Hallo* sweetheart, glad you could come and be with us tonight." He motioned to his companion, "Harvy, do you remember Lizabeth?"

I nodded and smiled. "Yes, we met last summer at the Troika."

Lizabeth stayed seated and put out her hand to take mine. "Yes, Harvy, you remember well. Good to see you again." Her grip was gentle but not shy or retiring.

Dad and I sat. He smiled. "Lizabeth happened to be in Toronto on business the same time I needed to be here. We managed to connect and are staying here at the hotel together."

Oh! I wondered what "staying here ... together" meant. I held myself back from asking.

Lizabeth smiled. "You probably know, Harvy, that your father is a hard man to say no to. I had other plans for tonight, but he insisted we have supper together."

I wish he had told me. And I wish Lizabeth would have said no to Dad.

I kept my eyes on her. "How do you two know each other?" I was getting onto ground I usually avoided, but I needed to know something about their connection. I suspected my mother didn't know about this woman.

Dad came in. "We met about a year ago. Aras introduced us. Lizabeth's company does business with Aras's appliance and furniture distributorship."

Lizabeth looked at my father as he talked. Her expression was soft as she held her cigarette delicately between her fingers and near her face. Dad said nothing more about their connection, nor did she.

I hope she won't be with us for the whole evening.

My father looked at me. "What would you like to drink? Your usual rum and Coke; or do you want a screwdriver this time?" He grinned. "I know you like the sweet stuff."

"Rum and Coke is fine, Dad." The darker concoction was a better match for my mood.

My father raised his hand, attracted the waiter quickly in this near-empty bar, and he put in the order.

Lizabeth turned to me. "So your father tells me you've been working for Procter & Gamble since last September. How's that going, working for a big company like that?"

Maybe Dad's purpose for having Lizabeth with us was for her to pinch hit for him. Dad knew I didn't like to be questioned much by him—like I didn't ask him questions about his personal life. He thus needed others to ask questions on his behalf.

I smiled a bit. "Things are going well; I'm learning a lot about making soap, detergent, and other consumer products."

Lizabeth smiled and winked. "Ever get any free samples?"

I smiled wryly. "When I arrived at P&G last year, I got a complimentary basket of their products. But it's considered stealing if anyone takes product home from the factory, even wasted product."

I went on, keeping my eyes on Lizabeth. "Recently, a thirty-year veteran of the company was caught by plant security for trying to smuggle out bars of soap in the false bottom of his large lunch box. Though he was one of the company's model employees, and everybody looked up to him, he was reported to the police and immediately fired."

"Wow, that's extreme," she said. She turned to my father. "Would you do such a thing without considering the circumstances?"

"Of course!" he said without losing a beat. But I knew my father might offer an employee—especially one he liked—a second chance once he gave them an earful of "Don't ever fucking steal from me again!"

Lizabeth turned back to me. "What do you do at P&G, Harvy? Your father couldn't explain it completely." She glanced at him with a small smile.

That's because he never asks me.

I gave her my usual line. "I'm a process-control-instrumentation specialist. I help to design and install new systems to help our Hamilton plant save money on the electricity and steam energy they use in their production." I grinned. "It may sound a bit dull and boring, but it's not a bad starting job for a new graduate engineer."

"Yes, your father told me you got your master's degree from MIT last year. Good for you!" She sounded sincere. She took a puff of her cigarette and pushed her big glasses higher on her nose. "Your job doesn't sound boring, Harvy. What do you like most about it?"

I thought for a moment. "The free car washes," I quipped.

She looked confused. "I'm not sure what you mean."

I glanced at my father who seemed to be perturbed as he looked at me out of the corner of his eye. I smiled. "Once in a while the plant's detergent or soap operation goes a little haywire, and soap bubbles are sent into the air and land on the cars in the plant's parking lot. If it happens to rain that day, employees' cars get a free cleaning."

I paused for a moment to let that sink in, and then I continued. "But even if it doesn't rain, I don't mind the dried soap bubbles. It holds down the fine layer of black soot that comes floating down from the adjacent steel mills." I chuckled, but I was the only one.

I wasn't sure if Lizabeth was relating to my quirky humour, but I didn't care. My response was for my father. If he was going to surprise me with an unexpected guest and have her ask me questions on his behalf, he shouldn't expect straight answers.

My drink arrived. Dad said, "Chin-chin" as he raised his vodka on the rocks to salute Lizabeth first and then me. Lizabeth had a glass of wine in front of her. She and I followed suit, she with a sip and I with a big gulp. She half-smiled, perhaps not knowing what to make of my answers to her questions.

Dad changed the subject. "So how do you like living in Hamilton, son? I know you have a lot less snow than we do in Montreal. Was the winter mild this year?"

I was polite with my father. "The winters are a lot easier in Hamilton compared to Montreal. There's as much rain as there is snow, so the snow doesn't last long."

I looked at Lizabeth. "With Hamilton's steel mills and other factories, people think that it's very dirty and polluted. But once you move away from the industrial harbour area, it's quite nice."

"How so, Harvy?" Lizabeth seemed to regain her footing.

I raised my hand to head height. "I live high up in an apartment building on the Niagara Escarpment, right behind the city center. I can walk the few blocks into the city where there are a wonderful performing arts theatre and a three-season farmer's market."

I lowered my hand. "Hamilton also has a very nice botanical garden at its west end, with lots of hiking trails. The city works to keep its buildings and streets clean; no junk or garbage is lying around."

"Sounds nice, Harvy," Lizabeth said. "Do you get a view of the Niagara Escarpment from your apartment?"

I pointed away from me. "I have a balcony that faces both the city's downtown on one side and the escarpment on the other. The escarpment goes for many, many miles east and west along the Niagara Peninsula. It's full of trees and parkland, like Mount Royal in Montreal. I get exercise by jogging through the area.

I took another sip of my drink. With no food in my stomach, the alcohol was quickly getting to my head. "If the wind is blowing in the right direction through the city, I can get a clear view of the harbour and the Queen Elizabeth Bridge to Toronto." I couldn't help myself. "But if it's blowing the wrong way, the smog can roll in from the harbour. It can then smell like rotten eggs even where I live." I didn't want Lizabeth and Dad to show up in Hamilton one day.

I didn't know if my defensive strategy was working. Lizabeth offered, "I hear there are good wineries along the escarpment, around St. Catharine's and Niagara-on-the-Lake." She turned to my father. "I'd love to go there sometime."

Maybe she's now sending me a message.

My dad smiled and raised his glass to her. "Sure, Lizabeth, you name the time. I'll be there."

Oh, oh.

I looked at my watch and turned to my father. "Let's have supper, Dad. It's nearly 7:30, and I'm starving."

"Sure son." He pointed toward the bar. "Behind us is the main restaurant. I'll pay the tab here, and we can bring over what's left of our drinks." Dad said that only for Lizabeth and me. He swigged the last of his vodka, set the glass on the table, and motioned to the waiter to give him the bill.

I figured Lizabeth was staying with us for the duration of the evening. I hoped she'd retire early and let Dad and I have time alone.

We moved over to the main restaurant.

Over T-bone steaks, I discovered that Lizabeth worked for a company that sold lamps, lampshades, and other kinds of lighting to home-goods distributorships like Aras's company. "Did you know that it costs next to nothing to make a lamp," she said. "What it costs to manufacture lighting products is about 15% the price you pay to buy it in a store. There are many middlemen in the food chain for these things. Every Tom, Dick, and Harry along the way takes a piece of the action."

Dad offered her a cigarette and lit it with his Dunhill. As she had done at the Troika, she gently put her hand on his arm. After taking a drag, she sweetly smiled at him.

I was glad we were in a big restaurant that was almost empty of other smoking patrons. I coughed a couple of times to give Dad a message. He moved the ashtray to the corner of the table between himself and Lizabeth, and they continued to puff away.

Dad offered, "Lizabeth, in my business, the manufacturing cost is higher than what you're talking about, something like 30-35% of the retail price to the consumer. But the manufacturing distributorships we work for, like RCA and Admiral, are one-by-one getting out of the console business."

He looked intently at her. "I'm already talking directly to the big retailers like Sears and Woolco through independent manufacturing reps—people like you, but in our industry. Because there will be only one other mouth to feed after us, the Canadian manufacturing cost will soon become 50% of the final cost to the consumer."

"It's different in your business, Johnny," Lizabeth said. "It's easier to cut out the middlemen with bigger, more expensive items like your console stereos. It'll be a while before that happens in my business, where there are more hands and mouths involved, especially since my products come from overseas." She raised a hand. "But I'm sure the day will come when you'll see consolidation in our industry too. The big retailers here will eventually buy directly from the manufacturers in Asia."

"Why is that?" I said. "Why will stores buy direct?"

My father looked at me with soft yet intense eyes. "It's because of cheap labour, son. JHS has already been buying our electrical components and radio chassis from Taiwan and Korea. Like with us, it's happening in every industry, and retailers will get into the act. They will make their products in countries where the labour is cheap."

He took a long breath. "Companies like JHS, at best, will only assemble components here into the final product. It's too costly to ship wooden cabinets from overseas." (Dad hadn't yet realized that technology would move the home entertainment industry to more compact components and then miniaturized devices over the next twenty-five years.)

"The market is demanding lower costs," Lizabeth added. "The middlemen importers, consolidators, and distributors eventually will be squeezed out. The good old days of everybody-can-make-a-buck will soon be gone."

Dad looked intently at Lizabeth and said something I hadn't expected. "Maybe you can come and work for me and be our retail sales agent? Our customers would love a fresh face."

Lizabeth laughed. "Johnny, you old fox. You just want to get me away from Aras's world. You know that's not possible. I know nothing about your kind of business and the players in it."

"You can learn my business," my father said. "I'll teach you."

Is this why my father wanted this woman here for supper, to entice her to work for him?

Lizabeth's eyebrows rose. "Thanks, Johnny, but I've been in my industry a long time. And what would Aras say if you tried to steal me away from doing business with him?" She grinned like a mother to a mischievous boy she revered. "And I don't think I can work for a guy like you."

"Hey! What do you mean?" My father looked at her as if he were an innocent child, his eyelids raised.

"I know you too well, Johnny. Working for you would be hard. Aras tells me you drive hard bargains and are tough with your employees. I'd rather be good friends with you than work for you." She gave him a small wink from behind her glasses. I wondered what she meant by "good friends."

They both chuckled. Dad nodded and took another sip of his third, or maybe fourth, vodka of the evening. Lizabeth matched Dad with her white wine. *What the hell!* I took a swig out of my third rum and Coke that the waiter had just placed on the table. Dad's paying for this supper; I might as well stay hitched to whatever kind of ride this evening was going to be.

Lizabeth seemed to be a smart lady. I listened closely—as much as my fuzzy mind would allow. She and Dad continued to go back and forth on business and the people they knew in Aras' circles. I asked more questions and got answers from either my father or Lizabeth.

Later in the conversation, she turned to me. "Harvy, you seem to be interested in what your father and I are saying. Do you ever see yourself heading back to school for a business degree?"

For a moment, everything was quiet at our table. Maybe Lizabeth was asking her question out of curiosity, but I bet my father had had a hand in it. He was like an old bird dog coming around the bush from a different direction until he got the right angle to flush out its catch.

As Lizabeth had said earlier in the evening, it was hard to say no to my father's haranguing. It didn't matter if it came directly from him or through his surrogates.

Though I now supported myself, I still felt dependent. I would need Dad if I were to continue my education. Deep down I knew he would eventually lasso me into B-school. I just wanted breathing room before jumping back into the degree-accumulation game.

"I'll go to business school at some point," I said. I repeated my usual line. "I want to get at least two years of work experience before considering more education." I was looking at her, but I meant my message for my father.

"You're a very intelligent guy, Harvy. I'm sure you would do well with whatever you chose." She stopped talking and took a sip of her drink.

This lady doesn't seem that bad. I bet Dad's getting hot under the collar in hearing her advice.

Dad spoke as he looked down at the drink in his hands. "I'm willing to support your continuing education, son. I think a place like Harvard Business School would be good for your future."

There he goes again!

He looked directly at me. I found it hard to meet his gaze as he continued. "But I also agree with Lizabeth; it has to be your decision."

Wow! Could Lizabeth's thinking be rubbing off on my father?

Lizabeth didn't give my father a chance to say more. "Any special girls in your life, Harvy, or are you out there playing the field?"

I paused for a moment. I searched for a simple answer. "I met a woman some months ago. She and I see each other once in a while."

Oh, oh. This ground was tricky. *My father knows the woman I've been seeing, but he doesn't know that I've been seeing her.*

* * *

My girlfriend and I had met in Jamaica over the recent New Year's holidays. Dad had taken our whole family there for a week's vacation. A half-dozen of our friends and relatives had come with us on that trip.

Among our group were Dad's bachelor half-brother Edo and Edo's cousin Alex who had recently separated from his wife. They shared a room. There was another family of four that were with us; close family friends from Montreal. My father liked to vacation with an entourage, and he had made the arrangements. He received one free stay for himself when he booked a group of ten, the exact number we had on this trip.

The beach hotel we stayed at was rustic. It had thatched wooden shacks and an open-air restaurant overlooking the blue Caribbean. There, Alex, my brother, and I paired with three available women who we met at that island oasis. My new friend, Madeline, was a short, slender, dark-eyed, perm-out-to-here brunette. She was also on the lookout for more than dinner conversation.

Madeline and I met on New Year's Eve. It started by Alex prodding me through supper. "Harvy, let's go and visit with those two nice ladies sitting by themselves at the other end of the restaurant."

After Alex had made repeated requests, he and I sauntered to their table after we had finished our main course. We asked if we could sit with them. They accepted, complete with pretty smiles and a little eyelid batting.

Madeline and Karen were high school teacher-consultants from Cambridge, Ontario, which was only an hour's drive from where I lived in Hamilton. Madeline, a divorcee with two kids, was nearly ten years my elder. Her big afro-like hairdo, slim physique, and round, full-cheeks made her look like my contemporary.

Days later, she'd tell me, "Harvy, your three-piece red suit at New Year's was an eye-catcher." She gave me a big smile. "When I saw your outfit, and the open collar showing your manly chest, I said to Karen, 'I never saw anything like that before! That young guy must be hot stuff." She laughed. "He and his friend better get over here before the night is out, else they'll miss out on two hot babes.'"

After we talked a bit at their table, Alex and I brought Madeline and Karen over to our family's table to toast in the New Year. The twelve of us must have gone through half a case of champagne that Dad put on his tab. At midnight, Alex and Karen, and Madeline and I wrapped arms around each other's waists as we stood barefoot on the beach and looked up at fireworks.

The remainder of that week, we hung out together and separately. We negotiated many a room key for a mid-afternoon or late-night rendezvous. I was with Madeline, Alex with Karen, and Steve got lucky by finding a twenty-something woman named Susan.

Many times that week, my mother asked me where Alex and I had disappeared to for hours at a time. My father interrupted her, saying, "Don't worry; leave them alone; they're just having a good time."

Steve and Susan got it on too. She was by herself at our beach hotel—something about her husband having passed away. Steve and she had long evenings together, though it sounded as if they did more talking than anything else. Afterward, Steve came back to our shared shack. He told me, "I didn't want to overstay my welcome with her."

"What a schmuck you are, Steve," I told him on our flight back to Montreal. "Your politeness with Susan wreaked havoc for the rest of us. Every night we had to figure out where we could go for a few hours of privacy."

Steve looked at me, shrugged, and said nothing.

* * *

Shameful Evening

At the Blue Sky, I didn't want to talk about Madeline. I didn't want my father to know that I was still seeing her, an older single Mom with two young kids. He might have seen her getting in the way of my going back to grad school.

Bringing up Madeline's name could lead to how I had met her in Jamaica, which could lead to a conversation about our whole family, months earlier, having been in Jamaica for vacation. That would be awkward with Lizabeth here. Then again, who and what was I trying to protect?

As we completed our main course, Lizabeth looked at me as if she were sincerely interested. "Is your friend a local girl?"

"She lives about an hour from me," I said. "We get together every two or three weeks, either in her town, or in Hamilton, or here in Toronto." I didn't want to lie, but I didn't want to reveal.

"I see you play things close to your vest, Harvy; like your father does." Lizabeth chuckled and looked at him.

I smiled and glanced at Dad. He stayed quiet as he twirled the ice in his empty vodka glass.

I tried to bury my thoughts of my mother, who was probably alone this evening watching television from her favourite living-room chair. The thought of her there and me and Dad here with Lizabeth was like a slow burning acid in my gut.

Taking gulps of my drink, I worked to drown my throat's recurring dryness and alleviate my upset stomach. A part of me wanted to act as if I were having a nice evening with my father and his woman friend. Our conversation was certainly more pleasant and interesting than my mother's crying over the phone.

So why are my head aching and gut burning?

For the remainder of the evening, Dad and Lizabeth shared notes about restaurants and nightlife places they had been to in Toronto—though adequate, never as good as the scene in Montreal. We shared a cherries jubilee dessert—not as scrumptious as Dad's Troika fare but still delectable.

Dad then said, "Harvy, go get your things from your car, and we can go to our rooms." He offered something unexpected. "I got you a separate room next to ours." He pointed casually at himself and Lizabeth when he had said: "next to ours."

Did I hear Dad right? Were the two of them going to be in one room together?

My mind was fuzzy from the alcohol. I needed a moment to clear my head. "I'll get my things and be back soon."

I stood on wobbly legs, grabbed my jacket, and walked out of the restaurant as upright as my limbs allowed. My head whirled. I had to hold onto the backs of chairs as I meandered my way back through the bar area. I focused on getting to my car, which was just outside the building's back entrance. I was glad that hardly anyone was around. Someone might stop me if they thought I was going to drive away half drunk.

It was still spitting rain outside as I exited the building into the parking lot. The cold air hit me like a slap of Mennen Skin Bracer aftershave. Like in that product's TV advertising, I mumbled, "Thanks, I needed that!"

I fumbled with the sleeves of my jacket to get the damned thing on my back before I walked into the weather. I pulled the collar over my head and walked as quickly as I could. Thank goodness I had parked nearby; otherwise, I'd get soaked or maybe not find my car.

I unlocked the car and opened the rear door to grab my overnight bag. But instead of pulling my bag off the seat, I got in and sat next to it. I shivered in the frigid November air that filled my car.

What the fuck is happening here? Who is this Lizabeth with whom Dad is going to share a room? *What's he thinking?* I came here to see him, and he makes no mention of her until I see her here, and then I can't back out.

I took deep breaths. I tried to focus my eyes outside of the car.

What the hell is Dad doing? He's playing it as if nothing is going on and they are the best of friends. I covered my face with my hands. *What the heck am I doing?* Am I going to go back in there and pretend that nothing disconcerting was going on between them?

I sat for another moment. *I'm a little drunk. Maybe I misheard Dad.* Perhaps he said it's him and I who are sharing a room, as he had said in our phone call earlier in the day, and Lizabeth has the separate room.

I worked to focus my eyes on my car's dashboard. *Why is my father putting me in this position?* I'm in no condition to go home. *My God! What am I going to say or do?*

I'm sure that if I confront Dad about what he's doing, he'll play it like there's no problem, or that I misunderstood him, and that nothing's wrong.

Why did he even want me to come here tonight? I should have suspected he'd pull something like this. *God, what should I do?*

I can't stay in my Datsun much longer; they'll wonder what happened to me, and it is cold as crap in my can of a car. *Doesn't my frigging father realize what he's doing?*

Through the fog and ice in my head came an image of my mother. If she had known about this woman, she would have screamed or cried about her to me.

Why does Dad do such bullshit? Was he on his way out the door again with Mom? If I came across too strong with him and Lizabeth, might I precipitate another separation between my parents?

Oh God; oh God! Give me a sign. I can't figure this out on my own.

For a moment I gazed around outside and inside my car. My mind was racing about Dad, Lizabeth, my mother, me, but I was blank about what to do next.

I turned to my overnight bag, put my hands around its handles, opened the car door, and stepped out into the spitting night. I walked back as steadily as I could through the hotel's lobby to where I had left Dad and Lizabeth. I was wet, cold, and livid. I wanted to scream but didn't.

When I got close to the restaurant, Dad and Lizabeth were sitting outside the bar area as they waited for me. They were talking, cigarettes in hand. Dad said. "Where have you been? Got lost finding your car?"

I half smiled. "I had to stop at the men's room. I guess I had too much to drink."

"You look tired, son. Let's get you to bed. I took care of everything at the restaurant."

Dad looked at Lizabeth, "Are you ready to go?"

"As ready as your son looks," she kidded.

They stubbed out their smokes, stood, and lead the way toward the elevators. I followed behind them, my head down. Through the lobby, up the elevator, and down the hallway to our rooms, I stayed quiet while my head battled with itself.

One side screamed: *What the fuck are you doing, Harvy? Say something. You can't let him share a room with her. What are they thinking?*

The other side spoke calmly: *It's only one night. Maybe you heard him wrong. Wait and see what will happen.*

My insides were shaking. I tried to stay collected. I didn't say a word. Was I afraid of making Dad feel bad? Upsetting Lizabeth? Speaking up for myself? *Why am I not saying anything?*

I was tired and tipsy as I lumbered down the hallway. I tried to walk a straight line but had to put my hand up against a wall to keep my balance. I couldn't wait to close my eyes and nod off from this nightmare.

When we reached one room, Dad unlocked the door and said, "Son, this is your room. I'll be in the room right next door." He pointed down the hallway and smiled. "See you in the morning, around eight o'clock in the breakfast room. Is that time okay?"

That answers one of my questions.

I took a deep breath. "I'm really tired, Dad. I'm going straight to sleep. Goodnight to you and Lizabeth."

I'll feel better in the morning. No need to make a fuss. It's too late to say anything. Just bear with this craziness and get straight to bed. I was in a daze. *I'll be out of this nightmare soon.*

"Good night, son. See you in the morning," my father said with a smile.

Lizabeth added, "Goodnight, Harvy. Nice having supper with you."

I nodded and tacked on as much of a smile as I could. I didn't kiss my father goodnight as I usually did but headed into my room. I didn't wait to see if Dad and Lizabeth entered the next room together.

As quickly as I could, I unpacked what I needed and headed to the bathroom. I couldn't bear to look at myself in the mirror as I brushed my teeth and washed my face.

In a few long minutes, I was done and headed to bed. I pulled the covers over my still swirling head. *God, please let me sleep through this senseless night.*

Years later, I thought about how much that hotel episode reflected my life with dad. I let him get away with his infidelities without saying a word. I think he wanted me to be accepting of (maybe learn from?) his MO with women and in business. But I continued to wonder what kind of father pulls such stupid stuff with their son, or anyone? And why had I been so goddamned afraid to confront him about his infidelities?

It would take me decades to considered that Dad might have wanted me to be his alibi that evening. Perhaps he wanted to say to Mom that he came to Toronto on a Friday to spend time with me after he completed some business there. He might have said to her, "Harvy and I were together for the evening," and he wouldn't have been lying.

What a conniver my father was! And what an enabler I had been! It sickens me even today.

* * *

Lying in my Blue Sky bed, I thought about Dad's other women who I had heard about over the years. After I had entered high school, my mother alluded to Dad's affairs. She offered names but few specifics—either she didn't know or wouldn't say.

Late one night, Dad was out with his business buddies. In a fit of despair, Mom told me about two Hungarian sisters, Margit and Edit. Her eyes filled with tears. "Margit had worked for your father as a forelady," she offered.

I nodded but said nothing. As a kid, I had met Margit when she supervised Montreal Phono's electronic amplifier department. She once patted my head as if I were her own. Years later, Dad told me that she had committed suicide. He said he didn't know why.

I listened to my mother's rendition. She cried, "Margit didn't have a car, so your father picked her up and took her home every day from work. They got friendly. Your father was going to leave me for her. They planned it for over a year. He was just waiting until you boys got a little older."

I didn't want to believe her. "How do you know that, Mom?"

"I know who to call when it comes to your father," she said scornfully. She added nothing about her source.

She raised her hands to wipe her soaking eyes. "But your father slept with Margit's younger sister, Edit." She banged the table with her fist. "That Edit was a tramp! She was trying to prove to her older sister that your father didn't love her. When Margit later found out from Edit what she and your father had done, Margit took sleeping pills and killed herself."

Mom took a long breath. "Luckily your father wasn't implicated in Margit's death." She ended the story there.

My mother put her palms on her face. "I'm the only one in the world who loves your father. I would stand by him through anything. All these other women will never love him the way I do. I never played tricks on him and I never would."

My chest pounded from my mother's story. I couldn't accept what she had said. I didn't share with her the little that Dad had told me about his forewoman's suicide.

I stood from the table, walked out of the kitchen, and went to bed. I couldn't believe my father would be doubly unfaithful, to both Mom and Margit. My mother, or her source, must have had it wrong.

* * *

I had pushed those awful thoughts out of my head for years. They now flooded back as I lay in my bed at the Blue Sky Hotel. Dad and Lizabeth perhaps lay only a few yards away, only a wall between us.

I now knew my father's infidelities first hand. Could he have driven that Margit woman to commit suicide? What kind of sick man was he? And what about this Lizabeth; who the hell was she to him, and what might happen to her?

To hell with her! Let Lizabeth survive her transgression with my father in whatever way works for her, as I'm trying to survive him by seeing and saying no evil. I wanted to idolize my father, to love him, to be first in line regarding his legacy. I didn't want him to abandon me the way he had abandoned my mother, now twice. Maybe the writing was now on the wall for Dad's third departure from her.

I didn't want my father to complain about me as he did about my brother. Perhaps I didn't want to forgo Dad's generosity with me. Maybe I didn't want to relinquish the offshore money with which he had enticed me, the knowledge of with he had entrusted me. *Oh God! What was I becoming?*

Speaking of God, he hadn't helped me out this night. Might I have made a devilish deal with my father about his clandestine money and affairs? Was I now obtaining a punishment I deserved? I pulled the bed sheet higher over my head. *If this is a test from the Almighty, I'm failing like a son-of-a-bastard.*

But wait! Nothing bad has happened as far as I know. Maybe Dad and Lizabeth have separate rooms down the hall. Then again, why wouldn't Dad have stayed with me as we did when we travelled on family trips? *Maybe I can leave quietly in the morning and forget I ever was here.*

I shut my eyes, ignored the dryness in my mouth, disregarded the knot in my intestines, and pretended that nothing inappropriate was going on. I'll go my cheery way in the morning. *God, if you can't tell me what to do, then let me get to sleep so that I get through this nightmare.*

Something startled me awake. My eyes opened into blackness. I saw nothing because my head was under my bed covers, but I thought I had heard noises.

Where am I? Did I hear something? What time is it?

I remembered where I was. I pulled down the bed covers from my eyes, but it was pitch black in the room because the curtains were closed. I heard nothing more, yet thoughts of my father and Lizabeth raced through my mind. *What the heck are they doing and what the f... am I doing here?*

I shivered under my covers. The next few minutes passed as if I was locked in a dark, tight prison cell. Could they be doing something next door? *Am I too naïve to think they're not?*

I closed my eyes and lay as still as I could, but my mind wouldn't cooperate. I couldn't get back to sleep. I turned my head more and looked over at the digital clock next to my bed. It read after 2:00.

I lay there a while longer. My mind was racing as my heart had been. *How will I be able to look at Dad or Lizabeth in the morning?*

My head felt as if it would explode. I wondered what kind of Catholic my father was and how many commandments he might have broken this night.

I pulled the covers off me and sat up in bed. I stayed still for a moment, stared into the darkness, and listened for any sign of what might be going on next door. *I must be going crazy. I have to get out of here!*

As quietly as I could, I turned on a light, put my clothes back on, and packed my bag. I stood to go to the bathroom. Thank goodness I was now sober and steady on my feet, but my mouth was parched and my heart pounding.

When I got into the bathroom, I turned on the light. Once more, I was not able to look at myself in the mirror.

How did I let myself get into this? And who was this frigging woman? Why did Dad pretend nothing was going on, that their relationship was only an innocent friendship?

I don't get it. What's he thinking? The bastard! He's acting as if I'm not here, as if he isn't married, and as if he can do anything he wants when he wants.

I left the bathroom and reached out and fumbled for the front door handle. If Dad happened to hear me through a wall, and then came out into the hallway, I'd tell him I couldn't sleep, that I was going out for a walk and would be back soon.

I grabbed the door handle and turned it slowly and gently. *Click.* I swung it open. I stepped into the hallway and let the spring-loaded door close behind me. I cushioned it from closing too fast. It still shut with a loud *click*.

I stood in the hallway for a few seconds. I heard no sounds coming from anywhere. *I'm safe now. I'm getting the hell out of here!*

I walked toward the elevators. On a table, I noticed a couple of pads of paper and pens. I felt I needed to leave a note for Dad. Though I was livid, it would be cruel not to say anything to him. I knew he would worry about me when he saw me gone in the morning.

I grabbed a pen and wrote: *I'm sorry, Dad, but I can't stay. I don't want to see her again.* In my mind, she no longer had a name.

I folded the paper in two and wrote "Mr. Simkovits" on the outside. I tried not to make a sound as I walked down the hallway back to the room where my father said he was staying. I slipped the note under the door and then headed for the elevators.

Usually, I liked to take a hotel pen and notepad with me as a souvenir. This time, I left those things on the table. There was no way I wanted to remember this night.

I'm never letting my frigging father do something like this to me again!

I walked through a deserted lobby. A man was standing behind the reception counter. He glanced at me as I walked passed him. I didn't look directly at him but glanced at the clock above the desk.

Gosh! It's nearly three o'clock. I bet they've seen a lot of Johns and Janes in this place. Hope they don't think I'm one, but I know two who were.

I headed for my car. *What am I going to do now?*

I was supposed to meet my Toronto friend for a squash game later that day.

It had stopped raining outside, but it was still cold and dark as the hell I had gone through inside.

I considered going to another hotel or driving back to Hamilton and then returning to see my friend.

I'm so frigging tired! Hell if I can drive home safely at this hour. Hell if I'm going to spend my money because of my father's indiscretion.

I got in my car and drove fifteen minutes to get into the neighbourhood where my friend lived. I drove along quiet streets. *What am I looking for?* God, at least help me find me a place to hang out.

I spotted a corner-strip-mall with a donut shop. I parked in the lot, the only car there, and kept my engine running. I got out, walked over, and saw that the donut place opened at 7:00. If a cop saw me hanging around here, I'd tell him I'm waiting for the shop to open. I look around. *I can't stay in this lot. My car is the only one here, and the street and lot lights are too bright.*

I drove around the block to an adjacent street. I parked, got out of the driver's side and got back into the passenger seat. I locked the doors, turned off my engine, zipped my coat, and leaned my seat back. *Maybe I can get sleep while I'm waiting like a vagabond on this god-forsaken street.*

The car's clock was approaching 3:30. I tried hard to keep the night's events out of my mind. I closed my eyes. Images of Dad and that woman came back: about how pleasant they were at dinner, and how Dad made their relationship seem so innocent. *Did he think I was hopelessly naïve?*

A voice screamed in my head. *How could he be so blatantly indiscreet, as if I were an oblivious child?!* My eyes were tearing, and my mind was livid. Let him realize what he's done when he sees that I'm gone. I don't give a crap about him and them. There's nothing he can say to absolve himself from his flagrant transgression.

I opened my eyes and looked down the dark, empty street. I refocused my mind on the donuts I'd have for breakfast: chocolate glazed, Boston cream, and chocolate frosted. Though I struggled to get him and her out of my head, at least I was miles away from them.

The cold outside air permeated into my little Datsun. Sleep finally overtook me.

I woke with a start. There was light outside. I could hear a car pass.

Where am I?

My mind raced; I looked around. *Oh crap, the world hasn't ended? Oh, shit; after last night, maybe mine has.*

I was still on that cold Toronto suburban street, and so too was my miserable life right there with me. My eyes burned as I tried to rub tiredness out of them.

What the heck's the time? The car's clock showed 7:30. Thank goodness I had slept some. Now, where's that damned donut shop?

The next couple of hours passed like maple sap in a Canadian winter. I sat in the shop, had four donuts and a pot of coffee, and read anything I could get my hands on, even the local real estate journal. I walked around the block.

At a quarter to ten, from a corner pay phone, I called my friend, Ellen. I asked if we could meet earlier than planned. I didn't tell her why.

She offered, "C'mon over anytime. Hardly anyone ever plays on the court in my apartment building's basement. What time do expect to get here?"

"How's eleven o'clock?" I didn't tell her that I was only a few minutes down the road from her apartment. Let her believe I was driving in from Hamilton.

I said nothing to Ellen about the previous night. During our games, I didn't play particularly well, but playing together was only an excuse to get exercise and to see each other.

Afterward, I talked to her about my work at P&G: "It's okay for now, but I'm not sure I could work in a soap- and detergent-making factory my whole life."

I talked to her about Madeline. "We get together at different places every few weekends. She wants to take me to Grand Bend on Lake Huron when the weather is warm. It's a funky town with a great beach."

"She sounds special. I'm happy for you, Harvy," Ellen said. "Hope I get to meet her sometime."

Ellen talked to me about what was going on in her life, but I remembered nothing she said. If she thought I was distracted, she didn't mention it.

Will I ever tell anybody about what happened? If I did, I'd feel ashamed that I hadn't questioned or confronted my father. I was distraught that I allowed him to draw me into a lurid situation. I pretended that the previous night never occurred; that I wasn't at the Blue Sky; that the other woman never existed;

that my father was never in Toronto. No one needed to know how he lured stupid me into his thoughtless vices.

After sandwiches at her apartment, I said, "I should get going." A thought came to my mind. "Before I leave, can I use your phone to call my answering machine at home?"

"Sure. The phone's on the wall in the kitchen." She pointed to it.

I left the dining room table, picked up the phone, and dialed.

I had four messages. All but one were from Dad.

As the first one started, I turned my back to Ellen. *Click.* "Harvy, son, I'm sorry. I'm still here in Toronto, and I want to see you before I go home."

His voice was contrite. "Lizebeth has left and gone back to Montreal. I'm at Jeff Peters' home. You know where it is. Can you come over to see me? I want to know you are okay." His voice was also on edge. "Please come. Please call me here. You know the number. I love you." *Click.*

Does he now want my sympathy after what he did? Just go back to Montreal and leave me alone.

The second message started. *Click.* "Son, it's Dad again. Please call me. Please come over. I need to talk to you. I can't leave Toronto without seeing you. Can you please call me at Jeff's? *Click.*

Can't you just go home! I don't want to see you.

I stood in Ellen's kitchen, my heart pounding. I made no sound as the messages clicked on.

The next message was from someone unexpected. *Click.* "Hi Harvy; it's Jeff. Your father wants to see you. Please come over if you can. He's been smoking cigarettes non-stop since he got here. He can't sit still. He's a nervous wreck. If you can't come over, then call at least. You know the number." *Click.*

As usual, Dad rallied his troops for his cause. *God, maybe I should see him. But what am I going to say? I want to forget about last night, not talk about it.*

The last message was from Dad again. *Click.* "Harvy, I can't leave Toronto until I see you. Please call me or come over. I'm truly sorry about last night. Please don't punish me. I want to talk to you and explain." *Click.*

I turned to Ellen. "Is it okay if I make another call? I need to go see someone."

"Sure, Harvy, help yourself. *Mi casa es tu casa.*"

I dialed Jeff's number. He answered. I said, "Hi Jeff; it's Harvy."

Jeff seemed relieved. "Harvy, we thought you fell into a deep hole. Your father's very upset. Let me get him and put him on."

"Wait, Jeff! Tell him I'll be there in half an hour."

"Okay, Harvy. I don't know what happened between the two of you, but I have to tell you I've never seen your father this upset." He took a breath. "Do you remember where we live?"

"Yes. Give me thirty minutes."

"Sure, kiddo. I'll tell him."

I said goodbye to Ellen and drove to Jeff's.

My insides felt empty. My esophagus hurt as if it were in a fiery hell. *I don't want to talk to that shameless bum.*

Maybe I'll listen to what he has to say and then leave. He's lucky I'm nice, showing up to help him out of his misery. I want to forget last night and have him leave me out of his bullshit.

I knocked on Jeff's front door, and he came to greet me. "Your father's in the den. Did I tell you that he hasn't moved from there or stopped smoking since he got here hours ago?"

I nodded.

"You know where to go. You can close the door behind you for privacy."

I walked into the den and shut the door. Dad was sitting down in a chair, his elbows on his knees, his face in his hands. A cigarette was burning between his fingers. The curtains were drawn shut. The room lighting was dim. The air stank of cigarette smoke and scotch.

Dad looked up. He stood and rushed toward me. His face was wet with tears; one of the few times I had ever seen or heard him cry. He hugged me, but I didn't return the gesture. "Harvy, please, please forgive me. I'm sorry; Lizabeth is gone; she went home." His voice was shaking. "But I couldn't leave before I could tell you how sorry I am. Please forgive me."

"Okay, Dad." I paused for a moment. The toxicity was still in my blood. "I can't talk more about this now. I'd like to go home."

He looked at me, but I couldn't meet his eyes. "Why didn't you say something last night about what bothered you? Why didn't you stand up and scream at us?"

I looked away, "I don't scream as you do. I wish I would have said something, but I couldn't." I looked back at his face but avoided his eyes. "What the heck were you thinking, Dad?"

"Please, son; it's not my fault. She wanted to be with me. It was nothing."

Ya, right! I stared at my father and felt nothing but resentment.

He looked at me. "Harvy, I promise that it will never happen again. I'm sorry. Can you find it in your heart to forgive me?"

"Okay, Dad. I'm sorry too. *For what, I'm not sure.* You should go home now, and please let me go home too."

"Okay, son; whatever you say." Dad grabbed me and hugged me again. "You and Stevie are the only ones I live for. I don't want you to hate me or to worry about Lizabeth anymore."

My father's apology seemed sincere. I didn't want him to suffer more than he had to. I gave him a small hug. *Hell if I was going to cry.*

"I don't hate you, Dad," I said without emotion. "I just need to get over it. Can I please go now? I'm really tired. I need time and some more sleep. I want to go home. You should go home too."

My eyes began to tear, but I worked to ignore it. This moment might have been an opportune time to ask my father about his intentions with my mother, but I wasn't in the mood to place more of our family's follies on the floor in front of us.

"Sure, son. I appreciate you coming here. I'll go home. I'll talk to you next week." He smiled through his tears. "I love you. I would do anything for you. Please don't forget that."

I could barely look at him. "Sure, Dad," I said. But I wondered if I could ever be sure of anything with my father. *Would I ever be able to forgive him?*

I kissed him on the cheek as I usually did, turned around and left the room. I didn't see Jeff or Wendy anywhere, not even their dogs, and I didn't want to. I walked out the way I had come in. I wanted to go to bed, to sleep and not wake until I was in my next life.

Just *Lassen* to Me!

Why couldn't God have given me a bloody normal family?

* * *

"No! Stop! Go away!" I lunged upright in bed. It was dark. *Where am I?*

The clock read 6:30, and Madeline had awoken next to me. "Harvy, sweetie, what's the matter? You were moaning and screaming in your sleep."

It was the weekend after I had seen Dad in Toronto. He and I hadn't talked since our Blue Sky Hotel altercation. I was now in Cambridge, Ontario with Madeline. Over supper the previous evening, I told Madeline that my father and I had had a big upset.

The day after I had left Dad at the Peter's home, during my usual Sunday evening call with my mother, I told Mom that everything had been uneventful in my supper and night with him. I couldn't tell her the truth, and thus be the one to break up my parents' marriage. It was easier to pretend that everything was fine.

I also hadn't told Madeline the details. I just said that I wanted to put it out of my mind, to forget about it.

I stared down at the bed. "It was just a bad dream."

"About your father?"

"I guess so. But it's gone now."

She rubbed my back. "Want to talk about it?"

I slowly shook my head. "Not really. It's over. I'm okay."

"Are you sure?"

"Yes; I'm fine now." I wasn't sure. I didn't understand it fully then, but I didn't want to talk about my shame in having been drawn into my father's vices and then not having stood up for myself.

After another moment of her scratching and rubbing my back, my muscles relaxed. I felt better and smiled. She nuzzled against me. "By the way," she said, "I've meant to talk to you about a little trip I had in mind for us. How does California in late June sound to you, once my school district is out for the summer?"

I looked at her and smiled. "Yah! Now you're talking."

She kissed me on the cheek. "Enough talk now." She smiled too. "Now let me help you take your mind off your father."

* * *

My father and I never spoke again about our evening with Lizabeth. We carried on as if that night at the Blue Sky had never occurred.

Dad never told me what happened to his lady friend, and I never asked. I wondered if she too had been innocently and unexpectedly ensnared into a situation of my father's making. She seemed like an intelligent woman; what was she thinking in sharing a bed with Dad while I was next door? Hopefully, she found a way to live with her choices as I lived with mine.

For forty years, I never told anyone about that night, not a girlfriend or spouse or therapist. Thinking about it continued to give me headaches and heartache.

Maybe it was just an f'ing bad dream.

* * *

Years after my father's passing, Ned Meyer's wife, Mimi, told me more about what had happened between my father and his former supervisor, Margit, and her sister, Edit. The over ninety-year-old widow made me supper in her Toronto apartment. Over her meal, I asked her to tell me what she knew about Margit and my father.

She complied. "Ned told me everything about Johnny. Your father confided in him like one would to a trusted big brother." She knew that my brother and I weren't close. "Ned lost his kid brother to World War II, so helping your father was as if he were helping his own."

Mimi's tone was matter-of-fact. "During the time she worked for Johnny, Margit and your father fell in love, but you and Stevie were still small kids back then." She took a long breath. "Your father told Margit that he couldn't leave your mother, or even have a love affair with her until you two kids were much older." She raised a hand. "Ned told me that Margit very much loved Johnny, so she decided to wait until the time your father would leave your mother."

Mimi raised an index finger, and her voice got edgy. "But her sister, Edit, wanted to prove to Margit that Johnny couldn't be faithful. Edit had a bit of a reputation for playing around, and she put that to use with your father.

"One night she got your father drunk and asked him to come back to her apartment. There she seduced him. The next day, Edit ran to her older sister to say that Johnny was not reliable because he had slept with her."

I cringed inside for the pain my father had stupidly inflicted by following what was in his pants instead of what was on his shoulders—as if there was a difference between the two for that man.

I kept quiet and let Mimi continue. She took a deep breath. "Margit was devastated by what your father did, but she continued to work for him."

She drew another long breath. "Sometime after that, she and Johnny had a fight about her salary. Because he balked at giving her a raise, she went home, took pills, and killed herself." Mimi guided her index finger across her throat.

"Wow!" Could my father be that callous, even cruel? Might he have seen Margit's salary increase request as blackmail for what she knew about his infidelities? "How did my dad find out she killed herself?" I asked.

Mimi talked as if the incident had occurred just the previous week. "Margit lived in an apartment building in the city. Ned's boss, Aras, owned the building."

She looked at me, and her voice rose. "You remember Aras, your father's long-time Troika companion?" She pointed her index finger upward and shook it in the air. "Aras and your father were inseparable in Russian vodka, Cossack music, and loose *vimen.*" She emphasized the last word in a heavy Romanian Jewish accent.

"Yes, of course; I remember Aras. He died the same year as my father did."

"*Dat's rrright!* They lived the Montreal nightlife together, and then they died together." Her finger pointed to the ceiling then down to the floor. "I don't know if they went up or down, but I'm sure they are there together."

Mimi calmed her voice and continued. "Your father and Aras became good friends because Aras could keep up with him at the Hungarian Tokay, the Russian Troika, and the Slovak Koliba on St. Helen Island. (The latter was a traditional Eastern European shepherd's log-house restaurant that was built and operated at the Montreal's Expo 67 site.) My Ned didn't like to drink, so he never went with them to those places. But your father called Ned whenever he got into trouble and needed help."

Ned had been a fixture in our family's life all through my childhood. I felt a twinge of loss of his presence after my father left my mother for a final time. I missed Ned and Mimi's smiling faces and them being with us in Florida during the winter vacations of my childhood. Ned loved to talk about the latest and greatest cars, and he always offered a listening ear and encouraging words. His and Mimi's energy had been fresh air to the foul odors that had hung around my parents for most of their marriage.

I stayed on our original track. "So what happened with Margit?" I asked.

Mimi batted her hand at me. "Yes, yes, I'm getting *dere;* be patient with an old *voman.*" She took a sip of water. "Your father had previously arranged with Aras to give Margit an apartment for low rent in one of the buildings Aras owned."

Mimi took a sip of water from a glass. "When Margit didn't show for work the next day, Johnny called Aras and asked him to check on her." Her voice elevated. "Aras soon called back; his voice was shaking. He had found Margit dead in her apartment, and he told Johnny to get down there right away."

My eyes widened. Mimi's voice steadied. "Your father immediately called Ned, and they rushed down to try to figure out with Aras what had happened. They searched the apartment and found a suicide note."

Her voice rose again. "Luckily, the note didn't implicate your father. It said that her suicide was not anybody's fault but her decision. It said she was tired of life and felt she had nothing more for which to live. The note didn't mention Johnny."

My ears were ringing in disbelief. "What happened next? Did anybody call the police?"

Mimi pawed her hand at me as if she wanted me to stay calm. "Ned, your father, and Aras left everything as they found it, her body and the note too. After Johnny and Ned had departed the apartment, Aras called the police. He told them he was checking on Margit because Johnny had called to say she didn't show up at work."

She raised one hand. "The police went to interview your father, but he said he knew nothing about why she wanted to kill herself." She looked pensive. "Maybe Edit told the police about your father and Margit's relationship, but they had no evidence to determine if your father was responsible for Margit's death."

Mimi looked like an aged grandmother who wanted to get the weight off her chest before her death. "Ned came home and told me everything," she offered. "It then remained unspoken for decades; until I told you today."

I was speechless. I imagined Margit lying motionless in the bed she had hoped to share with my father. I imagined my father looking down at her lifeless body, his eyes glassy, a *Hesus Maria* emanating from his mouth. But did he feel any responsibility for what she had done? Might he have blamed Edit, or Margit herself, for her fate?

For me, this was one more example of the painful secrets that were perhaps better left buried in our family's history. What was it about my father that attracted such damaged women to him? Though he acted cruelly with someone he had said he loved, Margit and Edit certainly had played their parts in this Johnny Simkovits soap opera.

Mimi's face looked relieved at divulging the story, but my own heart ached from hearing it. How did my father let his vices so easily drag him astray? Even more so, how did I come to admire and revere this man so much—as my mother had—that I sacrificed my conscience for him? My heart ached again.

Mimi looked at me. "But your father did do one nice thing for Margit."

"What was that?" I asked.

"He paid for her funeral," she said dryly.

She looked away and ended the story there.

* * * *

33

What Business School Doesn't Teach

In 1978, after a year at P&G, I received both my Ontario Professional Engineering certification and a job promotion. I was tapped to be the next head of P&G's Hamilton instrumentation installation and maintenance department. Though I had a mind for process engineering, the new job required me to supervise a crew of instrumentation techs and manage a set of outside maintenance contractors.

In addition to having installed new process controls successfully in our Hamilton plant, my peers knew me as a likable fellow. People told me I had an easy smile and enthusiastic laugh. But the tech group I inherited from a former, long-time supervisor had severe morale issues that dampened my mood.

One tech was on six-month probation for insubordination with my predecessor. Some months later, another disgruntled tech was observed throwing expensive pipe valves over a fence. A security guard saw him retrieve those items after work, probably to sell on an underground market for such things. But the guard waited until the next morning to report the crime and make an arrest.

The tech realized that someone had been watching him. The next day, the sly guy found a job at one of the adjacent steel mills. Because he didn't show for work at P&G, he couldn't be investigated, charged, and fired by management for stealing, which allowed his formal record to stay clean.

Our 1,000-employee Hamilton plant had many large closets and utility rooms in which one could hide out of sight. Other supervisors caught some of my instrumentation techs sleeping on the job in some of those nooks. It was my techs' way of catching up on rest after performing extra night or weekend shifts.

Another tech complained chronically about safety issues. The fellow once called a department supervisor and me to a problem situation. He pointed, "To replace the faulty level sensor in that tank, I have to stick my head into the tank to get to the sensor. I won't do it, and I'll bring it up with my employee rep if you make me go in there!"

The experienced department supervisor demonstrated—in less than thirty seconds—how the tech could get his arm into the tank to reach the sensor without having to put his head into the fumes. The tech then did his job begrudgingly.

Some of my guys complained about too much weekend overtime while others said there wasn't enough. Some didn't get along with their peers. A senior guy felt that management had overlooked him for promotion—he had wanted my supervisory position.

It was my job to help rebuild the spirit of this dispirited team. I was the new kid on the plant block, just one year out of engineering school. I wasn't sure I was cut out to fix these people problems that had festered from well before I had gotten there.

My immediate boss had been with the company for many years, but he was also new to his position. He wanted to see the people I managed either shape up or ship out. I was young and worked to please everybody—a sure formula for sleepless nights.

I soon became overwhelmed by the people issues. I sympathized with our plant manager who was once overheard saying, "My biggest problems in this plant are the ones that have two legs."

My previous work experience had been in my father's company where everybody knew who I was, and where I felt important and respected. At P&G, I was one of many new engineers and supervisors working to get noticed in a big corporation. After nine months in my supervisory position, my father's MBA offer started to look more enticing.

Dad continued to push business school like the salesman he was. "Harvy, don't get lost in that big company. Go to Harvard and then into business for yourself where you can be the boss." I knew his real message: *Get your MBA and then come to work for me where I would tell you what to do.*

Because I struggled with my demoralized and demoralizing P&G staff, I applied to both Harvard and Stanford MBA programs. I never thought I would get into either one of them, especially since I had, two years earlier, been rejected by both of them.

When the letters came, Stanford wait-listed me while Harvard Business School accepted me into the Class of '81. In addition to my good grades at MIT and high GMAT test scores, I surmised that my acceptance had to do with my two years of work experience. P&G had punched an important B-school entry ticket that helped me to leave that corporation with my head raised, though my job there had tied my stomach in knots.

I left P&G to enter Harvard in September of 1979. Dad said, "You made the right decision, son." He put his hand on my shoulder. "*Lassen* to me! A much bigger world and new opportunities will be open to you at Harvard."

He didn't know that my choice was more about running away from P&G than rushing toward his Harvard dream for me.

* * *

Before I departed Canada for Boston, Dad put a bank draft into my hand. It was for $100,000USD, made out in my name. (Unlike in the U.S., there were no limits in Canada on monetary gifts.) That amount of money was five times more than my most recent annual P&G salary and bonus.

Dad offered, "Use this money to pay for your Harvard studies. Open an account and deposit the draft into the Boston branch of the Canadian Regal Bank. Tell them to invest the cash in short-term CDs." His voice was considerate. "Then use the interest income to pay for your tuition and your room and board expenses. Keep the principle intact."

It felt good that Dad entrusted me with such a large sum. I followed his instructions, putting the money into laddered certificates that paid 5-6% interest annually, enough to cover my business school tuition and living costs. My savings from my two-years at P&G would cover my car expenses and what social life I'd have at Harvard. I'd have no debts afterward.

Dad added, "You won't have to pay much if any taxes on that interest income. Not only are you in a low tax bracket, but your Harvard tuition will be fully deductible against your Canadian income." He pointed to himself. "If the bank interest were to come directly to me, I'd have to give more than half the income to the government because of my high tax bracket."

He pointed at me and smiled. "This way, the Canadian government is giving you the gift of paying for nearly half of your MBA degree."

I nodded my understanding and was glad that Dad was getting a tax break for my Harvard education. But I didn't divulge how worried I was about partaking in an unfamiliar course of study.

I wondered if my MIT problem-set mind could break the code of Harvard Business School's case study method. Did I now have enough work experience to contribute to class discussions? Would my stock rise or fall during my time at the B-school?

* * *

It took me less than a month at Harvard to realize that the business school might not work out for me. My head ached from having to read and analyze the required three business cases each weeknight. My heart raced from the expectation and competition of raising my hand in class to impress each professor.

The cloudy subjects of marketing and international economics precipitated sleepless nights for my engineering-trained mind. My brain was good at solving complex mathematical problems that had one right or best answer.

In our business cases, we had to sift through a plethora of text and statistics, much of it extraneous, and then promote a strategy or recommendation for the presented situation. There could be more than one strategy or approach one could defend. I became quickly overwhelmed.

Because of the start of the 1979-1980 recession, a record number of applicants had applied to the B-school that year. I heard from the classmates that the professors considered our entering class among the best and the brightest.

Some professors saw this as a licence to be exceedingly demanding on the students. Others confounded us with their Socratic teaching method. They wanted us to figure out things on our own, so they answered questions with questions or gave few complete answers.

At any moment, a professor could call on any one of the 80 students in my class section. They might let us squirm in our seats as we scrambled to say something half-intelligent in front of our colleagues, all of whom seemed smarter than I.

One day, a young professor threw a chalkboard eraser on the ground near the feet of a student. The professor then demanded the student leave the classroom. The student had struggled with a question about the organizational impact of a senior manager getting fired.

The room fell silent. At first, I thought the professor was kidding about demanding the student depart the class. He looked the student in the eye, pointed to the door, and told him to gather his books and leave.

Another classmate came to the student's aid, saying the student didn't have to go. But the professor glared at the second student too and demanded his departure along with his peer. As both students gathered their books and walked toward the door, the professor looked at them and said, "As you leave, please reflect on what it's like to be dismissed and not know why."

Along with the rest of my classmates, I held my breath. It was as if a piece of each one of us was going out the door with our peers, possibly wondering who was next on our professor's hit list.

After class, our student section leader talked to the professor (maybe the subject head too) about his provocative approach. The professor came back to the next class and apologized both to the two students and to the whole class regarding his methods. He stated, "I wanted to give the class the experience of how it feels to have colleagues dismissed without cause, as can happen in some of today's organizations. I regret my class experiment failed its intended purpose."

The directly affected students, grim-faced, accepted the professor's apology. The rest of us sat in our seats, looking on and saying nothing. Though I felt some relief, I still felt sweat under my collar.

My 25th birthday fell on Columbus Day weekend in October of 1979. I didn't go home because I didn't want to see my parents. I stayed at Harvard to keep up with my classwork. Over lunch in the school cafeteria, I heard a fellow student talk about a thirty-something business school professor that had committed suicide.

I hadn't heard him say when the death had happened, but the statement shook me into my bone marrow. I imagined a successful Harvard professional who had a bright future, but I imagined that something about the pressure of his career made him take his life.

Weeks earlier, I had read in the Harvard Crimson that over a quarter of Harvard's students sought help through Harvard's Mental Health Services during their time at the school. Since I felt I was at Harvard more for my father than for myself, I sought professional counselling for the first time in my life. I was recommended to meet with an outside psychologist named Max.

At our first session, I found myself cold and shaking. I shared, "I'm worried about making it through the MBA program. I'm finding the material overwhelming. I'm anxious about raising my hand in class. For the first time in my life, I feel stupid compared to my classmates." Later on in the session, I admitted, "I feel like I'm at Harvard to please my father rather than being here for myself."

Max listened. He asked questions and nodded to my responses. His voice was deep and calm. "Harvy, don't be so concerned about feeling stupid. Most of the students feel that way—it's the nature of B-school."

He suggested, "Try to stick it out for another month or two to be sure whether or not Harvard is right for you. Come and see me every week and we can work to help you through it. If you leave now or a month from now, it won't make much difference."

He raised his hand off his lap and smiled. "It doesn't make sense to disappoint your father right out of the Harvard gate. And, don't worry about him so much. It's your life and career we are talking about, not his."

I felt comforted by my psychologist's words but still found it hard to concentrate on my classwork. I did what I could to prepare every evening, engaging in the requisite three thick cases for the next day, and getting to sleep before midnight.

During class, I worked to stay inconspicuous behind my cardboard name-card, avoiding the professor's eyes so he or she wouldn't call on me. When a professor called upon me, shudders went through me as if my life depended on what came out of my mouth. I stammered out answers.

In many subjects, I felt unsure of myself and what I was saying. It felt as if I were so far out in the B-school ocean water that the next wave of cases or professor's questions could drown me.

Halfway through our first semester, near the end of a class, my organization behavior professor looked at me. His face was serious as he spoke to me in front of our whole class section. "Harvy, at our next session, I want you to lead us in a review of our organization behavior class work so far this semester."

My jaw dropped, and my heart galloped. *I've hardly said a thing in class, and the prof now wants me to lead a discussion???*

That night, I stayed glued to my desk in my cold dorm room and frantically scoured through my case notes. I sweated as if I were going to be hung on the blackboard the next day.

At our next session, after his introductory remarks, the professor approached me and put his chalk into my hand. "Okay, Harvy, the class is yours." I stood and walked to the board as he took my seat.

My heart was racing again, my collar was wet with sweat, but I surprised myself. Notes in hand, I drew a flowchart on the blackboard that outlined the sets of cases we had gone through that semester and the connections I saw between them. I offered something half-intelligent about each set of cases. I then faced the class and asked if any students had questions or comments.

As students raised their hands, I picked a few to speak. I didn't try to address what they said but acted as the professor did. I looked up at the student that looked down at me. "Good comment!" I offered. I then looked around the room. "What do others think about that?" More students raised their hands.

As the professor had done in prior classes, I facilitated a discussion. After about ten more minutes—which seemed like an all-eyes-on-me eternity—the professor rose from my chair. He nodded and smiled. "Thank you, Harvy, for that review." I went back to my seat but remained with no memory of what I said or what any of the students had offered.

When our morning sessions were over, a couple of my classmates came to me. "That was pretty good, Harvy. I bet you were sweating bullets down there in the pit." I smiled back nervously and just nodded. I felt as if I had dodged a blackboard hanging for the moment.

Six weeks later, after the semester ended, that professor wrote me a note on my returned exam booklet: "Harvy, I thought I had gotten you turned around and out of your shell. You pretty much stopped talking in class for the rest of the semester. I wonder what happened."

I never responded to him, another sign of how I felt over my head at Harvard.

Outside of speaking each week to my psychologist, I wrote to Madeline in Ontario and told her my Harvard trials and tribulations. Because I was far away, we had decided to end our intimate relationship but remain friends.

She wrote back. "Get that Johnny out of your pretty head and hang in there. You are a smart guy and a honey!" Her words put a smile on my face.

But my head stayed heavy and my chest tight at the thought of disappointing both my father and myself.

The only other person I talked to about my business school ambivalence was my dorm roommate. He told me, "You have to want to be here at Harvard to make it through what they throw at you."

Something else was bothering me, which I shared with no one but Max. I told him, "My parents' relationship seems to be at an all-time low. I heard from my mother that my father is hardly at home. He sleeps on the couch when he does get home, after midnight most nights."

My voice was breaking as I added, "She seems exceedingly anxious whenever we talk. She whispers to me as if she were afraid of being overheard, but she's the only one there."

Max offered, "Harvy, try to stay focused on Harvard. Don't think too much about what's happening at home." His voice stayed calm and quiet. "What has been happening there has been going on for a long time. There's little you can do from here." He gestured toward me. "You need to make yourself your first concern."

Over the next weeks, I worked to stay on top of my studies. As fall crept into winter, it became harder for me to sleep soundly in my never-warm-enough business school dorm room.

* * *

In early December, I did something I had never done before. I called my father and asked him to come to see me for an evening. I wanted to talk to him about my angst about being at Harvard.

Dad flew in from Montreal on a Saturday afternoon and met me for supper at the Union Oyster House. I could hardly hug him hello. I was shaking inside as we ordered our meal at a private booth. I had on a thick wool sweater, but I had to keep my hands between my legs to warm my ice-cold fingers.

After we had ordered our meal, I started to talk. "I feel torn up inside about being here. I'm not enjoying Harvard as I did MIT. I don't feel good about myself." I took a deep breath. "I'm sorry to say this, but I feel as if I'm here more for you than for me."

Dad looked at me, but I couldn't meet his eyes. "I'm so sorry you are feeling bad, son." His voice was quiet and calm, but his hands were gripping the table. "How are your classes going and how are your grades so far? What's burning for you?"

I obliged. "We've had mid-term exams on several subjects. So far, my grades are about middle-of-the-road. I'm not failing anything, but I'm not excelling in much either. I'm passing all subjects, though it seems barely in some."

Dad stayed quiet as I yammered on. "I'm doing okay in subjects like decision science and operations management, which fit better with my training at MIT and my work experiences at P&G and JHS." I looked down at the table. "But I hate marketing and international economics. The case reading is overwhelming, and I'm finding those subjects hard to grasp."

I didn't say that I thought my female marketing professor was a hard-ass who spoke to the students as if we were ground chuck churned out of the Harvard meat grinder. She had rote clichés: "This is what you people need to know!" and "You need to adjust to what we are trying to do here," and "Everyone goes through a rough time in their first months here." There was no warmth from that woman. Many of the other students had trouble with her too, but that didn't assuage my angst.

I took a breath as I looked at my father's chest. "In the rest of the subjects, like organizational behavior and accounting, I guess I'm doing fine. But it's all new stuff for me, like having to learn Chinese, and I feel overwhelmed most of the time. It's been a lot of reading. The other students seem to be on top of it more than I am."

What I didn't tell him was that I was trying to do the classwork on my own. I hadn't teamed with other students—as others did every evening—to pool knowledge and understandings about each case. I had been mostly a loner student at MIT, but that approach didn't work well at the B-school.

My eyes watered as I looked out a frosty window. "You know that I was almost a straight-A student at MIT. I feel as if I know nothing here. Almost everything feels foreign. I don't know if I can handle it much longer." Though I had a good mind for technical things, I hadn't cracked the code at Harvard. I didn't know if I could succeed there.

Unusual for him, Dad didn't offer anything until he heard what I had to say. I looked at his hands that were still gripping the table. I continued. "The professors here are not like the ones at MIT. There the professors had teaching assistants who helped you outside of class if you needed it; though most of the time, I understood things without their help. Here there are no teaching assistants, and many of the professors talk to you as if you are a small cog in a big Harvard wheel."

I held my hands together on the edge of the table. "They all say the same things about managing your time on cases, not trying to do everything perfectly, working through the stress of being here, and staying engaged in the classroom." I pointed to my forehead. "It feels as if some of them are trying to cram the cases into our heads. I don't feel good about myself here."

I looked away again and then back at my father's chest, still avoiding his eyes. I had no idea what expression was on his face. I continued. "The students here are very competitive. Many are out to impress the professors in class to get a good participation grade. At MIT, it was about learning the subject material and not about needing to look good. I don't have a knack for this kind of showmanship."

Dad put his hand on mine. He spoke calmly. "Son, please don't get sick over it." His tone remained subdued. "Try to take in as much as you can. Be here as long as you can." He took in a long breath. "You can always come home and work for me—like your brother did after he left Queen's—if you don't want to remain here."

Dad seemed understanding, but I knew he wanted me to remain at Harvard. I didn't want to be a big disappointment. I knew he wanted me to obtain the education that had been beyond his reach when he had started out in the world. I sensed he wanted me to carry on the success he had built in Montreal over the last three decades. I felt as if I were letting him down badly, and myself too.

Our waitress came to gather our empty dishes. I glanced at my father's gold Omega watch that he had bought in Zurich, the city where he had opened his first hidden bank account. The watch reminded me of our recent Harvard corporate ethics cases.

Recent Wall Street Journal articles had mentioned several American corporate scandals. They questioned whether business schools like Harvard were teaching enough about corporate ethics.

Within days of those news items, the school presented students with cases on truth in advertising, shareholder and public disclosures, and ethical accounting practices. I struggled to make sense of our academic discussions in light of what I knew about my father's real world of underhanded business.

I said nothing to Dad about my ambivalence regarding his business MO. I said nothing about my mother's condition at home. I didn't want him to get mad at her for complaining to me about her unhappy life at home. What I did say was, "I'll do what I can to stick it out for as long as I can."

Before Dad got into a taxi to head back to the airport, he held my shoulders and kissed me on my cheeks. I did my best to look at his face. He offered, "*Lassen* to me, son. Don't be so hard on yourself."

He blinked a few times. "See you at home for Christmas. I'm sure you'll feel better after time away from here."

"Okay, Dad," I said, but I wasn't sure if I would.

On the subway ride back to Harvard Square, I stared out the window and into the dark tunnel. I thought of the Godfather movie I had seen years earlier with my father. I wondered if I could be like the Don's youngest son, Michael, who took over the family's business syndicate after initially wanting to have nothing to do with his father's straight and crooked businesses. I also wondered if my dad wanted me, as an MIT and Harvard graduate, to become a legit front for his illicit financial finagling and fortune.

I shook my head and blinked my eyes. *How am I going to survive Harvard?* Maybe the deeper truth was: *How was I going to survive my father?* My only comfort was that Dad was now on notice that I might quit business school, and thus jeopardize his aspiration for this son-of-the-boss.

* * *

Those Christmas and New Year's holidays were one of the only times when my father neither planned nor suggested a southerly vacation trip for our family. It was a sign of how bad things had gotten between him and my mother.

The last place I wanted to be for the holidays was with my family. I went first to Ontario to visit Madeline for a few days around Christmas. Though she and I were no longer a couple, we still cared about each other.

Madeline's two children were pre-teens. When I had visited Madeline in Cambridge, I took her and her kids to the first *Star Wars* movie. Driving to their home after the show, we pretended to be Jedi Knights fighting the Galactic Empire. The two kids bobbed in the back seat as they imagined the headlights from oncoming cars were lightsaber attacks that needed to be dodged or repelled.

Madeline laughed as I played along. I cowered behind the car steering wheel as vehicles passed us. From that point forward, her kids voted me their mom's "*bestest* man-friend."

Spending time with Madeline and her brood took my mind off Harvard. She made home-cooked meals, and we played Monopoly and Scrabble until late at night.

For every moment of joy I had during those days, a pang of dread filled my body regarding my upcoming time at home in Montreal. Would Mom cry and Dad yell? Would she run out of her kitchen and into the bedroom after a fight with him? Would he walk out of the house and slam the front door? Would I retreat under my bed covers, bang my head against a wall, or jump out a window and run away?

My despair became so dark that I couldn't make the six-hour drive from Madeline's house to my Montreal home in one day. Two hours before reaching Montreal, as the short winter day turned to icy dusk, my body started to shake. My head felt heavy and achy.

I stopped overnight in a motel so I could pull myself together for reuniting with my family. My Harvard psychologist felt very far away.

I called my parents and told them where I was. Mom said, "I'll be happy when you are finally home." Dad offered, "Do what you need to do, and we'll see you tomorrow."

What transpired the next few days in Montreal remained mostly a blank in my mind. I remembered my brother rushing out every day to ride his horse in Hudson. We said only a few words to each other in passing.

For the whole time I was home, my mother was sick to her stomach from having drunk soured eggnog on Christmas Eve. "I'm so happy to have you home, son," she said. "Look at you; you look so thin. Go to the fridge; there are things I made for you." Her eyes turned away. "Sorry I can't sit with you. I'm not feeling well." She spent most of the time in bed.

I hardly saw my father. When he was present, he headed for the couch to watch TV and get sleep. It had been a busy end-of-year for his factory, especially since the current economic downturn had forced him to cut staff. He and others in his company had done double duty to get production out before Christmas. He did ask me if I wanted to come with him to holiday parties. I wasn't in a celebratory mood, so I declined.

Though I was home with my family, I felt alone and lonely as ever. I had no idea what I was going to do come January, and I had no one to talk to about it. I couldn't even call my therapist because he was away for the holidays. My high school chums were away too. Even if they had been around, I was feeling no compulsion to see them while in my depressed state.

Dad did say he hoped I would stick it out in Boston, but I only nodded and said, "Okay." By the time New Year's came and went, I figured it was best for me to pack my bags and head back to Harvard.

The day I left, my body felt as if it were a 175-pound weight that I had to drag out of the house along with my suitcase. Mom stayed in bed. Steve and Dad were off doing their things. No one sent me off. I felt hopeless and helpless, as my mother might say about her life with Dad.

One day earlier than I had to, I got into my clunky Datsun and drove back to Boston. I knew my way back to Harvard, but I felt ever so lost. Though my father's route in the world hadn't been straight and narrow, he was driven and determined to find a path as a successful businessman.

I admired my dad for building a business from nothing with his big personality and sheer will. I desperately wanted to make him proud of me. I wanted to follow in his entrepreneurial footsteps. I wanted him to see me as the prime beneficiary of his legacy and fortunes. He was paying for me to get the best education that his money could buy. He wished for me to become a bigger man than he—without the war and post-war traumas he went through. I was failing, and I couldn't understand why.

During my drive back to Harvard, my gut felt empty, my heart was heavy, and my head ached from my not knowing what to do. I couldn't stay on the course I was heading, and I couldn't see where else I could go.

I questioned whether I could survive my fate as the son of Johnny Simkovits. I considered veering off the highway, smashing into a tree, and dying on the spot.

Something inside me kept my two hands on the wheel, guiding myself back to my Harvard Business School albatross.

* * *

One morning, after a week back at school, and a night of shivering under double blankets in my igloo of a dorm room, I opened my eyes and looked at my roommate. "I'm not feeling well this morning. I don't think I'm going to class." A moment later I added, "I may not go to any more classes and leave this place for good."

Knowing that I had been having trouble, my roommate offered, "You have to do what feels right. I'll still respect you, Harvy, no matter what you decide."

It occurred to me that the most distant strangers might understand you better and be kinder to you than your own family could. Though my father had shown me sympathy when we met before the holidays, I didn't think he understood my plight, especially regarding him.

After my roommate had left for class, I tried to get back to sleep, but my shaking wouldn't stop. I had no control over my body. I couldn't get the rest I desperately wanted.

I thought about the Harvard professor who had taken his life. I understood his pain. *Might I do something as rash as he did?* I felt my eyes were burning and stomach churning. Not able to sleep, I got out of bed and got dressed. I found a phone and called Max. I reached him quickly; he had an opening in his schedule that morning.

I was the only student in the campus dining hall as I worked to put down some breakfast. Though this building was warmer than my dorm, I still felt as if I needed to shake the chill out of my body and the cobwebs out of my head.

As my appointment time approached, I left campus and walked over the North Harvard Street Bridge into Cambridge. I lumbered over the frozen Charles River. I stayed vigilant on the ice- and snow-covered sidewalk. Had I not, I might have jumped into the river or fallen into road traffic.

I didn't know if it was the January air or my confounded mind that was making me shake. I felt my career was over, that I had no life left, and that I had nothing for which to hope.

About halfway through my session with Max, a big part of the root of my trembling surfaced. I had told him about the fun time I had with Madeline and her kids, and then the painful time I had at home in Montreal before coming back to Boston. But I hadn't told him about the torn loyalty I felt concerning my father's dishonesty in business and his playing around on my mother. Perhaps I wasn't fully aware of my self-torment in holding my father's secrets.

Max told me, "Deep down inside you, Harvy, it seems your body is lamenting that you never had a childhood as good and normal as what you recently experienced with Madeline and her children. You never received unconditional love, full attention, and complete understanding from your parents, something you seem to long for." Though his words sounded like a cliché, I felt its truth in my aching head and pounding heart.

Max looked at me with a soft expression in his eyes. He spoke in a calm, deep voice. "Harvy, if you can accept that your childhood, though turbulent and unfulfilling, is now behind you. If you could learn to bring to others what you sorely missed as a kid, then there would be hope and purpose for you as a guide or mentor."

What he said made profound sense. I felt my chest expand and my shaking stop. My body started to warm. I felt better and said so.

Max cautioned me to be kind to myself and not take to heart what was going on at home. "Harvy, the unhealthiness in your family has been there for a very long time. There is little you can do about it here and now. You need to focus on making yourself stronger. The rest can surely wait."

I felt a huge weight come off my head and shoulders. I left the session with more energy in my stride and a more sure breath than I had had in over a month. I nearly galloped back to the business school and my classes. I kept my eyes forward and didn't look at the frozen river or icy road.

When my roommate saw me come out of my last class that day, he came up to me, shrugged his shoulders, and said, "What are you doing here?"

"I'm trying to stick it out a little longer," I said.

The following Sunday evening, I spoke with my mother as I usually did. She was now out of bed from her illness. She offered, "After you had left to go back to school, I got worse and thought I was going to die. I lay in bed waiting for my last breath. I couldn't eat and only got up to go to the bathroom."

She spoke in whispers, her voice more frenetic than ever. She added, "I kept the bedroom TV on, with the volume low so I didn't have to turn it off. After two weeks of laying down sick as a horse," she murmured, "I felt better than before, so I got out of bed."

Mom's voice sounded like a non-stop train whistle that tooted in short spurts rather than hooted in long bursts. She continued. "Your father only comes into our bedroom to get his clothes. He sleeps on the couch. I run away into another room every time he comes home. I can't look at him or be with him in the same room."

"What about Steve?" I asked. "Can't he help you?"

Mom continued to speak fast and in whispers. "Steve's never home but always at work or riding his horse. I'm here alone all the time." Her train switched tracks. "I leave the house only on Thursday afternoon to buy food at the shopping centre. Then I rush back here without talking to anyone. When are you coming home, son?"

"Did you go see your doctor?" was all I could ask.

Her tone turned a touch terse. "Yes, I did that before, but my doctor is now an old fogey; he does nothing for me. He listens to me crying about your father and then sends me home." Her voice hardened. "I don't want to go out in the cold weather and see him for no reason."

My tone turned a touch desperate. "Mom, you can't sit in the house by yourself. Please talk to Steve and do something." I wasn't sure what. I had course finals coming in late-January and couldn't offer more than a weekly voice on the phone.

I wondered why my brother, who was usually there for our mother, wasn't seeing her distress and helping her. I found myself ticked off at him.

I wondered if Steve had become desensitized to Mom's suffering and Dad's neglect of her. Was he like a frog in water that's heated slowly? Before the amphibian knows it, it's cooked. Living with Mom and working for Dad could have deadened my brother's senses.

I hadn't the strength to call Steve or Dad to see what they could do about Mom. I reminded myself of what my therapist had said. I had to forget about what was happening at home, focus on myself, get stronger, and endure my situation. I wondered and worried if my mother would survive her life with Dad. Then again, might I be in the same boat as she was?

* * *

I don't remember how it started, but on another cold Friday morning later that month, my body was shaking again. My temples got into it this time; my mind felt as if it were going to explode. I couldn't get out of bed for class or breakfast.

I called my psychologist, and he called me back within an hour. After talking for a few minutes, he told me, "Harvy, get yourself to the Mt. Auburn Hospital. Tell them you're a patient of mine. See the psychiatrist on duty and then have them call me after they admit you."

Psychiatrist? I must be going insane!

After our call, I sat on my bed for the longest time, my head down and my arms in my lap. I wondered if I were losing my future. Might the world tag me with mental illness that would follow me for the rest of my life? Was I a promising protégé who then turned into a nothing and nobody; a bright star that fizzled out fast?

I felt the heat rise in me. *I don't fucking care anymore! Let them lock me up in a psych ward and throw away the goddamn key.*

I had had it with being the good son, the smart one, the one with promise, the one Dad has his eye on and his hopes for, the one who one day would inherit his treasure and kingdom.

I got myself to the emergency room at Mt. Auburn Hospital. I waited over an hour to be seen, keeping my winter coat wrapped around me the whole time. Every few minutes, my shaking legs wanted to run out of the place, but my shuddering body had no place to go.

When I finally met with the admitting nurse and intern, I was short with them. "How am I feeling? Like shit I suppose. My head is killing me. My body can't stop shaking."

"No, I don't know when I started feeling this way: today, yesterday, last week, last month, when I was nine years old, my whole goddamned life!"

"No, I have never taken drugs or put any needles in my arm. Do I look like the type?"

"No, I never tried to hurt myself." *What kind of f'ing question is that?*

"Yah, I think about being put out of my miserable suffering every goddamned day."

"Here's the name and number of my therapist. Call and ask him yourself!"

I waited for what seemed like hours—the waiting itself enough to make a sane person turn mad. The attending physician then admitted me for three days of observation.

For the rest of that first day, I gave short answers to the doctor and nurse's questions. I slept as much as I could with the hope of never waking. I called no one, not my parents, not my roommate, not even my therapist. My future had disintegrated. My life was over. I might as well live the rest of my life in a frigging mental institution.

When I woke on Saturday morning, I was still there. What had come apart in my head the previous day had snapped back into place overnight. The nurse had given me codeine to help me sleep. My body had stopped trembling, and the hammer had stopped banging in my head. I thanked God I was feeling better, away from school, my parents, and my life.

But what the hell am I going to do now?

Over the next hours, the nurses, the intern, and the attending psychiatrist came to see me. I apologized for being short with them the previous day. I answered their questions politely about what I think happened to me: "My parents are having problems at home. ...I guess that they—and me being here at Harvard—had gotten to me. ...I must have had a breakdown."

I held my hands in my lap as I sat up in bed. "Yesterday, I hated myself and everyone around me. I wanted to give up. I wanted to die." I hung my head. "I feel terrible about it. I can't believe I was that way." I felt my eyes tear.

The hospital psychiatrist had called my psychologist. Later that day, Max came to visit. He asked me how I felt and what I wanted to do. I said, "I guess I'm okay, but I'm scared. I don't know what I'm going to do on Monday." My voice trembled. "I don't know if I'm going to try to stay at Harvard or not."

I pushed the future out of my head as best I could. My eyes watered. "I'm so glad that I'm feeling better today than I did yesterday."

He looked at me with his caring eyes. "Harvy, with your mind a little clearer, maybe a thought will come to you about what you want to do next."

Max left me and went to confer with the attending psychiatrist. I sat in bed watching television to keep my mind off myself.

Max came back and sat down next to me. "The hospital wants to keep you here until Monday morning. If things are looking good with you tomorrow, they'll let you go out for a walk in the local area."

He put his hand on the edge of my bed. "But they want you back here for Sunday night. They want to be sure you are okay before they send you off on Monday."

My eyes got wet. I nodded. "Sure, doc, whatever they say. I'll be good and follow orders." I tried to smile. I wondered if being good and following my father's orders was a part of my problem.

Max looked at me. "I wouldn't call your parents until after the weekend. There's no sense worrying them, especially since you're feeling better now." And there was no sense getting myself distraught again by my mother's condition or my father's pending disappointment in me.

"Call me on Monday afternoon and tell me how you're doing," he added. "If you want an appointment during the week to make more sense of this, I'll make myself available."

"Thanks, doc—for everything."

"My pleasure, Harvy; I'll see you soon." He smiled, nodded, and walked out the door.

On Sunday afternoon, as planned, the attending psychiatrist permitted me to venture out of the hospital. It was a sunny and warm day. The snow was melting.

Unlike Montreal, where the snow and ice set in for the whole winter, Boston had mid-winter thaws. I was grateful that I could unzip my coat. I took in the non-biting air as I walked around the high-end Brattle Square area of Cambridge.

I sat on a park bench and looked at the big, beautiful, expensive houses surrounding me. I hoped that one day I might have a home like one of these, and have a normal life with a wife and kids.

At the same time, I wondered what craziness lurked behind those wrought-iron fences, well-pruned bushes, and stately colonial structures. I stared at the ground. I wondered if the people living in those highbrow homes fought the way my parents did. Do their children end up in a hospital psych ward the way I did?

My head rose suddenly. I looked down the quiet street on this church-going day. A new thought sent a quake through my spine.

I stood and started to walk back and forth briskly. Instead of looking at the houses around me, I examined something housed inside me. I suddenly knew what I had to do: about Harvard, about my parents and brother, about what was next in my life.

I continued to walk around in a rush, stopping here and standing there as I asked myself over and over again, *Are you sure, Harvy? Is that realistic? Will it work?*

My excitement built. That instant, I made up my mind.

I had been running away from my family throughout my adult life. I had tried to keep my distance from them at MIT, at Procter & Gamble, and now at Harvard. I had been waiting for the day that I could fully jettison Mom, Dad, and Steve from my existence.

I was now sure that I was going to make a 180-degree turn and go back to Montreal to do something worthwhile for my family.

Expunging my family from my psyche hadn't worked. I should, must, and needed to turn toward what I had been avoiding all these years. I was going home to try to make a useful difference: to help my mother through her sickness, to make a worthwhile impact in my father's business and financial affairs, to build a relationship with my brother.

Maybe I was unrealistic, but I had to try for the sake of my sanity. Based on how things turned out, I'd figure out what to do next.

I was shivering again but not with dread but with hopeful anticipation. I was scared, but I was certain that this was what I had to do. It wasn't going to be easy, but I had to try.

Though I hadn't set foot in a church in nearly eight years, I said to myself, *God, who- and what- and wherever you are, you'd want me to do this, wouldn't you?*

* * *

I dropped out of Harvard at the end of January of 1980. Daylight was getting longer in the sky, but the dreary days of New England winter were still sending their chill through me.

My student advisor was surprised to see me go. He told me, "Harvy, your first semester grades are fairly middle-of-the-road, nothing to be too concerned about."

He didn't try to stop me from leaving—I hadn't been the first HBS student at his door this year in this way. He added, "You can come back to Harvard, but you'd have to start the program from the beginning. You haven't completed enough of the classes to obtain any course credit."

"I understand," I replied. I didn't expect to see him or Harvard again.

I went to visit my organizational behaviour (OB) professor, the one who had me lead a course review in front of my class section. OB was one of the few subjects at Harvard that I enjoyed. Though the class material was very foreign to my technical mind, it revealed to me my interest in the people side of business management.

I told the professor, "I'm leaving Harvard and going back to help my family's business." I asked him if he had any advice for me.

He said, "Family businesses are unique animals in the business world. They follow the whims and notions of their founders whose choices aren't always coherent or rational."

I smiled but said nothing.

The professor rummaged through his shelves. He handed me a couple of recent articles about leading and managing family businesses. He was the co-author of one of the articles.

He then offered me the name of an American practitioner in the field of family business consulting and told me to look up the fellow's work and writings. I thanked him and said goodbye.

I called my therapist and told him of my departure. He offered, "Good luck, Harvy. Call me from Montreal if you need to talk." I thanked him but figured I'd find a person like him in Montreal, or I'd call the guy to whom my OB professor had referred me.

In my dorm room at the end of that day, my roommate offered, "I understand your decision, Harvy. I wish you well, and best of luck in trying to make a difference in your Dad's business." He then turned back to his desk to focus on his cases for the next day.

My closest classmates insisted on taking me to supper so that they could say their farewells. They took me to a fun place, the Averof, a Greek restaurant in Cambridge that had a male bouzouki musician and a female belly dancer.

As our meal and the music ended, my mates, one by one, wished me good luck and offered their goodbyes. When the last one departed, I suddenly felt unplugged from Harvard. I worked to focus my mind on what I needed to do back home.

That week, there was an article in the *Harvard Crimson* about an interview with the newly installed Dean of the business school. He had said something like, "By the time business school students are half-way through their first year at the Harvard B-school, they've acquired most of what they needed to learn."

I had been at Harvard for five months. I hoped that would be good enough for what I would be up against in Montreal.

I was trying to look on the bright side of my choice. Leaving Harvard would give me a chance to have a positive effect on my father's business and to serve my family. I had to help them to survive them. If I couldn't make an impact, then I would know I had tried, and I'd move on.

The day I decided to leave Harvard, I called my father and told him I was coming home. I didn't tell him about the three days I had spent in the hospital psych ward. I kept my voice as confident and assured as I could.

After a moment of dead silence, he offered, "Okay, son." He took a long breath. "You know I'll be happy to have you here at JHS as soon as you get yourself resettled. There are many things I could teach you. I'll make a list and show it to you when you come to the office."

I was glad that my brother had set a "leave college *sans* diploma" path ahead of me. I hoped there'd be things I could teach my father too, but this wasn't the time to raise that notion.

I called my mother and told her about my plans. I didn't say anything about my breakdown—it would have made her more anxious. I couldn't tell if she was happy to have me come home or worried about what my father would think.

I told her. "Dad knows already. It'll be okay, Mom."

"I hope so," she said.

* * *

Eight years after departing Harvard, when I visited Boston with my then steady girlfriend, I had a chance meet-up with a B-school classmate from my class year, a guy named Joe. My girlfriend knew the fellow, and she introduced us. I hadn't known the guy during our time at Harvard, but I found his words a revelation.

Joe told me, "You weren't the only one to leave the program under the pressure those HBS professors put on us back then. A record number of students left the first year we were there. Others didn't return for the second year."

He looked away and then back at me. "I made it through only because I realized what had been going on between the professors and the students." There was a hint of bitterness in his voice, and there was determination. "Though they had been putting it to us in class, I decided I wouldn't let them get the better of me."

He took a long breath. "Two years after that fiasco year, HBS changed the program, making the class requirements less onerous. Among other things, they cut back on the number of cases students had to prepare each week. And all incoming students were required to have a minimum of two years of work experience."

Joe looked right at me as he switched gears. "Do you remember two guys from our class, Sims and Hart?

I shook my head.

He continued. "They were close buddies at the B-school. They were in different class sections though they studied together at night." He smiled. "They had this little thing going where each of them would invoke the other's name at least once each school day during the year. Sims would attribute Hart's name to ideas they came up with regarding the cases they discussed, and Hart would do the same for Sims."

His grin widened. "That way, each of them would consciously sing the praises of the other. They believed that their mutual commendation would build the reputation of their chum, and vice versa."

He chuckled. "Well, it seemed to have worked. Both of those guys got better known because of their tactics. They certainly found a way to take advantage of the B-school's culture of working to stand out in a competitive crowd."

I stayed straight-faced. I hadn't figured out the lay of the B-school land as quickly and clearly as my former classmate and some of his cohorts. I also didn't consider myself a gamesman like Sims and Hart, though one could argue that I was wrapped up in my father's game plan for my career.

Joe's comments did help me feel more justified in having left Harvard midstream. Granted, it wasn't just what happened at the B-school that caused me to leave the program. My mother's illness, the growing distance between my parents, and my inability to reconcile my father's questionable ethics contrary to what I was learning at Harvard had all contributed to my decision to cut short my MBA degree.

For the previous years before and subsequent years after my talk with Joe, I was and continued to be plagued by recurring dreams about not keeping up at that business school. I envisioned missing classes, missing assignments, missing grades, or not understanding anything about a professor's lecture. Similar dreams came back over and over again. Those dreams only stopped after I had completed keyboarding this chapter of my life.

Thirty-seven years after I left Harvard, as I was completing this book, the professor who had ejected two students from a class session was still working at the business school. I contacted him, and he graciously took my call. I was amazed that he remembered me from 1979. He even remembered the HBS class section in which I had been a member.

He confirmed that my first year had been a tough year at HBS, especially for my section. Several of my classmates had experienced strained relationships with HBS faculty members. He offered, "There were also a few tough personalities in your section." He mentioned a couple of names, and I recognized one of them as a prominent political pundit, someone clearly on the opposite side of the political fence than I was.

The professor was philosophical about the classroom incident involving him. Unlike my recollections, he said that, before our class session ended, he had chased after and brought back the students he had expelled, and he then apologized to them.

He offered that a teaching case had been written and published about the "classroom learning experience" he had orchestrated with our section. He said that what he had tried that day didn't go off as he had planned, but that it had provided poignant learning for everyone.

* * * *

34

B-School Loose Ends

As I was packing to leave for Montreal, after having said goodbye to my Harvard classmates, Dad made an unusual request of me. It was regarding the money he had given me for my Harvard tuition and expenses.

I was thankful that my fingers, so far, had remained clean of Dad's unclean Cayman sandbox. On the other hand, there had been one Christmas vacation back in '76 (my grad year at MIT, soon after Dad had come back to Mom a second time) when he took our family to Cancun, Mexico.

Dad had booked a small, inexpensive hotel in town. We then spent our days at different seashore resorts, enjoying their pools and beaches. My father told us, "We'll buy dinner and drinks at the resort's restaurant, and we'll spend the afternoon there. If we act as if we belong, then no one will know otherwise."

Even on vacation, Dad was Dad. Mom went along, and no hotel security guard busted us.

One morning, in the middle of our Cancun week, Dad announced, "Harvy, let's go play golf while Mom and Steve go to the beach." Dad turned to Mom. "We'll join you after we finish playing."

My mother and brother seemed fine with that.

When my father and I got into a cab to head to the public golf club, he changed course. He told the driver, "Take us to the local Cancun airstrip just outside of town." He turned to me. "Our going to play golf is a pretense. I want us to fly to Cayman."

He looked at me and pointed outside. "The other day, I saw many Piper planes as we passed by the private airport. I have some business I need to do in Cayman. I don't want your mother or brother to know about it."

I was taken aback by my father's plan. I glanced out the taxi window and into the sky. It was mostly clear, but large puffy clouds filled the skies. Many of those clouds had dark undersides. They were moving quickly toward the horizon. "You want to fly over the Caribbean in a little plane?" I asked.

"Sure, son! Why not? Many people fly these pipers. I flew a plane like that after the war; don't you remember me telling you about that?"

I looked for a fissure in my father's flight plan. "Don't we need our passports to go to Cayman?"

He smiled. "I have them." He pulled both his and my documents out of his windbreaker pocket.

My stomach was starting to feel airsick, but I said what I usually did to my father's crazy ideas, "Fine, Dad. If you think it's okay." I didn't want my father to think I was frightened about bopping around the Caribbean sky in a little prop plane.

When we got to the airstrip, Dad talked to the owner and pilot of an air transport service. "What do you charge to take us to Cayman and then return here today?"

The dark-tanned, leathery-skinned Mexican raised an eyebrow and looked us up and down. "Cayman? You mean Grand Cayman Island?"

My father nodded. "Yes, George Town."

The man's face looked blank. "I never get this kind of request. Give me a minute to check my map." He looked at my father and me again. "When would you like to leave?"

"Right now," Dad said unequivocally. "Can you take us there, and for how much?"

The pilot rolled out a big map that completely covered the office counter. In the center of the chart was Cancun. According to the mileage scale, the east-west extremities went out over 300 nautical miles in either direction.

We looked at the map's eastern edge. Grand Cayman Island wasn't present on the chart.

Dad offered, "It's supposed to be right about here, less than 350 land miles due east from Cancun, just south and a little east of Havana Cuba." Havana showed on the map, and Dad pointed to where Cayman should be. "You should be able to fly there easily."

The pilot thought for a moment and then shook his head. "Our planes have an air range of over 400 nautical miles. Its ground range is dependent on wind speed and direction, and how much weight we have on the plane."

He pointed to his map. "This is the only chart I have. Grand Cayman must be just off the edge of it. I'd like to make the $500 U.S. it would cost you to rent my plane for the day. But unless I know exactly where Cayman is, I don't think I want to take the chance to go there. I don't want to run out of fuel." He didn't say, "and crash into the sea."

My father thought for a moment then turned to me. "Well, son; I guess we can't go there today. Maybe we can do it another time."

Dad changed course as quickly as when a Greek car rental agent had told him that it would be dangerous to take their rental car into Turkey. My dad had changed direction and instead drove our family to Sparta and then Belgrade.

I wiped perspiration from my brow. "That's okay, Dad. We don't need to go to Cayman today."

We bused it back to the beach hotel where we knew Mom and Steve would be waiting. Dad turned to me. "Just tell them that we decided not to play golf because the wait was too long. They don't need to know anything else."

I nodded. "Sure; whatever you say." I didn't tell him how relieved I was not to have to dodge the clouds, and perhaps the Canadian government, because of the business my father had planned in Grand Cayman.

When we returned to Montreal, I checked an atlas map. Dad wasn't quite right about George Town's location. It was 330 nautical miles east-southeast of Cancun, not due east as he had said. We might have crashed into the sea, or been forced down in Cuban airspace, putting a communist crimp in Dad's off-the-cuff Cayman excursion. Might we have been thrown into a communist jail cell the way Dad had been thrown in a cell after the Soviets had taken control of Czechoslovakia back in '48?

How did Dad even think we'd be to Cayman and back, and conduct his money business there, in the time it took to do a round of golf? Wouldn't Mom and Steve wonder and worry about our whereabouts if we were not back before mid-afternoon that day?

While I was on the phone with Dad from a cramped booth in the basement of my Harvard dorm, he told me, "Harvy, I want you to transfer the $100,000 you have in your account in Boston to an account at another branch of the Canadian Regal Bank. The account has no name, only a number." His voice stayed steady. "The bank branch is in George Town on Grand Cayman."

I was apprehensive, but I said, "Okay Dad, whatever you want." It was his money, not mine. I felt in no position to do otherwise. One day I might gain benefit from those assets if I kept quiet and did as he told me. More importantly, I was still working to stay in his favour, feeling that his goodwill with me wasn't guaranteed.

When I went to the bank, I felt uneasy about having my signature on the money transfer request. I now had a pen stroke associated with my father's offshore stash. I wondered if one day I would be approached by Revenue Canada for my money misdeed. Might I have to make up the jail time that my father had skirted?

My father-son dilemma wrenched my gut.

* * *

A week after I had returned to Montreal, I received a letter from the Boston branch of the Canadian Regal Bank. It contained a receipt for the Cayman money transaction I had made.

The slip showed not only the amount of the cash transfer but also the account number and Cayman branch where the bank had transferred the money. My armpits got wet as I stared at the receipt. Had Dad been careless about this transfer? Would this receipt be trouble for him and me?

Early the next morning, I went to my father at his factory office. "Dad, can I see you privately for a minute?" We went to his back office where I gave him the paper. "I received this receipt yesterday from the Canadian Regal Bank branch in Boston and thought you should see it."

His face tightened as he stared at the slip. "Son of a bitch," he said. He didn't look at me but immediately yelled out the door to his secretary. "Helen, get me Roger Delliard on the phone right away. He's usually in his office early in the morning."

Dad lit a cigarette. He paced the room, receipt in hand, waiting for Helen's page to pick up the phone when Roger would be on the line. I sat and waited in silence, wondering why my father was calling Roger. I didn't ask.

When Helen had Roger on the phone, Dad's voice was edgy as he spoke to his accountant. "Roger, Harvy today handed me a bank receipt from Boston showing a $100,000 money transfer I asked him to make for me to Cayman. I don't want Revenue Canada to know about my money over there. Am I in trouble?"

Dad repeated his advisor's words out loud: "It's just an internal bank document. ...It's one in a million of such slips of paper that get generated by the bank every day. ...It would never be picked up by the Canadian tax authorities."

Holding the phone to his ear, my father looked at me. "Harvy, did you get anything else?"

I shook my head and pointed. "No; that slip was all I got."

Dad relayed the information to Roger.

After a moment of more back and forth, he said, "Okay, thanks," into the phone and put down the receiver. He tore the receipt into many pieces and placed it in the trash under his desk. "The receipt is no problem, Harvy. Don't worry about it." His voice and demeanor were calm.

It hit me like a brick falling off JHS's factory building. Dad's new accountant was complicit in his money-hiding. How could Roger and his high-end, bigwig accounting firm allow my father to hide his money offshore?

I had hoped that my father would keep his fingers clean after staving off Revenue Canada corporate tax fraud charges in 1975. Had he become more brazen because Revenue Canada had given him a pass regarding his offshore money back then? Dad told me that he had promised the government agents that he would declare the income each year from the money he claimed to have come with him in 1949 from Czechoslovakia.

Perhaps professionals like Roger were in cahoots with rich business people like Dad to help them conceal their cash. Or maybe Dad twisted Roger's arm, as he had done with Mel Mozer, saying, "Either you are with me, or you can *foot-scoff*."

I wondered about the Canadian Regal Bank. Was one of Canada's biggest banks in on this offshore money game? They did have a branch in Cayman! Were they keeping their eyes closed, letting people like my father hide undeclared money and defraud the government of income taxes?

Something in my gut didn't feel right, but I only watched and listened to Dad's conversation with Roger. I didn't say anything to him after he hung up the phone.

What else could I do? Squeal on my father over at Revenue Canada? Tell my mother and my brother? Raise a ruckus with Dad? Roger was clearly in the know and supported my father. I decided to say nothing for now and bide my time.

A few days after that conversation, I found a quiet, end-of-day moment when no one but my father and I were in his front office. I kept my voice calm and collected as I spoke. "Dad, can I ask you something?"

He looked up from his desk. "Sure, son."

I took a deep breath. "Why do you need to do this Cayman stuff?"

Dad glared at me. His strong, confident voice responded with the well-engrained refrain I had heard before: "Because I don't trust the bloody Quebec government." He closed his fist and placed it on his desk. "The communists took everything I had in '48. I want to make sure that the Quebec separatists will never put me in that same position."

His tone was definitive and defiant. "If *le Parti Québécois* tries to separate Quebec from Canada, the rest of the country just might let them go. There are lots of English Canadians who hate the Quebec French and would like to kick their asses goodbye."

His closed fist remained firmly on his desk. "When their time comes, the separatists could nationalize every business in the province, as the Soviets did to me in Czechoslovakia." He ended in a loud crescendo. "Don't be so naïve, Harvy. We need to protect ourselves because the Canadian government might never fully protect us from what's happening here in Quebec."

I took a pace backward from my father's fury. After seeing my reaction, his voice quieted. "What the government knows is that I brought money out of Czechoslovakia with me when I had escaped from there in '49."

That was his carefully crafted story, invented by Mel Mozer and sold by Dad's hired-gun lawyer to the judge that presided over Montreal Phono's Revenue Canada court case four years earlier. That argument had convinced the federal government to divert their attention away from my fathers' offshore money. That argument was now Dad's reality.

My father's eyes softened. "*Lassen* to me, son. Please don't worry about this." He batted his open palm at me as if he were a parent quieting an anxious child. "Nobody here knows about it besides you, me, and Roger. Not even your brother knows what you know." And my mother wasn't privileged to know such things, but that went without Dad having to say it.

I looked down. "Okay, Dad." I was afraid to pry further. I wondered how Dad had re-hidden his offshore stash after revealing it to Revenue Canada four years ago. Maybe he moved his money to a different Cayman bank account and pretended it no longer existed, or he claimed he lost the cash in offshore business or land deals.

Was my father becoming increasingly shrewd or exceedingly flagrant? I hoped he wasn't becoming extremely reckless.

* * *

A decade after my father's death, I contacted and met with the over 80-year-old Roger. I wanted to know what he had known about my father's offshore money—if he'd give me details.

Over a deli sandwich, he and I spent time catching up on the years. He asked what my brother and I were now doing. I asked how he was keeping busy and engaged. He told me he sat on boards of business and non-profit organizations. Roger wore his age well; he seemed as sharp as the days he had worked for JHS.

I came to my line of inquiry. "Roger, you worked over a decade as an auditor and advisor for JHS. What did you know about my father's business and personal finances?"

He eyes looked away and then came back. "I'm sorry, Harvy; I don't remember much." He scratched his head. "I can't remember anything about how big his company was financially, or about how much money your father had personally or within his business."

He shook his head. "And those records are probably long gone now. I don't believe my former firm or the government would keep such records for this long."

I felt let down, but I pressed on. "Roger, I need to ask you something specific."

"Sure, Harvy." His back was straight and his hands flat on the table between us.

I looked him in the eyes. I spoke quietly so no one around us would hear. "How much did you know about my father's offshore money?"

Roger thought for a moment then spoke softly. "I did have an inkling about it, but I didn't know for sure." His voice came across straight and true.

I reminded Roger of the phone call he had had with my father in February of 1980 after my return to Montreal from Harvard. I offered, "I was there when you and he spoke about a $100,000 U.S. transfer I had made from the Canadian Regal Bank in Boston to my father's account in their Cayman branch."

Roger leaned lower in his seat as he pointed his finger at me. "Now that you mention it, it might have been that specific conversation that had given me the inkling about your father's money over there."

Roger brushed his hand along the table and toward me. "However, for your father, $100,000 U.S. was small potatoes. If that was all he had had offshore, then it was little to worry about."

I said nothing; I knew much differently.

* * * *

Part VII:

Homecoming

35

Family and Business Reentry

At the end of January of 1980, on my first night home from Harvard, Dad began telling me about the things he'd teach me about his business. I'd learn how he designed console models, calculated material and labour costs, controlled plant labour expenses, planned production, and more. He never questioned me about my decision to leave business school.

I hardly said a word to my brother about my abrupt grad school exit. I suspected he knew what it was like to come home feeling downtrodden by not finishing a university degree.

One evening during supper with Mom, Steve told me his college story. "When I entered Queen's six years ago," he started, "the Dean of the engineering school stood in front of our entering class and said, 'I want all of you freshmen to look to the person to your right and then to the person to your left.'

"We did." My brother smiled as he spoke. "The Dean then offered, 'One of the three of you won't be graduating from here within the next four years.'"

Perhaps my brother was implying how he hadn't known (or maybe he did realize) the Dean had been referring to him. Steve and I now shared that same sense of failure, but it remained unspoken among us Simkovitses.

Steve continued. "If you come with me into the factory tomorrow morning, Harvy, I can use your help to rewrite the operating manuals for some of JHS's console models." His voice was calm and flat, like a pastor talking to a church member. "I'll show you what to do so you don't have to start from scratch. I could use a person who can write."

Because I had written both my bachelor's and master's theses, and I had taken a couple of writing courses during my time at MIT and P&G, a writing project could be good to get me going. It would ease me into my father's business, and it would give my brother and me a chance to do something together. "Okay, Steve," I peeped.

Giving me my first assignment at JHS was the nicest thing my brother ever did for me. Dad had talked about teaching me things, but Steve dug in and got me started.

* * *

Two-and-a-half years had passed since I last worked at JHS. Seven chunky wood desks still stood in JHS's large, rectangular front office. To the left of the entryway, Helen still sat at her L-shaped secretarial desk. Near to her, Dad's front-office desk continued to sit in the middle of the room. From that perch, my father could see everything going on in the office.

Immediately behind Dad, Steve still sat at his desk that faced the factory wall. The company bookkeeper, Jane, still had her desk at the other end of the room, to the right of the entryway. That location offered her a slightly quieter place to work, though she was still in my father's view.

When I came into the office, my brother sat me at an empty desk closer to Jane. It was the desk where our former shipping and distribution supervisor, Danny, had been. Because JHS's business was down from its 1970s peak, Dad had let Danny go and distributed his work between Helen and Steve. Maybe that was why Steve wanted to delegate a piece of his job to me.

I was glad to be sitting a distance away from most of the office staff. As a casualty of Harvard, I could hardly look anyone in the eyes, even my brother. I didn't want anyone to look at me as if I were a fallen Simkovits son.

My brother got down to business the moment I sat down. He looked over my shoulder as he showed me an outdated console stereo manual of twenty to thirty pages in length. He was matter-of-fact. "Start with this manual we have from JHS's last year's model."

After more explaining, Steve motioned for me to follow him. "Come with me into the showroom," he said. He led me to the other end of the company's offices, past Dad's private office, into a larger room where JHS's consoles were on display.

He took me through the functions of the console unit for which I was rewriting the manual. He offered, "Make careful note of the additional and altered functions of the radio, cassette, and record player that you see on this new model. Use a pencil for your edits in the old manual so we can adjust things later if we need to."

When we finished in the showroom, he walked me back to my desk. "I'll give your edits to the printer, and he'll come back within a few days with a printed proof. We'll look at that copy once more before approving it for printing."

Steve smiled. "Once you finish with this model, and if you like what you are doing, I can give you a couple more manuals to work on." He pointed to himself. "Your work would save me a lot of time. I'm probably the only other one in the company who can write English well enough to do this work."

Because JHS was a melting pot of immigrants, my brother was being practical. He added, "Recheck your work a couple of times. Any errors or omissions would force us to reprint everything, and that's costly. We print a thousand of these manuals at one time, so don't rush your work."

I nodded. Though editing line by line in an existing booklet seemed cumbersome, I could do it. I didn't mention it, but I was grateful for Steve's attention and guidance. He had reached out to me. I wanted to contribute in a useful way both to him and to JHS.

Because there were no partitions in the front office, I could overhear and see everything that was happening there.

Dad practically lived the whole workday at his desk. From there, he dictated orders, invoices, and correspondence to Helen. He had face-to-face meetings with his foremen. He cradled his black rotary phone against his ear to talk to JHS's customers and suppliers and his lawyer and accountant.

My father opened every package and piece of mail. He had once told me, "I open everything that comes in and then distribute it where it needs to go. That way I get to know about and stay in control of what's going on."

The short, stout Helen continually refilled Dad's Styrofoam coffee cup. A cigarette always burned somewhere around him. When his ashtray became full, he turned to Helen, smiled, and calmly asked, "Please get me a clean *arsh-tray.*" Helen smiled and did as he had asked.

My brother's desk was within spitting distance of our father's. On the floor next to Steve was a big metal box on four wheels. It was a Kardex filing system, the box filled with inventory sheets. Steve used those Kardex cards to keep track of the raw material the company purchased and warehoused.

Steve updated the Kardex sheets daily, each card being larger than legal-sized paper. He wrote meticulously on them, accounting for the merchandise ordered from suppliers, received by the factory and put into inventory, or released for production. Dad called the Kardex system "the company's production bible." Steve turned to those cards so often that the box seemed to be an extension of his arm.

Once or twice a year, Steve did actual physical counts of factory merchandise to make sure the cards reflected what was actually in the JHS warehouse. (During my summer stints at Montreal Phono, I too had helped in that counting.) That count could take days to complete, for JHS's merchandise—stacked to the ceiling beams—occupied nearly a quarter of the factory's 50,000 square feet.

When Steve wasn't attached to his Kardex, he was connected to his phone, ordering and expediting merchandise from suppliers across the country. (Dad still handled the big merchandise orders from England, Korea, and Taiwan.) My brother regularly stepped into the plant to check on supplies and to make sure the foremen had what they required to meet the production schedule set by Dad.

I soon realized that walking into the factory offered my brother a bit of respite from the ringing telephones, cigarette smoke, coffee smell, and phone chatter that filled the front office. Unlike Dad and Helen, whose teeth were permanently yellowed from their daily coffee and smoking routines, Steve shunned those vices. He preferred his diversion coming from the Coke & Sprite vending machine standing next to the other side of the door that led into the factory.

A small blackboard hung on the wall next to my brother's desk. There, Steve maintained a material shortage list—merchandise due to arrive for upcoming production runs. That visual allowed Steve (and, of course, Dad) to kept track of last-minute merchandise deliveries needed for production.

On Wednesday, Dad pointed to the board and asked, "Steve, what's happening with the special grill fabric we ordered for our production run next week for Sears? Has it arrived?"

Steve answered, "Not yet, but it will be here any day now."

"Get on the phone right away and chase those guys," Dad retorted. "We can't afford to wait any longer."

Steve responded curtly but not crossly. "It's under control, Dad. That item was originally due in today, but the supplier promised me yesterday to have it to us by the end of the week."

"We'll see," Dad said. He took a puff of his cigarette then went back to his paperwork.

Steve was usually right about those deliveries, but sometimes he wasn't. That Friday at noon, Dad came back to my brother. "Didn't I tell you to chase after that supplier? Get on the phone right now. I don't want to have to change our production schedule at the last minute."

He pointed to Steve, then to himself, and raised his voice. "If you can't get a straight answer from those guys, then give me the phone, and I'll talk to them." Dad gestured with his hand. "You have to be on top of every fucking thing, Steve, or else you'll get it into your behind."

From the time Steve departed college seven years earlier to work at JHS, such skirmishes became commonplace between him and our dad. For good and bad, Steve trusted his suppliers. He spoke politely and calmly to them. He threw in a forced laugh here and there to keep the mood light. Steve preferred his sugar to Dad's vinegar.

It was as if Steve wanted to prove that his kinder words and gentler approach worked better than Dad's harsh barbs. After he had called the supplier, Steve turned to our father, "Dad, they had transport problems, but they promise to have the fabric here by the end of today or first thing Monday morning."

Dad's face was tight as he responded, "The suppliers always feed you their bullshit, Steve. You are such a gullible guy that you put salt on their explanations and eat it up."

The fabric didn't arrive by the end of that day. The supplier called to say it would arrive at eight o'clock on Monday morning, thirty minutes before JHS's production was going to begin. Dad raised his voice once more. "Those guys are screwing us. They better be at our door first thing on Monday, or I'm going to be on their ass."

All weekend, I hoped that my brother would be proven right. When he and I arrived for work at 8:00 a.m. on Monday, an hour after Dad had gotten there, the fabric supplier's truck was nowhere in sight.

As we walked into the office, Dad was on the phone with the supplier. He was doing more screaming than talking. "What! You want me to change my whole fucking production around because of you? You promised us the material by last week, and then by eight o'clock this morning. When I make a commitment, I keep it. I won't take this bullshit from you or anybody."

His face was red. "If you can't get that merchandise here within the hour, then I'll deduct my rescheduling costs from your invoice, and I'll find another supplier to work with next time."

The fabric didn't arrive until noon. In the factory, stereo consoles had to be stacked on pallets waiting for the grill material to be cut and stapled onto the front of the cabinet. All morning, Dad sucked on cigarettes and bellowed smoke because of the delay.

Weeks later, Dad acted on his threat to cut the payment to the supplier for the extra work the factory had to do. He subsequently received a lawyer's letter from the vendor for non-payment. He called the sales manager of the fabric company. "What! You guys are now sending me love letters?!" His voice rose, "Why should I pay you? You make promises, but you don't deliver."

After a tense back and forth, Dad worked to settle. He gained not only a discount on the invoice but also a price break on a future purchase. It looked to me as if my father enjoyed these supplier skirmishes, and he didn't seem to care how it made my brother look.

After Dad had ended his conversation with the supplier, he turned to Steve, "I've been doing purchasing since before you were born!"

Out of the corner of his eye, our father glanced at me across the room, but he still pointed his finger at my brother and raised his voice. "In business, every penny and every minute count!"

Steve stood and then looked around the room. "I'm getting a drink from the Coke machine. Anybody want anything?" He was out the factory door before anyone could respond.

I kept my eyes glued to my manual writing job. I got Dad's message that trust never successfully ran a business, and that one had to fight for profit every single work day. His ways probably were successful on JHS's financial statements, but his brash bravado sent shudders through my thin skin and into my spine.

Dad wanted Steve and me to grasp his business survival lessons. But I wasn't quite sure that they were the kind of lessons I wanted to learn.

One afternoon later that same week, Steve left early to ride his horse. Dad spoke to me after everyone else had left the office. "The suppliers love your brother," he bellowed. He raised a fist. "He's working for them more than for our company. If he keeps on believing their baloney, we'll go bust fast."

Dad pointed to the factory door. "We can't always control our labour costs, but we need to control our cost of merchandise and its delivery. That's how I've survived in business these last thirty years."

As the new son on the JHS block, I nodded at my father as his words rang loudly in my ears.

Another part of me sympathized with my brother for taking the brunt of Dad's criticisms. From the time he had left college seven years earlier, Steve had to sit within barking and biting distance of Dad. I now understood why he took months off every year or two to go on an outdoor trekking trip to western Canada or the U.S. He needed breathing space from Dad's smoke and fire.

My brother and I never talked about our father's berating ways. Maybe we thought that ignoring Dad's ire would make it feel as if it had never flared.

I wondered why my brother didn't walk out of the company and find another job. Was he feeling dependent on our father for a living, or did he feel that Dad owed him a job? Maybe Steve had convinced himself that he was on a mission to change my father's MO. *Might I be here for a similar reason?*

Though I felt bruised by my abbreviated Harvard stint, I hoped that my cut short B-school training could help JHS become a better business and help my father cut back on his bellowing.

For the moment, I kept my head down and continued to wait, watch, and write. I wondered what learning I would take away over the ensuing months and years from my defiant brother and belligerent father.

* * *

During my first weeks back at JHS, many of Dad's business colleagues came to visit. I heard my father tell them, "Our big retail customers are squeezing us dry. Every year they want more blood from us, expecting discounts and extra service as if it costs us nothing."

He huffed. "JHS is now making more money on its money in the bank than from our production operations. Thank goodness we don't have any debt. But we need to find other lines of business; otherwise, we'll become sunk in a few years."

A few days later, during a quiet moment after work, I approached my father. "Dad, I heard you speak to your friends about the company. Where do you think JHS's future is heading?"

He looked at me with a long face. "Son, since 1975, Canada's major console stereo manufacturers, like RCA, Admiral, and Philco, have one-by-one gotten out of the console stereo business." His voice was somber. "JHS is now selling directly to the major department stores like Sears and Woolco, and we now use independent sales reps as go-betweens to those companies."

He looked at me, his eyes penetrating as if he wanted me to get the importance of what he was saying. "We're lucky that JHS is a low-cost producer and can stay in business by selling to the department stores." He pointed his finger my way. "But the market is moving in the direction of Japanese and Korean component systems. One day soon, our product will become passé."

He took a drag from his cigarette. "As long as we can keep our costs down, and buy components for a good price from Korea and Taiwan, we can still make money for a while."

Being young and new to the business world, I never considered my dad forced out of the console business. Though he had worked hard to build his company, he was right; consoles were going the way of the buggy whip. In a maturing market, a cash cow held only so much milk before it ran dry. No wonder my father was fighting for every penny of profit.

Dad looked at me, his eyes a little glum. "I had a chance some years ago to get into the stereo component business. People from Hitachi asked me if I'd be willing to be the distributor of their line in Canada." He glanced down. "I stupidly said no because I wanted to stay loyal to RCA and our other major customers. They had been loyal to me for many years, so I didn't want to compete against them."

He looked and pointed directly at me. "I let the Hitachi deal go and gave it over to a business friend of mine. Now JHS is suffering for it, and my friend's company is growing like gangbusters."

The previous year, Dad had to retire his former production scheduler and coordinator. Herb had come to JHS after RCA curtailed its Canadian console business. For several years, he had been my father's right-hand man, and he had sat at the desk opposite Dad.

I was sorry that the former RCA'er was gone. He was level-headed and rarely raised his voice, a good counterbalance to the boss's volatility. I wondered if I might be able to become like Herb, my father's right-hand son.

Even with Dad's explanation, I didn't fully grasp the company's long-term predicament. I kept my eyes on manual writing and other things my brother asked me to do. I figured my father would find ways to obtain more business.

I vowed to help JHS become more efficient, to save the company money, and to do it with less yelling and screaming. I wanted Dad to get a good return on the five-and-a-half years of MIT and Harvard education for which he had paid.

* * *

There was another important member of my father's front office staff, the company's designer, François. He was another former RCA'er and an immigrant from France. He designed and engineered JHS's console's cabinets to make most efficient use of purchased materials and factory labour.

François created blueprints for the production foremen. (My father then employed his electronics skills to configure component spacing and wiring.) François then put together parts lists for Steve, from which my brother could order the hardwood, pressed wood, plastic grills, grill fabric, etc., that were needed to produce the more than dozen stereo models JHS built each year.

I liked François because, like Herb, he rarely lost his cool. He was a soft-spoken man who used many a "please" and "thank you" while speaking. He was one of the few JHS staff members to whom Dad rarely raised his voice.

If François needed anything from the boss, he approached my father's desk slowly, his hands clasped together below his heart. He never interrupted the boss while he was busy on the phone or concentrating on paperwork. He stood patiently a few feet from my father's desk until Dad raised his head or got off the phone and asked, "Yes, François?" It was rare for the mild-mannered Frenchman to walk away empty-handed.

I found out from Steve that François had been diagnosed with lung cancer a year earlier. His doctors had given him five years to live. My father subsequently told François he could work at JHS for as long as he wanted to, and as much as he could.

François was grateful. He never complained about Dad's impulsive anger or coarse language, except when Dad directed it at him unjustifiably. If necessary, he could go toe to toe with Dad, saying, "Johnny, don't speak to me like that! If you have a problem, you talk to me like a fellow human being, and we'll fix it." My father usually calmed down, saying, "Okay, François," but he rarely apologized for his bluster.

I admired François for his gentle fortitude and the grace he showed regarding his death-sentence illness. He never complained about his growing cough and hoarse voice as his cancer progressed.

The only time I ever heard François show frailty was when he once told my father, "My wife is still in denial about my pending death. She's not willing to look at what we need to do to prepare her for when I will be gone."

Dad asked, "Gosh, François; is there anything I can do to help?"

"No, Johnny, but I thank you," François responded. "It's my problem to work out with my wife and family."

* * *

It wasn't always harsh hammers and sharp nails from Dad; he could be crudely charming. He liked to make lewd remarks with the salesmen who came to sell their wares.

My father was known for quips like, "That molded part [or peg, bolt, metal bracket, screw, or sheet of press wood] you sold us is *krucket* like my dick." He could easily get riled at those who tried to get one over on him, shouting, "If you are going to screw me good, at least do it from the front where I can see you."

Johnny Simkovits could endear people to him via his grainy lightheartedness. When another vendor demonstrated a new touch-up spray for wood parts, vigorously shaking the can before spraying, Dad smiled. "Shake it, Joe, but don't break it!"

Another time, when a rep lingered around the office when Dad needed to leave for an after-hours gathering, my father wisecracked, "Roberto, it's five thirty, time to close the whorehouse."

Dad's rough humor, accompanied by his boyish grin, wink, or hearty laugh, made me smile. When he winked at me as he said such things, I felt as if I were one of the guys.

Then there was Mr. Freid, a long-bearded, Hassidic Jewish salesman from a corrugated box company. Dad never missed an opportunity to joke around with the man. I didn't know the fellow's first name, for everyone called him Mr. Freid. He came almost weekly to Dad's office, selling boxes and packaging materials for every JHS console model.

Mr. Freid was a short, thin man. He had a wife and a brood of nine. He wore a black jacket, black pants, black shoes, black suspenders, and a black tie over a white shirt. A long white talisman hung from his waist to indicate his faith—if one couldn't tell from the rest of his attire.

One day, before getting down to business, my father jested with Freid. "I can't believe you now have nine kids. Don't you have anything better to do at night than to screw around with your wife?"

Dad seemed to enjoy the challenge of seeing how far he could go with the guy. We watched Mr. Freid's face turn beet red as Dad was "giving him the gears," as he liked to say.

Mr. Freid had known my father for years. He never got upset or irritated. To my father's jibe, he looked and pointed upward, then said, "Every year or two, both God and my wife bless me again with no chance of retirement."

Dad responded with a big smile and guffaw. From across the room, I smiled at their kibitzing. In addition to giving Mr. Freid JHS's corrugated box business, Dad offered Chanukah presents each year to the man's nine blessings.

For all his boisterousness in business, Dad made amends at Christmas. He shut down the production operation at noon. He invited his factory foremen, long-time employees, and important supplier reps to an afternoon office party to celebrate the year-end.

Helen ordered and arranged a big spread of deli food on the conference table in the showroom. Dad provided the fixings for everyone's favourite drinks: rum and Cokes, screwdrivers, Scotch and soda, Seven & Seven (Seagram's Crown Whiskey and 7-Up), or anything straight-up. For the coffee drinkers and teetotalers, Dad spiked the hot drinks with a little Drambuie or Grand Marnier for the men, and Tia Maria or Kahlua for the ladies.

Dad was in there with everyone, toasting the year that passed and the year to come. When I was home from college, I participated too, having one or two mixed drinks. I never saw my brother have more than a soft drink.

Dad liked to play Santa Claus, but he had a hefty factory man dress as Saint Nick. With big grins, the saint and Dad passed out wrapped cartons of cigarettes, decorative ashtrays, or bottles of liquor to all the guys. Women who smoked got cigarettes too, and they received packages of nylon stockings or colourful imported scarves that the boss had bought on one of his overseas trips.

Everyone sported a smile and said thank you to Johnny. There were happy faces in the room, a far contrast to the day-to-day drudgery of JHS factory life.

* * *

315

One Monday morning, a few months after my JHS re-entry, Dad's bookkeeper, Jean, didn't show for work. Late that afternoon, after everyone else had left for the day, Dad told Steve and me what had happened. He offered, "Our accountant, Roger Delliard, recently started his annual audit. He found out Jean was taking money from the company."

He pointed to his head. "It looked like Jean went coo-coo after her and her husband separated last year. She wrote extra payroll cheques to herself."

He took a puff from his cigarette and pointed it at us. "When Roger confronted her about it last Friday, she realized she was caught. I wanted to give her shit when she got in this morning, but I guess she decided not to show."

His eyes narrowed as he pointed a finger. His voice stayed aggravated. "I didn't even get the satisfaction of kicking her ass out of here. It goes to show you that you have to watch people all the time, or they will take advantage of you."

Steve and I nodded but said nothing. I liked Jean, and she had a nice figure. (At the time, I was still my chauvinist father's son.) I agreed that what she had done was blatantly wrong, but I wondered if my father's overbearing demeanor had put her over an edge.

Within a week, and with Roger's help, JHS hired a new bookkeeper, Robert. The Quebec francophone was a short, mustached, easygoing fellow.

Like François and my brother, Robert rarely raised his voice, even when Dad yelled at him about incorrect entries into the company ledger, or about paying a wrong invoice amount. It wasn't long before Robert had to forcefully defend himself, saying, "Johnny, you have it wrong; I did 'this' and not 'that.'" The man never yelled as Dad did.

I didn't know whether it was Dad or Robert who was right in those altercations. What I did know was that Robert, as with Helen, became a JHS fixture, remaining with the company for decades.

Twenty years later, I'd ask Robert, "Why did you stay at JHS? How could you stand my father's berating ways for so long?"

He grinned, "In my family, I'm the youngest of twelve children." He fanned his hand. "Your father's ways were nothing compared to my bigger brothers. They always told me what to do and harassed me if I didn't. I had to learn to defend myself with them, and it was no different with your dad."

Helen too had to find her way with my father. On one occasion, he raised his voice, "Helen, why did you invoice such a low amount on this model we sold to Sears?" He was looking at a customer's statement that had come in with a cheque. "That's much less than what it should have been."

Helen walked over to my father's desk and looked at the invoice. "It was you who told me to put in the lower price. It was just before I mailed that invoice to Sears."

"NO, I DID NOT!" Dad shouted. He banged his fist on the table. "Because of your mistake, we're losing our shirts on that model run."

Lips pursed, Helen went to the company files, pulled out a carbon copy of the invoice, put it in front of my father, pointed to the writing on it, and said tersely, "Look here, Johnny. You wrote that lower price right on the invoice yourself, and I had you initial it."

Dad put on his reading glasses, looked down at the paper and then up at Helen. His voice was annoyed. "*Hesus Maria!* You bloody *vimen!* You think you know everything." He pushed the invoice back into her hand and turned back to the rest of the mail.

Helen's face stayed blank, but her lips were pressed tightly together. She put the document back into the file, walked to her desk, and sat down hard on her chair. I imagined her smirking inside a little for her small victory, though she got no apology from the boss.

Everyone had to find his or her way to deal with Johnny.

* * *

The winter weeks passed into spring. Over an office lunch one day, my brother told me about JHS's field service network. "Manufacturers like RCA had product repair centres across the country. JHS now maintains an independent service network for our retail customers, Sears and Woolco."

He pointed at himself and smiled proudly. "I single-handedly built our Canada-wide network of independent electronic repair centres."

"That's impressive, Steve. How did you arrange that?"

Having taken a bite of his sandwich, Steve raised a finger to have me wait a moment for his response. He then offered, "I called every Sears and Woolco store across Canada and got them to mail me the Yellow Pages phone book from their part of the country."

Using his index finger, he pretended to dial a rotary phone. "One by one, I called and signed up electronic repair shops until we had enough of them covering the territory surrounding every customer store in the country." He pointed to himself again. "I made all the contracts myself."

"That must have taken a while." I was absorbed.

He nodded. "Yes, many months; it was a big project. Now, occasionally we have to find a new service centre when one goes out of business or doesn't perform." He pointed upward. "I keep those old phone books stored in the stockroom upstairs."

My cut-short business training kicked in. "What are our customer service policies, and how do you keep track of customer warranties?"

Steve opened a drawer in his desk. It was full of white cards arranged by JHS model number. He pulled out one card at random. "Our policies are written on this warranty card that we put into each stereo unit."

He showed me the card then carefully placed it back in his drawer. "It's simple. If the customer mails us back their warranty card, we'll give them one year free parts and labour." He smiled. "No card, no warranty!" He took a breath. "The only exception is if the customer or repair shop mails us a copy of a dated register receipt from the store where the customer purchased the unit."

I kept up my questioning. "How do we get the spare parts to supply those service centres?"

My brother seemed to force a smile as he glanced a bit past me. I don't know why, but his grin appeared bigger than the situation called for, a kind of smile that could make one's face tire or stiffen if held too long. He continued. "With every electronic component purchase from our overseas suppliers, we pay a few percentage points more to get a set of standard spare parts." He pointed to the far corner of the office. "We use our telex machine there to order anything more we need."

I glanced over to see the waist-high metal machine that looked like a typewriter keyboard on a pedestal. I turned back to Steve. "Does JHS make any money on spare parts?"

He raised his finger again, indicating he wanted me to wait until he finished chewing on a bite of his sandwich. He spoke calmly and didn't rush his words. "Yes and no," he said. "If a unit is under warranty, we send the part out for free, plus pay for the labour to fix the unit. If it's out of warranty, then we charge the repair centres three to five times what the part costs us, plus shipping."

He raised a finger like a grade-school teacher might do with a student. "The lower the value of the part, the greater the multiple we use so that we can recoup our costs to pick, pack, and ship those parts across the country." He shrugged his shoulders. "It's a break-even proposition, at best."

He pointed at me and smiled again. "Maybe you can send telexes for me, Harvy."

Later that week, Steve showed me how to type and transmit overseas telexes. Though facsimile machines were now on the retail market, it would be a couple more years before Dad caught up with that technology—once the machine's price dropped below $1000.

Steve brought me to the telex device. "There is a dedicated phone number assigned to this machine," he started. "To take advantage of lower overseas phone rates we transmit telexes before seven a.m. or after five p.m."

He demonstrated how a message had to be typed into the noisy contraption before it could be transmitted. "When you push the teletype keys, the machine automatically punches holes in this tape ribbon that encrypts the message into code."

My brother took his time. He seemed pleased to show his MIT brother a technical thing or two. I was happy to learn.

Steve continued. "Once I type the message onto the tape ribbon, I use the telex's phone line to dial our Korean supplier's machine overseas. When the connection happens, I start the ribbon through the same hole-punching machine that produced it so that it could transmit the code over the line."

He pushed the start button. We watched the telex ribbon make its way through the device.

It was fascinating to see the coded ribbon transmit in less than one minute what took Steve fifteen minutes to type into the machine to produce the ribbon. At the same time, like a clacking automatic typewriter, the telex crunched out the ribbon's message onto the telex paper so one could see what the machine had transmitted. "That's neat," I said.

In addition to sending telexes, my brother asked me to file them. He said, "We need to maintain evidence of our communications in case any miscommunication occurs—like suppliers shipping us the wrong products or spare parts, which can happen."

He brought me to the filing cabinet where JHS stored telexes with the supplier purchase orders. He offered, "Electronic components and parts can take months to get to Montreal from Asia—via boat to Vancouver and then train to Montreal. Communication and ordering mistakes can be costly, so we have to keep good records."

I nodded my understanding and smiled to show him my appreciation for his teaching. I eagerly watched his instruction and followed his direction. I hoped he felt my gratitude.

Over another office lunch, Steve told me, "Telexes also help us to track merchandise deliveries, especially when an overseas supplier is late with a shipment. If Dad is pressed to get a console model out quickly, he'd have some of the merchandise air-shipped directly to Montreal."

Steve grinned as he raised his teaching finger. "Without good records of our supplier communications, we wouldn't be able to prove who was responsible—the supplier or us—for the expensive air freight charges."

Barring his scraps with Dad, it seemed that Steve knew much about the day-to-day workings of the company. I wondered how far he and I could go together in our father's business.

After I had learned to order and expedite spare parts, Steve asked me to work in the stockroom to organize the parts when they arrived. That room, situated above the JHS offices, was a barely head-high space that was fenced by chicken wire. It overlooked the electronics assembly area where I had worked many summer stints from the time Dad moved his company into the St. Laurent building in 1975.

Standing in the stockroom, I looked down on the production line. I considered how much water had gone under my career bridge—both at Procter & Gamble and the Harvard Business School—since I had worked at JHS during my high school and college summers.

Though I wondered where I might have gotten if I had remained at Harvard, I worked to put those contemplations aside. I had a job in front of me at JHS and needed to stay focused. I wanted to learn as much as I could and discover where I could make a useful impact on the business. I couldn't bear another failure.

Steve asked me to arrange postal shipments when JHS's field service centres ordered parts for stereo repair. In one corner of the stockroom was a stack of odd-size boxes, many filled with packaging peanuts. "Harvy, any time we receive a small package in the mail, I keep the box and packing materials so we can reuse it for our spare parts shipments." He smiled. "The fewer dollars we spend on that stuff, the more dollars go into the company's pocket."

Steve had learned my father's money-saving ways. He even took scrap company stationery, cut it in half on the woodshop's band saws, and stapled one end together with an industrial stapler. He offered that scrap paper to everyone in the office to use for notes. Dad kept one of Steve's makeshift pads right on his desk and used it every day. Dad's mantra was, "In business, we save every penny we can."

Though the company's stockroom was a little dusty and cramped, my new role got me out of the stuffy front office where Dad and Helen sucked on cigarettes and put down strong coffee all day. Unlike my brother, I did drink coffee. But the constant cigarette smoke made me cough.

My father didn't talk to me much during my first month back at his company. Perhaps he thought Steve was doing a decent job of getting me up and running. Then again, maybe Dad was trying to get used to his second son being a permanent JHS employee rather than becoming a promising Harvard businessman. In any case, I was glad I was working, getting a salary, and not having to think about school.

Near the end of my first month at work, Helen handed me my first JHS paycheque. As my father did with Steve, he had set my salary to a nominal amount, about $1250 per month (about two-thirds of my ending salary at P&G) before taxes and withholdings.

Dad put the check into my hand and told me quietly, "Use this as pocket money. It's about the same amount as your brother gets monthly. You and he will get more at end-of-year bonus time, depending on how well the company performs."

He winked. "And the bookkeeper, rather than Helen, will make out those checks. Because Helen does the general payroll, I don't want her to know about your bonuses."

Living at home, I had very few expenses, so I was okay with the amount. I was in no position to negotiate. And, if Dad wanted me to stay quiet about end-of-year bonuses, as the new son of the boss on the JHS block, it was certainly to my advantage to do so.

After I received my first paycheque, I used a portion of the proceeds to invest in a tabletop office air purifier. I placed it on a small, moveable stand against one wall near Dad and Helen. When I maneuvered it into place, my father raised his head from his paperwork. He asked facetiously, "Harvy, you don't like my smoking?"

I smiled. "Not at all, Dad!" I winked at Helen. "It's only Helen's smoking I mind."

Helen returned my smile. My father showed a small grin and returned to his paperwork.

The air purifier made a difference in filtering the thick office air. Because no one dismissed it, removed it, or scolded me about it, I knew I had fully arrived at JHS.

* * * *

36

Threading Together a Tattered Family

My mother had been sick with food poisoning when I had been home for the New Year holiday. Though her body had recovered, her mental health didn't get appreciably better during the month after I had arrived home from Harvard.

She continued to talk fast and in anxious whispers. When the phone rang, she jumped up with a start and then put her hand to her chin, her eyes searching as she questioned whether she should answer it.

When she saw Dad's car arrive home, or heard the automatic garage door open, she left supper simmering on the stove and hurried into the master bedroom. She later told me, "I'm scared to be around your daddy."

When I asked why she was scared, she couldn't explain. She turned around and went back to her sewing, cooking, cleaning, or ironing.

I didn't know what to make of her behaviour, but it wasn't normal for her. I became worried to see her this way. Could this be a lingering effect from her food poisoning over Christmas? I spoke slowly and calmly when I talked to her, hoping it might curtail her acting like a scared animal. It didn't. I was hoping my presence would help her get better on her own, but it didn't.

When I asked Mom to see her doctor, she batted her hand vigorously and said, "He does nothing for me except to listen to my crying."

Mom did make her usual Thursday food shopping trip to the nearby mall. Otherwise, she stayed at home and watched soap operas on television, as if those dramas might heal her. My brother and father seemed oblivious to her plight, and that worried me too.

Mom spent hours at her sewing machine mending clothes. She put many more hours into writing letters to her family overseas. She rarely called her friends. If they called her, she said she was too busy to talk and ended her conversations quickly.

I sensed I was the only one who saw my mother's distress.

Most nights, Dad came home late from a business gathering. He smelled of cigarettes, alcohol, and perfume. He found myriad business reasons to be away on the weekends. When he was home, he lay and slept on the living room couch in front of a blaring TV. Mom no longer sat in the big chair next to him. She ran off to the den or their bedroom.

Steve went off most evenings and Saturdays to care for his horse. On Sundays, he galloped to church services and then to church meetings. It looked like my brother was following in Dad's footsteps, choosing not to be around much, though his addictions were perhaps more subdued.

By the time March rolled in, I felt I had to do something. Seeing my mother continually in an agitated state caused me sleepless nights.

One late afternoon after work, I cornered my father and brother in the office. "We have to do something about Mom," I said. "She's not been herself since she had food poisoning at Christmas. And she doesn't want to go see her doctor." I felt I had to open their eyes to what was right in front of us.

Silence filled the room for a few seconds. Dad looked at Steve and then back at me, his face expressionless. "What if, one evening this week, you boys take your mother over to the emergency room of our local hospital? Go see what they could do to help her." He took a long breath and pointed. "It would be better if the two of you take her there. She'd listen to you."

For a moment, I was stunned. Dad just needed someone to point out what was happening to offer a possible solution. He was right that Mom would listen to her two sons rather than the husband she shunned.

I looked at Steve; he nodded and agreed right away. I wondered why it took this long to figure out a seemingly simple solution. I hoped Mom would let us take her to the hospital.

Over supper at home, Steve and I talked to her. "Mom, we're worried about you. You're not yourself. We want to take you to the hospital and see what they can do to help you."

She looked at one of us and then the other. "You don't think I'm crazy?"

"No, Mom," Steve said. "You're just not yourself."

"At the hospital, they can figure it out and make you better," I added. I didn't share how such a move had helped me at Harvard.

Mom didn't resist. She changed out of her house clothes, put on makeup, and we drove together to the local hospital. After waiting a couple of hours—both my brother and I quietly cursing the long waits inherent to Quebec's health care system—the psychiatrist-on-duty ushered Mom into an examining room to interview her.

After twenty minutes had passed, the female psychiatrist came to talk to my brother and me. She was a husky woman, perhaps fifty-something, and had unkempt hair and no makeup. She looked overworked. She introduced herself and said, "I would like to admit your mother for testing and observation. You should expect her to be here at least a week, maybe two."

"Does our mother agree to your plan?" I asked. I worried whether she might put up a fight or run out of the place—as I had considered doing six weeks earlier in Cambridge.

The woman nodded. "She fully accepts my request for her to stay here a while."

I remained with Mom during her admission. Steve went home to get her the things she'd need for her stay. While I waited with her until a private room was available, Mom turned to me. "Are you sure I'll be okay here?"

Though I didn't know for certain, I placed my hand gently on her arm and said, "This is the best place for you to be right now. They will do what they can to help you feel better."

Every subsequent day, Steve or I alternated to be with Mom. We took separate evening and weekend shifts so she wouldn't be alone all day. During my visits, Mom didn't say much for the first week or more. She sat in bed and leaned against the elevated back.

Her hands lay gently on the bed covers that blanketed her from the waist down. She nodded my way, but she remained quiet. After kissing her on the cheek, I sat by her side. When I placed my hand on her palm, she accepted my touch but didn't squeeze my hand. We didn't talk much, just watched (she stared at) whatever program was on television.

Mom's attending psychiatrist wasn't around the first few times Steve and I visited our mother. The nurses couldn't tell us about Mom's diagnosis or treatment plan. One nurse did offer, "We sedated Mrs. Simkovits for her protection. She won't be very animated."

Though we wondered whether the hospital was doing right by her, we decided to let them do their job. I don't know if Dad ever came to visit her—he never told us if he had, and Steve and I never asked him. Dad left Mom's care decisions up to Steve and me, though no one at the hospital asked for our opinions. Being 25 years old, I was simply relieved Mom was under professional care, and that Steve and I were there for her if she needed anything.

In the third week of her stay, Mom was back to her regular self. No more whispers, no more fast-talk, and no more jitters. I found the attending psychiatrist and asked her, "What happened to my mother? How did you make her better?"

The lady doctor looked as scruffy as ever. She spoke matter-of-factly. "We think it was her mix of medication, perhaps in conjunction with hormone imbalances, which are not uncommon for older women."

She offered, "Your mother has a slightly elevated sugar condition, pre-diabetic, on top of her having high blood pressure. Something in the mix of that and the medication she has been taking caused the change in her mental state."

Mom had once told me her two sisters had diabetes, and that the disease ran in the women of her family. I asked the doctor. "Could the food poisoning she had had at Christmas have contributed to her changes or imbalances?"

The doctor looked at me with a straight face. "We don't think so." She went back to her first track. "When your mother first arrived here, we took her off most of her medications and worked to get her stabilized, sedating her in the beginning to keep her calm. Then we tried different blood pressure and other medications. We added them slowly and monitored her carefully until we found the ones she can best tolerate with minimal side effects."

The doctor spoke in an unexpressive monotone. "We will give her new prescriptions to take with her when she leaves here. She should have them filled right away and continue with that regime. Her regular doctor should follow up with her within the next few weeks."

Mom's hospital discharge happened a full three weeks after her admission. Steve and I decided not to let her go back to her suburban doctor, her physician for over twenty years. We figured he was past his prime. Steve and I took her to see our younger doctor in the city.

Weeks later, while eating her stuffed cabbage and potato dumplings that she had simmered on the stove all afternoon, my mother unexpectedly turned to me. "Harvy, I want to thank you for coming home and saving my life. I don't know where I would be without you."

Her voice was calm and clear. "Your and Stevie's doctor is so much better than my old fogey doctor ever was." She didn't say anything about her hospital stay and her months of fast talk, jumpiness, and rushing away from Dad.

I nodded at her. I felt pleased about having helped my mother. I hoped that the recent dark period in her health would become a washed-out memory for all of us.

After Mom returned home from the hospital, she no longer ran away from Dad. They now shared quiet words when he occasionally came home for supper. She was back to reading letters to him from her family in Czechoslovakia while he ate her cooking from the coffee table in front of the living room television.

But those moments were few, and I knew that grave uncertainty still loomed in their marriage. Every night in bed, I wondered how much longer they'd remain together.

I wished for a miracle that would keep them wed. I wondered if there was anything I could do to prepare my mother for an eventuality to which she seemed oblivious. Or was my parent's relationship none of my business? If it wasn't, then what?

* * *

Once Mom was back to herself, and I was feeling better about myself, I wanted to take a larger stride with my brother. I didn't think it was healthy for him, at 26-years-old, nor for me, a year younger, to be living at home.

On a warm spring morning, I talked to him as he drove us to work. "Steve, I'm thinking of moving into an apartment here on the West Island." That area was the western extremity of the Island of Montreal, closer to where Steve stabled his horse. "Would you like to move with me? We could get a bigger place at a reasonable cost if we moved in together."

Steve thought for a moment. "Sure, Harvy, that sounds like a good idea." He hesitated. "But how would Mom feel about it?"

I had an answer. "Dad's hardly around. Mom doesn't need a big house out here in Dorval, especially with her Hungarian friends living closer to the city. If you and I move out, maybe she'll agree to have Dad sell the house and for them to move closer to her friends. Except for us, she's alone out here in the West Island, and she has no car."

Steve said, "Sounds good, Harvy. Let's talk to Mom at dinner tonight."

Mom sighed when we broke the news to her. "Your father is hardly home." Her eyes welled up, and her voice trembled. "And now the two of you are leaving me?!"

I considered asking Mom what she wanted for the future. I figured I knew her answer: "To grow old with your father! I love him and want to be with him until the day I die." She had told us those words many times after Dad had left her for other women.

I didn't think Mom's wish was realistic. I guessed my brother felt the same. No matter how hard it would be, and whether I saw it naively or not, I believed Mom had to find her life separate from Dad. It seemed as if her husband didn't want to be around her much anymore.

Even if Steve and I talked Dad into staying with her, I felt it wouldn't have made an iota of difference. For many years now, his attention hadn't been on his marriage.

I implored my mother. "Mom, a move closer to the city can give you a chance to be where your friends are. You always tell us how you feel stuck out here in Dorval. You and Dad don't need such a big house. If you accept the idea, we'll talk to him and see what he says."

Our mother's head hung down into her hands, her elbows propped up on the kitchen table. Though her and Dad's toxic screams and shouts had embossed these kitchen walls, this place had been her home and the center of her life for the last twenty-five years.

She raised her head. Her face became flushed and her eyes watered. She must have felt as if we were telling her that we no longer needed her in our lives and that she was going to lose us forever.

I offered, "We won't be far away, Mom. It will be good for Steve and me to get out on our own. He and I will be together, and we'll come to see you every week." I tried to stay confident and upbeat. "You won't be losing us; you'll be getting some freedom."

Her eyes looked down. "I hope you boys are right." She must have realized that Steve and I were serious, and what we proposed was right for us.

My mother may have wondered if she could survive alone in a country where our father had brought her with the promise of a future together. She had hoped he'd be by her side for the rest of her days. But it was becoming increasingly apparent to me—and perhaps to my brother as well—that she was becoming less and less a part of her husband's world.

My fifty-nine-year-old mother seemed deeply unsure of what new-found independence might bring her. I hoped it would give her a better life, without a focus on only Dad, Steve, and me. But freedom is a funny thing; one needs to know what to do with it.

Her eyes watered more. I could tell she was scared. Steve said, "We'll help you, Mom, as much as we can." The question remained, would she be able to help herself?

When I look back at that time, I regret that neither Dad, nor Steve, nor I recognized that she had never lived alone in her life. What we were asking her to do was beyond her ability to implement or even imagine.

Steve and I talked to Dad the next day, and he quickly agreed to the plan. By the end of April, my brother and I moved into a two-bedroom apartment one town west of our childhood home and one town closer to

Steve's horse. (I had mad that a part of the deal to encourage him to leave home, instead of us moving east and closer to the city.)

Soon afterward, Dad found his way to say to Mom, "Anna, you'll be better off in the city and out of Dorval." He then put our home on the market.

On a subsequent night, while I lay in bed, I wondered if my father would stick around with Mom after their move, or might he see our mutual moves as an opportune time to leave her again. Was there anything I could say or do to change things between them?

I had stitched together a plan for my father, mother, and brother that seemed to be heading in a better direction. But would this second son's thin thread be enough to hold together the frayed ends of our torn and tattered family?

* * * *

37

Whorehouse Business

After two months of sitting across the room from my father, he invited me to join his foreman production meetings, held every Tuesday at the end of the workday. Baptist, Georges, Guido, and François semi-circled the office's metal framed chairs to one side of my father's desk. Steve rolled his low-back secretarial chair a foot or two from his desk to be situated nearest to Dad.

I—the new guy—pulled up a metal chair at the far end of the semicircle, past François. "The boss" then held court from his high-back, tilt-and-swivel chair. Helen sat at her secretarial desk across from my father's. She took notes as Dad did most of the talking.

As she did every week, Helen had helped Dad prepare for his production meeting. Earlier in the day, she had given him weekly payroll figures from which he calculated the actual labour dollars spent in production. He compared those figures to the estimated labour costs that he had calculated when he had planned production months earlier. He started the meeting with, "We lost money on production labour again last week."

Our group sat in silence as we took in the discouraging information. Steve and the staff stared at different parts of the room as if they had heard the same line from Dad too many times before. I too stayed quiet after my father's declaration. I wanted to wait until I got a better handle on how Dad calculated his actual production labour costs and made his original labour estimates.

I felt bad for the lot, some of whom looked like "see, hear, and speak no evil." From my summers at JHS, I knew everyone worked hard at their jobs. My brother worked hard too—though he sometimes arrived late for no apparent reason, or left early to ride his horse.

After a moment of silence for the past week's production losses, Dad changed the subject to the following week's production plans.

After several production meetings, I moved myself to Herb's old desk, the one facing Dad. I sat there only for our weekly gatherings.

I felt a bit uncomfortable being in a spot reserved for Dad's former second-in-command, but nobody—not even Dad—said anything one way or another. To justify my need to place myself there, I put a pad of paper and a pen on the desk with which to write notes.

My father kept on delivering poor production news for most of the ensuing weeks. He stressed that the company continued to lose money on labour costs.

Near the end of a subsequent workday, I walked up to my father and caught his attention. "Dad, how do you estimate your labour costs and make your actual labour cost calculations?"

He looked at me and obliged. "Son, it's based on how much we spent in production labour each week compared to the labour estimates that François and I make for every JHS console model."

"Can you tell me more about how that works?"

"Sure." He grabbed a pencil and tapped the end of it on the desk. "At the end of every week, I compare our total week's factory payroll—the money we pay out to our factory workers—against what we estimated we should be spending on labour based on how many console units we produced that week."

I kept my voice calm as I dug a little deeper. "It's clear to me how you get the actual factory payroll numbers. I know Helen gives you those totals every Monday for the previous week." I took a breath. "But how do you calculate what we should be spending each week on labour?"

Dad was accommodating. He talked to me like a grade school teacher trying to explain how to multiply and divide. He pointed toward François's office. "One part of it comes from François' and my estimates for the factory to produce each console model—the hours needed to build and finish each cabinet and to assemble the electronics into it. I multiply those estimated labour hours by our average factory labour rate, which gives me the total dollars we should be paying our people to build each unit."

From his drawer, my father retrieved his last week's report, typed on half a sheet of paper. He pointed to his figures. "I then multiply the estimated labour-cost-per-unit by the units we completed the week before. He huffed. "Last week, we effectively lost $1,250 in labour. That means we spent that much more on labour costs than we had estimated." His face looked glum. "I'm not happy about that, but it's better than in other weeks."

I thought for a moment. My Harvard cost accounting cases kicked in. "But how do you account for work-in-progress?" I put my hand to my chin. "Your calculations only look at units coming off the end of the production line. You could be building work-in-progress and not have it reflected in your labour calculations."

Dad looked a bit peeved. "Harvy, I've been doing it this way for years. It works out over the long run. Work-in-progress can go up, and it can go down, but in the end, it is finished units that count."

I hadn't finished with my Harvard Socratic method. "Those labour dollars we are losing each week, how do you know if it's because it takes us longer to build a unit than what François' estimates? Or might it be because our average labour rate is higher than your estimates?"

The student was now trying to teach the professor a thing or two. Dad's voice became edgy. "To figure out our average labour rate, I do a big calculation at the end of every fiscal year to tell me what our actual hourly rate had been the previous year. I raise that number by inflation and use it in my estimates for the following year. My system is simple and works for me."

I had seen much more sophisticated methods in my Harvard production operations cases. What Dad had done did make sense, but it was too simplistic for an operation of his size, with three departments and several console models produced each month.

Because of my recent business school training, and a need to contribute, I was undeterred. I looked at my father. "What if I can do better for you, Dad?

What if I give the foreman worksheets for them to indicate how much employee time they're putting into each model we produce? Then we can more accurately determine what every model run costs us in labour, both in the time it takes to build each unit and the average dollars we pay our employees."

I spoke fast, perhaps not to give my father a chance to break my train of thought. "I can give us breakdowns for each production department: cabinet making, cabinet finishing, and electronic assembly. We'll get to know more precisely which areas are making or losing money for us." I pointed to his sheet. "Nothing wrong with your calculations, but they only look at the factory as a whole."

Dad's voice grew loud; his back arched a tad. "Okay, Harvy. Here, take the whole damn thing and do what you want with it." He pushed his sheet toward me. "See if you can do a better job."

He looked at his secretary who had overheard our conversation. "Helen, from now on give Harvy a copy of your weekly payroll report. He thinks he knows better how to do the weekly production report."

Perhaps Dad was annoyed because he didn't want to be shamed by his son in front of his secretary. Though I was taken aback by his irritability, and for his lack of recognition for what I had learned at business school, I wasn't fazed. I was at JHS to make a difference, and this was one place I could. If each foreman did his part, I could give my father and all of us a more detailed production analysis.

I suspected Helen wouldn't mind my new report because my calculations would bring to light the hard work of Georges, her husband, and the other foreman. I figured she'd prime the pump with Georges this evening during their car ride home. He'd be the first one I'd go to in the morning, once I designed a production reporting worksheet.

I looked at my father and stayed calm and focused. "Okay, Dad. Give me a few days to arrange this with the foremen. I'll need to get them to agree to do regular production reports to get the information I need to make this work."

I took a long breath. "Because we have a fair amount of work-in-progress around the plant, I'll get the cabinet making department to start collecting data for our next model produced."

Dad slouched a bit in his chair, turned back to other work on his desk, and grumbled something under his breath.

I chose to ignore his grumpiness. I was determined to show him that a little more sophistication in his production reporting would be valuable for the company. This analysis was a chance to show my B-school stuff.

Four weeks later, while again sitting at Herb's old desk during a production meeting, I passed out completed labour reports to Dad, Steve, François, and the three foremen. As a former RCA employee, François had immediately seen the value in my idea. The three foremen had cooperated by filling in daily production hours for each model their department produced in a given week.

My pitch to each of them had been, "The new reporting will give us a much better idea of how we are doing against our estimated labour costs." I offered my best argument. "This system will let us know if our weekly losses have to do with François's product labour estimates, my father's labour rate calculations, or with your own department's productivity."

I threw out my best argument. "François and my father have already agreed to do this. I just need you to fill out the reports every day, giving me the best data you can on how many work hours your people spend on each model we run through the factory." I had kept my face beckoning as if I were asking a big favour. "Would you be willing to try it out?"

When each foreman, in turn, took the worksheet out of my hand to examine it more closely, I knew I had convinced him.

The report I passed out to Dad and the foremen on that early spring day showed a summary and analysis of the data I had gathered in the past weeks, presented by console model. I said, "There's both good news and bad news in this report." I took a breath. "Let me start with the bad news first. Yes, we are continuing to lose money on production labour."

Though I was shaking inside, I tried to project an air of confidence, as I had done at Harvard when I had been called on by a professor. "On the report, you can see that actual labour dollars spent have exceeded estimates in our three departments and in the console models we produced these last weeks. We're about 15% over François and Dad's estimates of our labour costs during that period.

I took another breath as I watched my father's reactions. I shivered a bit inside while his eyes scanned my documents, but his serious mood didn't deter me. "However," I continued, "the good news is now we know exactly why."

Not a sound came from Dad or anyone. Every person had their eyes on my document. "If you turn the page, you'll see my charts and calculations by JHS model run."

Everyone turned the page.

I continued. "Regarding the labour hours needed per console model, we're not far off. On average, production labour hours are a few percentage points more than we expected, which isn't too bad."

I kept my voice firm. "However, we can probably do a better job working with François regarding the Model 8045 for Sears. With that model, we have underestimated actual labour hours per unit by 12%. We need to figure out why that model run took longer to build, and then fix the issues."

Georges piped in. "This is good to know, Harvy."

François pointed to the papers in his hand. "I was worried about the 8045. It's the first time we produced it. That console box is a bit more complicated than what we usually do, and I wasn't sure about my calculations."

"That's what I was hoping to hear," I responded. "And I couldn't have given us this good information without the three of you foremen filling out those labour worksheets."

"What else do you have?" Dad said a bit sternly. He turned to another page in my report.

I looked at him. "I'm glad you asked, Dad. The other big issue, shown on the next page, is that our average labour rate is almost 13% higher than our estimates. In other words, our factory people, on average, are costing us significantly more per hour than we had expected." I didn't dare add, "Their time is more expensive than what you, Dad, have calculated as JHS's average labour rate."

Dad looked closely at my charts and calculations that lay flat on his desk. His eyes shifted left and right. I stayed quiet as the wheels turned in his head.

When he was ready, he proclaimed, "Our people are too expensive because our production turnover is down from where it was last year. Having fewer console units to produce this year than last, we had to let our cheapest employees go. We've kept our most experienced people."

He looked at his foremen. "Our experienced people are more expensive." He turned back to me. "If we can't increase our sales orders, then we can't rehire our less expensive labourers, and then we'll never get our average labour rate down."

He placed his fist on his desk. "We have to find more business for the factory so we can hire back our cheaper people and lower our average labour costs."

I was impressed with my father's quick uptake on my analysis. "You hit the nail on the head Dad." I took a breath. "Our losing money on labour each week is not so much because we are inefficient in production. It has more to do with our paying our people more per hour than we had estimated."

I kept my momentum going. "And you are right about JHS trying to hold onto our most experienced people, which is the right thing to do. But if we can get more orders and hire back our lower-cost people, then we could stop losing money in production."

Steve raised his eyes off the report and looked at me. "I guess you learned something there at Harvard."

From the time I had come back through the JHS doors, no one else had ever mentioned Harvard or asked me about my time at business school. The fact that I had departed B-school seemed irrelevant now.

I kept my face serious and didn't address my brother's statement. I said, "My report is complete. I'll continue to do these calculations every week for us."

I sat down a little straighter in Herb's chair and allowed Dad to do the talking about next steps for François and the foremen. I didn't want to horn in on his role in addressing solutions to our production challenges.

After the meeting, Georges told me, "It's good what you are trying to do here." His words boosted my spirits.

Dad never thanked me for my production analysis. It hurt not to be acknowledged by him, but his not standing in the way of my efforts may have been acknowledgement enough.

Unlike Harvard's three business cases a day, JHS was one big case for me. The boss, for now, was letting me make small but significant changes to his way of doing business. If I worked not to seek the limelight in his domain, perhaps he'll let me make positive inroads in our family too.

Over the ensuing months, the foremen continued to fill out their production worksheets, and I continued to make my weekly reports. We had better weekly production meetings and worked to make the plant more efficient. I suspect we silently hoped my father could make more sales to fill the slack in our factory's capacity.

Had I been a little smarter, I might have gone out to seek more sales opportunities for JHS. But I was not an outgoing guy—the people schmoozer and night-time entertainer my father was. I felt more comfortable contributing to the company's inside operations than being on the road asking for factory orders.

For better or worse, in my mind, I had made it my father's job to go out and find more business for his company. I could then help him, and my brother, run the company more effectively and hopefully with fewer screams and shouts.

* * *

At another production meeting, Dad asked, "What's been the hold-up in production this week?" He was looking at Baptist, the electronics foreman.

Baptist replied, "I'm having trouble getting product fast enough from the woodshop and finishing departments." He kept his eyes on my father, though we all knew that it was the other foremen he was talking about. "My people have to sit idle, waiting until cabinets arrive one pallet at a time. That makes my department very inefficient."

Guido, our wood shop foreman, took Baptist's statement as a personal affront. Though he said nothing at the meeting, the next day, he went back and told his workers to "Fill up those guys!" His area then inundated the wood finishing and electronics departments with cabinets.

Within days, the front of the electronics assembly line got jammed. Extra people were needed to move cabinets around so they wouldn't block the production conveyor.

I disliked petty bickering among our foremen. I had seen it when I was at P&G. There, my inexperience and timidity had prevented me from stepping in. I had let squabbling molehills turn into mountain clashes among my direct reports.

My growing son-of-the-boss confidence had me rally the foremen outside my father's weekly meeting to discuss problems between the departments. I brought Guido, Georges, and Baptist together and told them, "Okay, guys, how are we going to solve this problem? Or do we need to talk about it at the next production meeting?"

In other words, *If we together cannot settle these differences, then I'll raise the issue at our next meeting with my father. Then you'll take your chances with the big boss.*

No one enjoyed Dad's ire. I believed the foremen would settle their skirmishes to keep my father off our backs, and it worked. Our production areas functioned more smoothly because of my efforts to improve communication. I spoke with each foreman every day to support them any way I could, and to relay messages, with my suggestions thrown in discreetly. I believed we all were better for it, especially JHS.

One evening, several weeks after I instituted my production reports, I brought my files and other materials over from my desk across the room. I made

Herb's old desk my own, and neither Dad nor anyone said a word about my move.

As the months passed, I saw myself as the company's de facto Director of Manufacturing. I didn't want a Director of Operations title because that would have Steve, the purchasing agent, report to me, and that might jeopardize our growing partnership.

Dad never bestowed on me the company's Director of Manufacturing title, nor was it ever put on my business card. Even so, everyone in the plant got to know me as JHS's manufacturing head, in addition to Johnny's MIT-graduate son—the H-word remaining unsaid. Best of all, my system for tracking and evaluating labour costs, and my way of including the foremen in informal production meetings, had everyone see me working for everyone's best interest, especially the company's.

* * *

Though Dad never told me I was doing a good job, he let me take on more responsibility.

In the electronics department, there was a young guy, Gary, who Steve and I felt was intelligent and trustworthy. We advanced him from assembly line worker to stockroom clerk. The previous clerk and shipping foreman, Danny, was long gone from the company. Dad had laid him off because, "The guy *foot-scoffed* [fucked off] with merchandise," though our father could never prove it.

My brother and I agreed that the stockroom needed a full-time person. We showed Gary how to arrange the area, how to release merchandise for production, how to sort and organize incoming supplier shipments, and how to pick, pack, and ship spare parts to our field service people.

Because Gary was physically strong, we had him help Baptist in the shipping and receiving area. In effect, Steve and I had Gary perform Don's previous position without incurring the higher expense of Don. Over time, Gary could grow to do more and get better pay. Though Dad grumbled about having one more position on the payroll, he didn't stand in the way of Steve's and my plan.

Baptist was pleased about having someone else handle merchandise shipments. He told me, "I always have to take a guy off the end of the production line to move merchandise in and out of the transport trucks. If it's a big shipment, I lose my guy for hours. It slows things down on the line and makes my production report look bad."

I was elated about Baptist's concern regarding his department's labour costs. It was another positive result of utilizing my production reporting system.

The re-establishment of the shipping/stockroom position proved that, together, Steve and I could make important company improvements. I was pleased to transfer my stockroom duties to Gary, for I was moving up in JHS.

I felt I was making headway in our family business, proving my value to Dad, with the hope that he might see my brother and me as worthy successors to run his company. And perhaps Dad's pleasure with his kids would spill over into our family, with his being nicer to Mom.

I secretly hoped I'd be right.

* * *

Once or twice a year, Jim Smyth, the head furniture and electronics buyer from Woolco, came to visit JHS from Toronto. He checked on our production schedule and talked about pending orders with Dad.

In the middle of one meeting held in JHS's front office, Mr. Smyth mentioned how Woolco's consumer services department had complained to him about JHS. It seemed it was taking too long to repair some customers' console units at JHS's repair centres. Smyth mentioned one particular customer who had called many times over months concerning the long wait to get his unit repaired.

Dad waved me over from across the room where I sat doing my production report. "Harvy, can you please come here?"

I stood and walked across the room. Dad continued, "Can you explain to Mr. Smyth about our parts service. He says a customer has been waiting a long time for a repair."

Because Steve involved me in JHS service functions, and my brother was out that day, Dad put me on the spot with Mr. Smyth. I figured my father would rather have me on the hook on a service issue than for him to look bad to the Woolco buyer.

Dad hadn't prepared me for his unexpected request, but I started to talk. "We have a lot of pieces to this parts service game." I took a big breath to keep me steady. "Not only do we have independent repair centres, which are contractors for JHS, but there's also Woolco's consumer service department working to please the customer."

I used my hands to draw a make-believe diagram in the air to show the different players involved. "If we are not in good communication with each other, misunderstandings can develop, which could be the case here."

I paused to see Mr. Smyth's reaction. His eyes stayed on me, but his face remained blank. I continued. "One of the wild cards in this whole equation is our overseas suppliers." I drew a new circle in the air, above the others I had drawn. "We buy a complete spare parts inventory based on both their recommendations and our experience as to what could break or get damaged in a stereo unit."

I looked directly at Smyth, keeping my voice calm and confident. "If you like, Mr. Smyth, I can take you upstairs to our stock room to show you our whole spare parts inventory."

"Not necessary for now," he responded. I surmised that just a word about our big inventory was enough to get him—someone who probably couldn't tell a radio chassis doohickey from a record player thingamajig—to be impressed yet decline my invitation.

I pressed on. "Sometimes, our overseas supplier or we guess wrong. Something unexpected breaks or we need a part for a discontinued model."

I kept up my pace. "Because our electronics suppliers are overseas, it usually makes little sense to ship just one part over here at a high cost. We group our spare part orders into monthly batches. It then takes a month or two to get the parts over here by boat and train."

I continued to talk briskly while I kept my eyes focused on Mr. Smyth. "Shipping by air is very expensive, only used when there's an emergency in getting our production out on time." I pointed to the factory door.

I looked again at Mr. Smyth and said sincerely, "I hope I'm making sense."

He nodded, "Yes, okay."

I worked to keep my voice even-keeled. "Once in a blue moon, even our overseas supplier doesn't have a particular part in stock, especially if they are no longer manufacturing a specific chassis model. They have to order the missing pieces from their vendors, which creates another delay." I took a breath. "It then could take many months before we obtain an obscure part."

I showed my open palms. "That seems to be what has happened here with your customer's unit."

I was making an educated guess about what was happening with that repair. I spoke with confidence, as I had learned to do in my Harvard classes, where some students followed the rubric: *If you can't dazzle them with your brilliance then baffle them with your baloney.* At least I wasn't throwing any ham into this conversation.

I kept my face straight and my tone steady, though a part of me was still shaking inside. "Unfortunately, we have none of those radio chassis in our inventory that we can cannibalize to get the specific part needed for your customer. So the customer's unit has to sit at the repair centre until we eventually receive the piece in question from overseas."

I looked at my father. He was listening and nodding his head. I raised my hand. "Now we could give the customer a whole new stereo of another model, but I think you would agree that it would be overkill for one missing part. Doing that on any regular basis would be costly."

I put my hand down on the edge of the desk. "I know having a unit sit in repair can feel frustrating for a customer, yet we can only do what we can do. Keeping an adequate spare parts inventory is an educated guess." I raised a hand to make my point. "Not having enough parts creates this kind of problem, but having too many creates other problems, like higher costs for everyone."

Mr. Smyth looked at me, a hand on his chin. He nodded, but his face still showed concern. I took another breath. "What we could do is be in better communication with your Woolco consumer services department. They should inform us directly about issues like this instead of bothering you. We can then respond to them better, and they, in turn, can respond better to the customer."

The Woolco buyer nodded again. He glanced at Dad and offered something I didn't expect. "What if Harvy meets with Joe Raymond, the head of our Canada-wide consumer service, the next time you visit us in Toronto?" He pointed my way. "Harvy can discuss the matter with Joe directly, and they can better figure out how to deal with such service situations."

I didn't know if I had impressed Mr. Smyth or if he was pushing the customer service buck elsewhere. I held my hands together to keep them from fidgeting. Dad jumped in, "Yes, that's a good idea, Jim. We'll be in Toronto next month. Harvy can meet with Joe then."

Mr. Smyth added, "When I go back to Toronto, I'll recommend that to Joe." He turned to me. "So what can we do now for this specific customer? This one nagging guy continues to complain to our consumer services department about his unit sitting in the shop."

I stood frozen for a moment. An idea came to me.

I pulled out my wallet. "Here; please take my card and give it to Mr. Raymond. Your consumer services people can give the customer my name and number and have him call me if he wishes. I'll explain the situation and ask for his patience until we can get the part for his unit."

I looked at Dad and then back at Mr. Smyth. "Though his unit is probably out of warranty, we can give him the part for free when we get it in stock, and save him a bit of money for the repair."

Dad looked at me and then Mr. Smyth. "Yes, we can do that, Jim."

Mr. Smyth leaned forward in his chair. "Okay, thanks for the explanation, Harvy, and for your consideration for this customer." He waved his hand and turned back to my father.

Dad looked at me and said, "Thank you, Harvy. You can go back to what you were doing."

The next afternoon, after the factory clock had buzzed five o'clock and JHS's employees left *en masse* for the day, I sat at my desk across from Dad. My father looked at me. "Last night, I had supper with Mr. Smyth. He said what a bright boy you are." He pointed west. "Jim said he'd talk to Joe Raymond and suggest that you and he have a meeting next time we are in Toronto."

"That was nice of Mr. Smyth to say," I responded. "And a meeting with Mr. Raymond would be good."

Dad stood, looked at me and smiled. "So let's close the whorehouse, and we can go home."

That fatherly smile was about as good as it got from Dad. I smiled back, knowing I had made a mark with him and an important customer. My father set the office alarm for the night, and we headed out the front office door, I following right behind him.

* * *

A month later, Dad and I headed to Toronto. While my father met with Mr. Smyth and other Woolco executives, I had dinner with Joe Raymond and Jeff Peters (our Woolco sales rep who lived in Toronto).

Mr. Raymond's tall, stick-thin stature was in sharp contrast to Jeff's short and rotund physique. I thought about how Jeff's wife kept him flush with delicious apple and cherry pies, baked with large sugar granules sprinkled on top. Every time we went to Toronto, Dad and I got to taste her great baking over another supper at the Peters' home. We were to gather there again this evening after we completed our respective business dealings for the day.

Joe, Jeff, and I went to a restaurant near Woolco's head office. There I took the service manager through the presentation I had given Mr. Smyth. When I was about halfway through, Joe said, "Let's order; I'm hungry."

After ordering, and for the remainder of our meal, Joe never returned to the customer service subject. Instead, he and Jeff started to talk about explicit sex videos they had recently watched.

After sharing details about titles and themes (oral, anal, 2-on-1, and other styles), Joe said, "It's nobody's business what people watch in the privacy of their home. If my wife and I get pleasure out of a good X-rated video, the government shouldn't interfere with that."

Jeff responded, "I wholeheartedly agree with you, Joe. By the way, did you see the one about….," and their conversation continued.

Not to feel left out, I piped in, "While I was a student at MIT, twice a year, at the beginning of each semester, the student union screened X-rated flicks."

The two men looked at me, their eyebrows raised. "I did not know they did such things at such a prestigious college," Jeff said.

"Kids under twenty-one years old shouldn't be exposed to such stuff," Joe added.

They turned back to each other and continued their sex video talk.

Unlike these two guys, I was not the kind of person who discussed what I liked or didn't like about sex films. I was here to talk about customer service issues and JHS's relationship with Woolco and its consumer services department.

I also felt I had to defer to Jeff's judgement about what Joe wanted to discuss. He knew Joe much better than I did, and our salesman seemed to be into this sex tape stuff.

When Jeff and I caught up with Dad for supper at Jeff's home, my father looked at both of us and asked, "So how did it go with Joe Raymond?"

Before I could say anything, Jeff came in. "Our meeting went fine. We talked about the usual stuff." He winked at me. "Joe was pleased Harvy came to see him, and he looks forward to staying in touch on important service matters."

I didn't know if Dad knew what "the usual stuff" was to Jeff and Joe, but I said nothing. Maybe Dad was right about JHS being in a whorehouse business.

* * * *

38

Sons of Simkovits

One Thursday, Dad asked me to join him for supper at the Troika with his close colleague and friend, Aras. I was pleased to be included in his evening business meeting, though I knew that it wasn't business that propelled these men to the Troika.

During the meal, neither Aras nor Dad mentioned my departure from Harvard. I was glad the memories of that trying time in my life were fading.

After a couple of drinks, Dad looked at Aras and started complaining. "Steve's working only for himself and not for the company."

I could mouth the words as Dad spoke them. "Steve comes in when he wants and leaves when he wants, caring more about his horse than about me or the business that supports him." His hand was in a fist and on the table. "He lets suppliers get away with bullshit explanations about why merchandise is late. It pisses me off."

Aras lifted a hand and said, "Johnny, you should talk to him."

Dad took a swig from his third glass of Scotch. "I do, but it doesn't change anything."

Dad's "talking" to Steve was more like screaming and chastising. I sat quietly and said nothing about it in front of my father's friend.

I had a hard time fully understanding my brother's motive back then, but I wanted to make things work better for Dad, Steve, and me. Even though a part of me shared my father's distaste for my brother's contradictory ways, I felt that Steve and I would be stronger if we worked better together at JHS, and if Dad wasn't on Steve's behind half the time.

At the end of the following day, after everyone left the office, I sat at my desk across from Dad. I looked at him while he was doing paperwork. "Dad, I'd like to talk to you about something."

He put down his pencil and looked at me. "Sure son; what is it?"

"It's about you and Steve." I stopped to look at his face. His eyes were open wide and on me. I continued. "From what I can tell, you never talk to him about how you feel without getting angry."

I kept my eyes on his jaw for it was hard to look him straight in the eyes. "What if you, he, and I meet every week or two to discuss important company issues and things that bother you?" I took a breath. "Maybe some things bother him too."

My father nodded, which spurred my courage to continue. "You need to be able to tell him what you want without shouting at him." I put my hands flat on the desk. "And you always let him get away with doing what he wants. If there are no consequences, he won't change."

Dad thought for a moment and said, "Okay; good idea, son."

My voice grew in its strength. "Dad, it would be better if you call the meeting among us rather than if I do it. Then Steve wouldn't think I'm trying to run our conversations."

Dad nodded, "Okay, son. That makes sense."

The three of us met after work the following Monday. I hoped my presence would help Dad not lose his temper. He looked at my brother, "Steve; the company needs you here during regular business hours. You shouldn't run away to your horse before the end of the day or to come in late in the morning because you have something more important to do at home."

Steve countered calmly, "If my job is getting done, I don't need to be around the whole time."

Dad came back, "I know, but our foremen need you here first thing in the morning. Please do what you can to be on time."

"They can call me at home if it's urgent," Steve retorted. "I always answer the phone."

I sat at Helen's desk, thinking it a more neutral place than my desk. I leaned forward, my hands clasped and on the desk, my eyes looking at the floor.

Initially, I said little while the verbal ping-pong ball went back and forth between these two hard heads. I didn't see it as my place to take sides or to speak for either of them at this first meeting of the Simkovits minds.

Whether I was spurred on by my P&G management training, or Harvard Business School case studies, or the books and articles I had read about family business, I did encourage each of them to talk calmly and clearly to each other.

I also made a suggestion. "Steve, what if you scheduled your time to be in the office earlier on days you plan to go see your horse. Then you can leave the office earlier on those days and not get stuck in rush-hour traffic. On alternate days, Dad will know you'll stay later. He can then schedule his production meeting, or these meetings among the three of us, for those late afternoons." I moved my hand in a circle to indicate the "the three of us" were one.

To my surprise, Steve agreed to my suggestion. For the next few weeks, he followed a more predictable schedule. But he eventually fell back to his timetable of arriving late and leaving early unpredictably.

I began to feel frustrated as Dad did, thinking it was easier to lead my brother's horse to water than Steve himself. When I asked Steve why he changed his ways, he offered, "It's not convenient for me to follow your suggestion." He delivered his words in a superior, big brother tone.

After work one day, I privately urged Dad to provide consequences for Steve's insubordination. Neither he nor I could think of anything short of firing my brother. Without anger, I suggested, "What if you let Steve go for a while until he agrees to change his behaviour? It may be better than letting him get away with his misbehaviour. He's not a good example for the rest of our people."

Dad looked down at his desk. "I can't do that to your brother, even if he is acting like a prima donna. Who would hire him without a college education?"

It was frustrating to see my usually tough father make a soft decision regarding his first son. Then again, I was his son too, and I was out for Dad's treasure buried in an offshore bank. But, contrary to what I saw Steve do, I was trying to earn my keep at JHS and not confront or defy my father at every turn.

Over the ensuing months, our father-son meetings continued, albeit infrequently. At the end of most of our three-ways, I left the office feeling frustrated.

Not much changed between Steve and Dad. And the little that did change, didn't last. I surmised there wasn't much I could do to alter what had been seeded deeply in those two. A tough survivor father had bred a hard-headed first son, an accord made by greater forces than any reconciliation this second son could provide. I imagined myself a sidewalk pedestrian observing two reckless car drivers speeding along the highway just before a crash.

On the other hand, I certainly wasn't detached from our family's drama. I had one eye fixed on Dad's hidden pot of money—perhaps my substitute for his attention and love.

But I had read in one of my family business books that it was important "to solve Dad's problems first." Unlike Steve, I decided to focus on finding reasonable solutions to JHS's issues, solutions that Dad would accept or tolerate. I wanted to endear myself to our father. It certainly was in my best interest, and perhaps in the best interest of our family.

There was a downside to my strategy with Dad. Steve may have viewed me as being continually on Dad's side. That perception may have stymied any influence I tried to muster with my brother.

Even though I usually stood a little closer to Dad on any issue, I tried not to dangle any bias in front of my brother. I didn't want overt competition between us in our early collaborations at JHS. I wanted to show Steve that having me in the company, and by our working together, we'd build our strength in facing our father. I couldn't understand why Steve couldn't see my value and why he and I couldn't get on the same sibling bandwagon.

Steve responded well to me only when I deferred to him, allowing him to take the lead with the JHS projects we took on. Even in our move into our apartment, I let him have more of a say in the furniture and fixtures we bought and in how we decorated the communal areas of our place.

I eventually realized, *Steve's just like Dad!* My brother wanted final say, his way or no way. Then again, maybe he was working with me only because he saw me filling in for him at JHS whenever he'd go on trips to far-off lands. My brother's motivations regarding me were never fully clear; perhaps as mine weren't fully clear to him.

Though I felt privileged in being closer to our father, I didn't realize that my greater harmony with Dad and my closed lips to his business and offshore shenanigans would cost me with my brother.

I may have become a superior son, but I wondered if I had been the better man.

* * *

In the summer of 1980, five months after I had come home from Harvard, and two months after Steve and I had moved in together, he and I made our boldest attempt to work on our relationship.

Steve and I had spent a few successful long weekends together, both biking in the Laurentian Mountains north of Montreal and hiking and camping in the Adirondacks of NY and the Green Mountains of VT. We had even arranged a house-warming party with his and my friends coming together. Because living together seemed to be working well, we decided to travel across Canada for a three-week holiday.

Dad initially tried to persuade us not to make the long trip. "The roads could be dangerous. Unlike in the U.S., there isn't a divided highway all the way across Canada."

Steve and I were unified and undeterred, a rarity for us.

Our father turned around a few days later and said, "Okay, how about going to visit every Sears and Woolco retail store and warehouse from here to Victoria, BC? If you can do that, and do it during our regular factory summer shutdown, JHS will pay your travel expenses." He pointed at us. "It will build goodwill with our biggest customers."

Though Dad's gesture was perhaps a bit over the top, I figured he smelled both a justifiable tax deduction for helping his boys and goodwill from his customers for providing them support in the field.

JHS was having nagging issues with several of its console models. One Korean chassis had an inherent aesthetic defect that had emerged unexpectedly in customer stores. Not only did that defect need to be fixed, but JHS's reputation with its customers also needed mending. Steve's and my adventure west could be billed as a product repair and customer relations trip to rebuild confidence with JHS and some of its consoles.

Steve and I talked about our father's offer, and we responded to him the next day. "Okay, Dad; we'll visit those stores as we head west. And to give us enough time to do that, we now need to be away for four weeks instead of three."

Our father's face grew tight, but he accepted our terms.

Before leaving Montreal on our work expedition, Steve and I armed ourselves with a box of tools and a bunch of spare chassis parts that had recently arrived from our Korean supplier. I had my AMX company credit card to cover travel expenses. Form Sears and Woolco, we obtained an updated list of their every department store and warehouse between Montreal and the Pacific.

In mid-July, my brother and I headed north and west in what would turn out to be an 8,000 km (5,000 miles) round trip in his roomy Mercedes 300D sedan. We'd visit customers during weekdays and spend long weekends sightseeing and visiting our high school and college friends who lived along the way. Steve would do most of the driving while I'd do most of the navigating.

Our first stop was Ottawa, where we visited Uncle Edo's cousin. Cousin Alex had escaped the Iron Curtain and immigrated with Edo to Canada in 1968.

Alex took us kayaking down the wide but shallow Ottawa River. Steve and I shared a double kayak. My brother took the lead position in guiding and steering us from the back of the boat.

He and I worked well together to paddle our kayak into the faster-moving water and to avoid grounding on the shallow parts. We grounded only once because I thought the water was deeper than it was. I tried to push us off the sand with my paddle, but Steve climbed out of the kayak and pulled us into a deeper channel. I could see his frustrated face, but he didn't say a word.

In the middle of nowhere in Ontario, we visited Steve's college friend, Brian, a mining engineer. He took us to the nickel-silver mine where he worked. We changed into orange overalls and put on heavy helmets with a miner's spotlight. We walked a large, steep underground incline, passing gigantic mining machines. Their humongous rubber tires were taller than if I were standing on my brother's shoulders. After walking downhill underground for forty-five minutes, we were thousands of feet below the surface.

We turned to look out through a large opening and into a vast vertical hole through which the midday sun was shining. Brian pointed up and offered, "This manmade hole is a mining stope. We are over two-and-a-half thousand feet below where the original strip mine ended above us."

As we stood at the opening, he now pointed down. "Rather than digging down from the top, the mine is now digging up from the bottom. The material is being taken from way below us and transported to the surface on a beltway."

He pointed down into the almost vertical wall pit. "So much material has been taken out that it's left this giant hole in the ground." He pointed across the pit. "At our depth, the resulting pit is wider than a Canadian football field is long."

My heart beat hard and fast as I bent over from the wall opening to determine if I could see the bottom of that stope or the sky above. I couldn't.

My head grew dizzy from the enormity of that hole in the ground. Any false move could send me falling a half mile straight down. I kept looking at Steve behind me to make sure that he wasn't close enough to push me over the edge.

That evening, I became friendly with Brian. He and I went beer for beer while my brother sipped 7-Up. Being graduate engineers, Brian and I sang the Engineer's Song for his girlfriend who had cooked us supper:

We are, we are, we are, we are, we are the engineers,
We can, we can, we can, we can demolish 40 beers,
Drink up, drink up, drink up my friends and come along with us,
For we don't give a damn for any ol' man who doesn't give a damn for us.

Brian sang a couple of verses from his days at Queens University. I offered a verse from my MIT days:

Princeton's run by Vassar, and Vassar's run by Yale.
And Yale's run by Wellesley, and Wellesley's run by tail.
And Harvard's run by stiff ones, the ones you raise by hand.
But MIT's run by engineers, the finest in the land.

Brian and I laughed. Steve's grin looked a little forced.

In Calgary, Steve and I joined my friends, the Lowell family. Six years earlier, I had met the Lowells through John, my high school friend, when he and I had made a similar cross-Canada trip. Over the years, I had stayed in touch with them, and it paid off.

The Lowells invited Steve and me for the weekend to their lakeside summer cottage in the middle of British Columbia. As it had been years earlier, when they had taught me to waterski, I got up on skis easily and glided effortlessly behind the speedboat.

Every time we went out on the lake, Steve sat in the back to spot me. We encouraged him to try to get up on skis, but he declined, saying, "I prefer my sports on hard ground."

During that weekend visit, he stayed more in the background. He might not have wanted to horn in on my fun with my friends. I later thought it might have been hard for him to be in a number two position with me—as I disliked being that way with him. I very much wanted Steve to share my friendships, but maybe he saw it differently.

Outside of our weekends of having fun with friends, Steve and I were all business during the weekdays. We visited several Woolco and Sears stores every day, and we drove in the evenings to get to our next destination. We stayed at roadside motels and ate at roadside restaurants, which I picked out using Canadian Automobile Association travel guidebooks. I was careful to look for only two- or three-star motels and reasonably-priced restaurants so that our father wouldn't see an exorbitant travel bill.

One evening, without asking my opinion, Steve stopped the car by the side of a mountain river. He decided to sleep overnight in the open air on the river bank. Because of the chilly mountain air, I slept in the car.

Steve kept a logbook about every store and warehouse we visited, and every department and warehouse manager to whom we had talked. With that, we could inform the merchandise buyers and customer service department managers at Woolco and Sears' head office about our visits and repair work.

Everything seemed to go according to plan until three weeks into our four-week trip. After finishing our visits to the Victoria Sears and Woolco stores on Vancouver Island, we drove to catch the ferry back to the mainland. I sat in the passenger seat, giving my brother directions. Halfway to the ferry, my brother stopped the car abruptly. He opened his door and bolted out of the vehicle.

Not knowing what was wrong, I exited on my side. Steve beat his fist on the roof and screamed, "Harvy, stop telling me what to do and where to go like I'm an idiot." I stood there startled by his anger.

Maybe the current incident had been small, but it seemed that something had been building within Steve. Perhaps he needed to blurt out his frustrations with a Johnny Simkovits vigour. He maintained his belligerent tone. "And I hate the way you drive my car! When you're behind the wheel, you abruptly switch gears from reverse to forward while the car is still rolling backward—it will kill the transmission!"

My eyelids rose, but I tried to keep my voice calm. I looked at my brother. "Okay Steve, I get it. I'm sorry you're feeling that way, but can you please calm down?" I was a little afraid to get back in the car with him as upset as he was. I didn't want to find myself in a car accident and then a hospital this far from home.

Though I had never seen Steve hit anyone, I had seen him break things. Once, in our teens, he broke a golf club over his knee when he was frustrated on a fairway, both with his play and with Dad's golfing pointers. Dad subsequently told him, "Gosh, Steve, you didn't have to do that. Can't you stay calm?"

Steve responded angrily to our father, his face contorted. "I hate this game! I'm never playing it again." He grabbed his clubs and marched in a huff straight to the clubhouse, leaving Dad and me to gape at him as he walked away. He never played the sport again.

On another occasion, during an evening at home in those same formative years, Steve tore every stamp in his prized Monaco stamp collection for reasons I never understood—he said not a word about it. More than once I saw him smash a toy model he had spent painstaking hours building in our basement.

His volatility was unpredictable and troubling; I wanted to stay clear of it. Perhaps because of his and our parents' explosiveness, my modus operandi was to do the opposite—to freeze in one spot, keep my cool, and try not to escalate the upset.

Fire still in his eyes for my bad navigating and poor driving, my brother responded to my suggestion of calming down. "Okay, Harvy, forget it." His tone was terse. "Let's go. Just get in the car."

I looked at him without moving a muscle. "Not if you are angry like this, Steve." I didn't want to provoke him further, but I was frightened by his display. "Can you let me drive? I'll be more careful in how I switch gears."

After another round of similar comments, Steve jumped back into the driver's seat and slammed his door shut. I remained still on the sidewalk as he put the car into gear and sped off. He didn't look back. The car's front end bounced as a wheel hit a curb. In a moment, he was gone down the road toward the ferry back to Vancouver.

I waited, alternately sitting and pacing in circles on the side of the road. I hoped Steve would come back when he cooled down. I kept on touching my wallet in my back pocket, glad I didn't store it in between the front bucket seats as my brother did.

It would be decades later before I understood what Steve did to me that day. It was like what my father had done to my mother, abandoning her by the side of a marriage road, caring little for what it was like for the one left behind.

The uncertainty of not knowing whether or not my brother would come back, or if I should wait or move on, was both debilitating and infuriating. I tried to understand what this meant for our sibling relationship. It became unequivocally clear that Johnny Simkovits lived within my brother, perhaps as much as other parts of our dad lived in me.

It would take me a very long time to understand Steve, just as it took me a very long time to make peace with my father. Maybe I still haven't forgiven either of them. Could it be because I haven't fully forgiven myself?

After nearly an hour standing and sitting by the roadside, I knew Steve had left me there for good. I had to find my way to Vancouver. I hitched a ride to the Victoria bus station and took a bus to the mainland, arriving at our pre-reserved hotel after seven o'clock that evening.

At 7:30, my brother arrived at our room. He knocked on the door just minutes after I had walked in. He entered, sat down, and said nothing of our altercation. Instead, he offered, "I called Mom and Dad and told them I'm flying back to Montreal the day after tomorrow."

What?!!

Steve's voice stayed calm and polite. "I'll help you tomorrow with the stores and warehouses we have left here in Vancouver, and then you can drive back to Montreal by yourself. You won't have many stops to make because we did most of the store visits on our way out here."

I raised my voice but only by a decibel or two. "Why the heck did you call Mom and Dad about a problem you and I are having?" I pointed to him and then myself. "Shouldn't you and I try to work this out first?"

Steve didn't respond. He did say, "I had a pleasant drive up the Vancouver Island coastline, taking the Nanaimo ferry to North Vancouver." He didn't say whether that drive was pleasant because of the island scenery or because he was without me.

At precisely eight o'clock (eleven o'clock Montreal time), Steve picked up the phone and called home. He reached our father and repeated the plan he had told me. He then mentioned when his flight was going to arrive in Montreal.

He already booked a flight?

Through the receiver, I heard my father talk loudly and vigorously. "Can you guys please get along?" After a few more similar statements, Dad calmed down. "Please cooperate with each other. Try to stick together."

Steve's voice was matter-of-fact. "It's too late, Dad. I'm coming home."

There was nothing our father could do from far away. I could tell that he was as frustrated as I was, and I was sure Mom was worried sick. I imagined her pacing the living room floor, her palm to her head as Dad spoke to Steve.

Dad repeated the same statements to me when my brother handed me the phone. Steve hardly looked my way as I turned my head toward him to make sure he overheard my words. "I hope Steve changes his mind. . . . Yes, I'm trying to talk to him about it. . . . No, I don't want to drive back to Montreal by myself."

Before our call ended, Dad offered, "Okay, call me tomorrow evening at the office to tell me what you guys decide. And please get along."

When our father hung up, I felt cold and alone.

Steve said, "I don't know about you, but I'm watching a little TV and then going to bed."

I laid on my bed and stared at the ceiling. *What the hell am I going to do?*

The next day, Steve and I performed our Sears and Woolco store and warehouse visits across Vancouver, doing a record six sites in one long day. I tried to apologize to Steve for what I had done to irk him.

He didn't respond. He said little to me outside the subject of our work assignment. He drove peacefully around the city while I navigated. I took great care with my words and tone.

After five o'clock, we stopped for supper at a roadside diner. Steve made his usual written record of our contacts and conversations with Woolco and Sears service and store managers. I offered my input cautiously about the things I felt he should include.

There was a payphone near our booth. Precisely at six o'clock (nine o'clock Montreal time), Steve walked over and called Dad collect.

I sat within earshot while Steve talked to our father. "Hi, Dad. I want to let you know I decided to stay with Harvy." My eyebrows rose as Steve continued. "We got along better today, and I've accepted his apology." They talked for a couple more minutes and then Steve hung up. I didn't get a word in with our father.

Taken aback a second time in two days, I asked, "How come you changed your mind, Steve?"

He hardly looked at me. "You were nicer today, and I started to feel bad about your driving back to Montreal by yourself."

Steve neither admitted to what he had done the day before nor apologized for his behavior. I sat in our booth and said nothing. My head ached, and my throat was dry and irritated. I didn't have the words or courage to express my despondency. I felt trapped. I needed Steve to help me get back home.

Steve and I never spoke about our Victoria incident during our three-day drive back to Montreal. I swallowed my irritation, along with aspirin for my aching head. We made it back without another sibling mishap. We talked cautiously to each other, and I drove his car carefully.

All the way back, I thought of how our family's die had been cast long ago by our father. Dad's pride in me, and perhaps my analytic, know-it-all attitude, had caused my brother to detest me deeply. It seemed to me as if

Steve had made a pact in his head that said if he couldn't be Dad's favourite, then he'd work continually to prove to Dad that he was the better man.

Little did Steve realize how much he turned out to be like our father, and little did our dad realize his part in creating Steve's MO, maybe mine too.

It was as if our father's water fountain poisoned any drink that Steve and I tried to share. Though the side effects of that well water were different for my brother and me, neither one of us could stop drinking it—me with my second-son loyalty to Dad, and Steve with his first-son defiance of him.

After our return to Montreal, Steve and I continued to be cordial with each other at both JHS and our apartment. But neither one of these Simkovits sons ever suggested another joint adventure.

From that point on, though I tried not to show it, I found myself reveling a little more in Dad's displeasures concerning my brother. When Dad got up in arms about Steve, I never had to add any fuel to that father-son fire because Steve was doing a good job of that himself.

To Dad's discontents, I usually nodded my understanding and said little. I did occasionally point out, "Dad, you complain continually about Steve, but you never do anything about it." Though an ugly part of me basked in my father's criticisms of my brother, I found it ironic that Dad never considered his part in creating Steve's way of operating.

When Steve and I arrived at our apartment from our four weeks away, my brother took his car and went to visit his horse. I took my car to Mom's to tell her we had made it across Canada in one piece.

When I rang her doorbell, Mom rushed to the door. I could see her eyes red from weeping. "Thank goodness you're home," she blabbered. Her voice was in agony, like a wounded animal, but with an edge. "Your father left me again for another whore woman!"

I was shocked and incredulous. I couldn't believe that Dad had done that to her so abruptly. "Mom, I'm sorry," I said with a gasp. "Please tell me what happened."

* * * *

39

My Tunnel's End Revisited

November 1999.

I walked out of the Elliot Trudell's elegant glass and mahogany wood doors for the second time. I was encouraged by my first meeting with my latest big-firm lawyer, Bernard. I was relieved to know about Revenue Canada's rules for making a "voluntary disclosure" concerning my father's offshore assets in Luxembourg.

From what I recalled of my father's Global Trade Bank statements, he hadn't made many offshore gains during the last few years. The decline of the Euro since its introduction some years earlier had degraded the value of Dad's hidden holdings. *Maybe we'd be lucky.* His estate might only have to pay the low end of the 30-40% percentage range Bernard had predicted for back taxes and interest on my father's undeclared offshore money.

I looked down at the floor next to the building's elevator doors. I wondered how I'd get my hands on three years of my father's offshore statements to figure out what that government cut might be. The only way was to have him request the statements from the bank. I didn't have an acceptable reason to ask Dad to do that for me.

I rode an empty elevator to the ground floor of the Bank of Commerce building. Other questions nagged at me. Might my father transfer full control of his offshore assets to me before he died? If he did, I could get started on the voluntary disclosure sooner.

I hadn't told Bernard that, years earlier, my father had given me power of attorney over one of his smaller Global Trade Bank accounts. Dad had wanted me to be his money mule if he ever needed cash fast and couldn't get it himself. I couldn't make a voluntary disclosure move with the solo account without risking my father exorcising me from the rest. The latter portion made up the bulk of what he had stashed over there in Luxembourg.

I liked the idea that my brother and I could say no to the government if we didn't like the deal Bernard would make with Revenue Canada. However, my honest, church-going confrere would never allow us to keep Dad's offshore money hidden from the tax authorities. More importantly, how was I going to tell Steve about Dad's offshore holdings without upsetting my brother?

Steve knew little about our father's black money ventures. If I told him too soon, he might jump on Dad for his offshore mischief, haranguing him to clean it up before his death. If Steve opened his mouth to anyone, especially the tax authorities, Dad would blame me. Our father then might bury his money in a different hideaway, energetically claim he had nothing offshore, and keep Steve and me from it forever.

It might be good to see those ill-gotten gains disappear. I was doing well enough in my consulting career to survive without my father's offshore wealth. But I had waited twenty-seven years for the day I could have my say over that money.

I knew my mother, now deceased, would have wanted her sons to obtain Dad's assets from which she had received nothing. I was hanging in there on her behalf in addition to mine. I no longer felt loyalty to my father for what he had done to her, to our family, and to me these last three decades.

I shook my head. I put my palm on my forehead to avoid seeing my reflection in the elevator's metal doors. Maybe I should take the easier route for now, following Dad's plan to keep his hidden money under wraps. Legitimizing those assets was perhaps too much to ask while Dad was still a distance from death.

He would turn 80 in a couple of months. It was over six years since he had had the stroke that debilitated half his body for a time. He now used a cane to help him drag his bad leg behind his good one. He might be in a wheelchair soon and then find himself underground.

I had played along with Dad's offshore games for over twenty-five years. I could allow his Global Trade Bank accounts to stay alive a little while longer until he was deceased. Though my stomach churned with that morbid thought, it might be my best option. I could even wait to tell my brother—sharing my knowledge with him later rather than sooner wouldn't hurt him.

My thinking sounded crass. But I was struggling for the best means to survive my father and get beyond my struggle with his secluded stash.

My mind remained unsettled as I exited the Bank of Commerce building. Other than having talked to a few lawyers, I felt very much alone in shouldering Dad's money secrets. Not even my wife of over five years knew anything about what had burdened me for over half my lifetime.

I had gotten sound legal advice so far. My U.S. attorney, Jay Henry, had told me to keep my distance from my father's suspect accounts. My high school chum, André, had said that Dad's suspect Independent University annuity agreement was not binding by estate law. André's colleague, Bernard, shared how he could conduct a voluntary disclosure to Revenue Canada that would involve cash penalties but no jail time.

But none of those advisors could tell me what I should do next.

I took deep breaths as I walked down the street toward my car. While looking down at the pavement, I nearly bumped into a pedestrian. *I have to bide my time.* Dad's hidden hoard was my load to bear alone. Given his state of health, time was on my side.

I climbed into my car, a Nissan Maxima, which I had parked on the street. Like my loyalty to my father, I had stayed loyal to the car brand ever since I had gotten my Datsun F10 in college. [By 1986, Nissan phased out the Datsun name.]

I turned on the ignition to warm the chilly November air, and stared out the window for a moment. My throat was dry from my decades of selfishness. I had kept my father's skeletons concealed from my mother and brother. I never demanded that Dad stop his offshore playing around with money or his onshore playing around in business and with women. *Would he have listened to me if I had told him to stop his finagling and fooling around?*

Maybe my brother had gotten what he deserved from our father, which was for Dad not to include Steve in what I knew about our father's offshore financial affairs. My brother never made anything easy for our patriarch. If Dad wanted to go west, Steve immediately went east, even for the simplest things.

One time, on a family outing to a movie, my twenty-something confrère was maneuvering our family's car in a crowded parking garage. Dad told him calmly, "How about turning here, son, into this lane."

My brother immediately barked. "I'm the one driving. I'll go the way I want to." He turned the car in the opposite direction.

From the back seat, I could see the red rise in my father's face. Steve continued to weave in and out of the rows of vehicles, looking for an open spot in which to park.

A long few minutes later, my brother found an opening. He may have done well enough to leave sleeping father dogs lay where they were. Instead, Steve chirped, "This looks like a good place; what do you think?"

It was Dad's turn to bark. "Why are you asking me? You just said that you're the one who's driving!"

Steve stayed silent as he parked; he acted as if Dad hadn't said anything. In the back seat, Mom and I kept our mouths shut. Such father versus first son scenes riddled our family life.

Steve had resisted me as much as he had opposed Dad. As teens, we bicycled along the streets of our hometown. Steve raced ahead to go off to a friend's home; he never included me in his rendezvous. I must have decided at an early age that if I couldn't be my brother's friend, then I'd do my best to become my father's favourite.

It was rare that Steve and I agreed on anything. Other than the years we worked together at Montreal Phono and JHS, and the few years we had lived together in a Montreal West Island apartment, we crossed paths only at our childhood home or in Dad's JHS office.

In spite of our father telling us, "I want you guys to get along," and "You two are stronger together than you are separate," Dad had been an unwitting instigator in our sibling dislike and distrust. He repeatedly complained to me about my brother. At many restaurant suppers, Dad banged the table with his hand and ranted, "Steve never puts me first. He always has more important things to do than having time for me. He treats me as if I'm the last on his list."

Over my years of working for Dad, I had advised my father to tell Steve how he felt about my brother's defiance without blowing his top at him, but my father didn't follow my advice. He continued to get angry or scream at Steve whenever his first son contradicted him at work. Or, in front of Steve, Dad would take out his anger on another office employee.

I entered my car outside the Bank of Commerce building. While sitting behind the wheel, I looked at my stained hands as they held firmly onto the steering wheel. I had been a part of Dad's divisive ways.

I was angry at my brother for having stranded me on Vancouver Island on our road trip across Canada. He later went off on outdoor adventures while I tried to make inroads at JHS. Perhaps I even resented the guy.

When Dad complained about Steve, instead of backing my confrère, I said to Dad, "Why are you tolerating his bad behavior? You're the one who's enabling him to get away with what he does."

Dad came back, "You're right, Harvy; I should be tougher on him. I keep on taking your brother's baloney without firing his ass." But Dad did no such firing, nor did he have any quiet tête-à-têtes with his first son. He just stopped his complaining for the moment and then restarted it on the next occasion.

I abhorred Steve waving his big-brother moralism in front of Dad and me. After Dad had closed his business and retired in 1984, putting Steve out of work for a while, my brother refused to collect unemployment benefits. Dad told him, "You and JHS have paid into unemployment for many years. You have every right to claim that benefit."

Steve's response was terse. "I don't need the money. I'm not like you, Dad. I don't take advantage of my situation." Steve's statement and decision meant my father could support Steve until Dad found him (not my brother found himself) a new job.

Steve's impudence about not collecting unemployment turned our father's face red once more. He threw his hand in the air. "Do what you want, Steve; but what you're doing is stupid." He turned and walked out of the room.

I knew my mind was preoccupied as I sat in my car outside the Bank of Commerce building. I looked out cautiously into oncoming traffic. Though my big brother could be one big pain in the butt, I couldn't blame him for our father's abusiveness or my failings. Although I never growled or roared like Dad, I'm sure Steve felt my sneers.

I wondered what my father might have said to my brother about me. Did Dad sing my MIT and graduate school praises until my brother retched? Steve never said anything about it to me, as I had said nothing to him of my discourse with our dad.

As time passed, Steve and I shared less and less about our lives. After I had no longer worked at JHS, we saw each other only on birthdays and major holidays, rarely without one of our parents present. Though we stayed cordial, the concrete block wall between us rose higher each passing year.

Steve and my relationship may have turned out differently had Dad had fewer fights with Mom, or if our father had spent more time at home when Steve and I were kids and teens, or if he hadn't abruptly left Mom high and dry after thirty years of tumultuous marriage. My brother and I might have become closer collaborators instead of constant competitors. It felt too late to have any hope for Steve and me.

I wondered again what I was going to tell my brother about Dad's hidden assets, and when I would tell him. Would he blame me for keeping him in the dark all these years? That fact could further strain our distant relationship.

Steve and I still had to work together—perhaps for many years—to deal with Dad's estate after his death. We would remain partners in Dad's JHS holding company; we'd have to deal with the properties amassed within the corporation. Whether I liked it or not, I'd have to work with my brother to unwind Dad's legitimate Canadian holdings. That could be a harder task if I were unfair to Steve regarding Dad's offshore empire.

I was tempted not to tell my brother anything about Dad's funds held at the Global Trade Bank. That would mean I'd have to continue deceiving not only Steve but also my wife, Revenue Canada, and the IRS (I was now a U.S. resident) after my father's death.

Might I then have to pass this weighty legacy to my son the way Dad had done with me? He was three years old, and my wife and I were trying for a second. Did I dare put any of my children into the covert money game I had grown to abhor? I despised the thought of stealing off to the Global Trade Bank to count, collect, or consort with the cash Dad had promised me.

Then again, I could carry out the voluntary disclosure on my own in the U.S., without my brother knowing about it. If I played the game right, maybe I could walk away with the whole after-tax proceeds from my father's secret stash.

I shook my mind back to reality as I continued to look out into the street from my car. Though Steve and I were more like distant relatives than close brothers, I didn't think I could pull off a government disclosure on my own outside my home country. I'd then have to keep my maneuver secret for the rest of my life. That modus operandi was my father's, not mine. It wasn't how I wanted to survive my father and be remembered by my heirs.

It was fair, ethical, and legal that my brother gained equal benefit from our father's offshore money. Steve didn't need to know all the details of my nearly three-decade history with Dad's ill-gotten gains. Maybe *mon frère* would be happy to get his half of Dad's offshore stockpile and walk away without any explanation.

I put my car into gear but left my foot on the brake. I knew I was distracted, so I again scanned the traffic. My body shivered. I hadn't been forthright with my brother, my late mother, my wife, or even myself. It didn't feel good, not one bit.

My father's fears of Quebec separation and business nationalization had not been realized. After several separation attempts and one very close vote, the people of Quebec had spoken. Quebec was staying in Canada.

I had read in the U.S. and Canadian newspapers that the IRS and Revenue Canada were focusing more resources on catching tax evaders. I wondered what would happen to Dad and me if his hidden money became known to tax authorities before I was ready to declare the lot. What would my professional colleagues and clients think about me? What would my wife say? What would my children think once they understood such things?

It would be devastating if Dad's and my names and pictures were spread across the Montreal newspapers for personal tax evasion. The papers had splashed Dad's Montreal Phono name across its business headlines in 1976, the year Revenue Canada convicted his company of corporate tax fraud. That thought brought shivers to my bones.

I pulled out into the street. I saw an old lady walking on the sidewalk with a scarf placed over her high hairdo. It reminded me of the way my mother used to wear her scarves. If I shortchanged my brother, then thoughts of my deprived and cast aside mother might haunt me for the rest of my days.

I smiled a bit. Though Mom had been born Jewish, she might find a way to let St. Peter know of my sins.

I blinked my eyes that seemed to be staring into space. Being honest and fair with my brother was the only way to make peace with my mother and perhaps with myself.

When Dad had arranged the Independent University annuity, he had told me, "I'm leaving you most of my pension money, but please help your brother if and when he needs it."

The thought of turning into a Johnny Simkovits replica, controlling the purse strings with his first son, repulsed me into my core. That would make Steve despise me even more. More so, it wasn't my job to be my brother's keeper. Could Steve and I possibly become better collaborators regarding Dad's onshore assets if I were fair to him about Dad's offshore stash after our father's passing?

I drove cautiously down the windblown street. *I have to stay realistic.* Not much could happen until our father was dead and buried, or if he became incapacitated. As long as he was alive and considered mentally fit, there was little I could do to straighten out his offshore money tangle.

I had to wait and see how the situation unfolded in Dad's waning years, months, or maybe even days. He dragged his stroke-affected leg more and more every time I saw him. A wheelchair was in his future.

I entered the highway leading back to my father's apartment; I was spending the night there. I hoped I could keep a guiltless look on my face. I couldn't risk a slip, unwittingly revealing my voluntary-disclosure intentions with my shameful eyes.

If Dad suspected, he could and would cut me off within a day. If my brother got wind of Dad's pile of offshore cash, he'd open his mouth and surely say or do something stupid.

I wished for a simple "Do the right thing" way out of the nagging predicament into which my father had put me. One thing I knew for sure: I didn't want to become the finagling, womanizing, vice-driven man that he had been all his adult life.

Though I had made a life and career different from my father's, I still wasn't free of him. I knew that I wouldn't be free until I separated myself from his tax-evading ways.

I glanced at the sky as my car followed the traffic. I prayed that my mother in heaven would help me keep my wits about me a little while longer. I didn't want to have another breakdown as I had had at Harvard Business School two decades earlier.

I needed to wait and hold myself together until the time would be ripe. I needed to act prudently on what I knew and what I held in my conspiring mind and tainted hands.

How I would do this remained unclear. That I would do it was not.

* * * *

Excerpt from

Just Lassen to Me!

Book Three: Survivor Learning

40

Chasing a New Life

The years leading up to Dad leaving Mom for a third time.

Albert Vidor was a short, thin, cigarette-smoking Polish Canadian. He had a hooked nose, a crooked smile, and a squeaky voice. He spoke Russian fluently, having been born and raised in the eastern half of Poland that, during times in history, had been a part of Russia.

One sunny summer day in 1978, Albert walked into the offices of Granite Real Estate in Champlain, NY. The firm was situated north of Lake Champlain, near the Vermont border. Behind the counter was Elaine Russ, a good-looking, dark-haired, 30-something woman.

Albert approached her and blurted out in his thick-accented voice, "I'm looking for the owner of this firm."

"That's my ex-husband," Elaine responded energetically. She eyed up and down this petite Pole who was inches shorter than she. But you can talk to me. What can I do for you, stranger?"

Albert stubbed out his cigarette in an ashtray on the counter. "My name is Vidor, Albert Vidor." His voice rose. "I'm looking to bring your firm business. I'm a real estate agent from Montreal, and I have rich clients who are looking for property around Lake Champlain. I can bring you lots of prospects if you are willing to work out an arrangement with me."

"Okay, let's talk," Elaine said. She stood and ushered Albert into her office. They reviewed real estate listings and made a commission deal for any business Albert would bring Elaine's way from across the border. For the rest of the day, they drove around the area to preview desirable properties.

A few Saturdays later, Albert returned to Champlain, NY with John Simkovits. Elaine showed them several properties, one of which was a ten-acre peninsula jutting out into Lake Champlain on the New York State side of the lake.

As they walked around, Albert did the talking. "Johnny, you see this land here. If you buy this estate, you can keep the main house for yourself and subdivide the property into one-acre lots." He swept his hand around, like a male version of Vanna White on *Wheel of Fortune*. "What you get for selling the pieces will pay for the whole property. It's like you'll get the house and what's under it for free."

My father said, "Okay, Albert, good idea. Let me think about it."

Elaine said nothing.

The following Monday, my father was in his Montreal office. His secretary, Helen, was on the phone with a call that had just come in. "Is it Mr. Simkovits senior or junior that you wish to speak to?" she asked the caller.

She got the answer and then turned to my father, "Johnny, I have a call for you on line two from an Elaine Russ."

He said, "Okay, Helen, it's about a property I'm looking at in New York State. I'll take the call in my private office."

A moment later, he was alone and on the phone. "Hello, Elaine. It's nice to hear from you. To what do I owe the pleasure of this call?"

"Mr. Simkovits, I'm sorry to bother you," she said. "I need to tell you about the large lakefront property I showed you the other day."

Her voice hesitated. "I like to be straight with my clients. I'm sorry to tell you this, but what Mr. Vidor said about the property is not true."

She pressed forward. "I was feeling bad about what he had told you, so I wanted to tell you myself that the property cannot be subdivided and the pieces sold off. There is no way the zoning there can change. No one can build anything more on that peninsula."

My father was quiet for a moment and then spoke calmly, "Thank you, Elaine, for telling me."

Elaine continued. "Mr. Simkovits, could you please not say anything to Mr. Vidor about this. I would feel bad if he knew I told you."

Dad took a long breath. "I understand, Elaine. And, please call me Johnny." He paused for a second or two. "By the way, in my appreciation for your honesty, please come and have supper with me one evening here in Montreal."

There was a pause at the other end of the phone. Then came, "Mr. Simkovits; Johnny; I make it a policy not to date my clients."

"Who says this is a date? And who says I'm your client?" He took a breath. "I just want to thank you for your honesty with me."

After another pause, "Okay, I could do that," she offered.

My father immediately added. "What about later this week? How's Thursday evening?"

A few moments later, Dad emerged from his back office. He shouted, "Helen, get me that schmuck Vidor on the line. I want to give him shit!"

Elaine told me that story years after my father's death. She added, "I had a policy about not dating married men. When I met your father for that supper, he told me he had separated from your mother."

She confessed. "I relocated to Montreal a half-year later; it was a big move for me. When I had gotten married to my first husband, I left Canada for Vermont and became an American citizen."

She looked away and then turned her eyes back to me. "In those days as a U.S. citizen, one could only hold a single passport. I renounced my Canadian citizenship when I moved south." She took a long breath. "When I came back to Canada after my divorce, I had to go through the Canadian Embassy in Boston to apply for Canadian landed immigrant status. It took nearly five months for the paperwork to come through."

She blinked a few times. "While I waited for the paperwork, I worked with my ex-husband in his real estate firm in upper New York State, right across the state line from where I lived in Vermont."

Elaine looked down. "To be honest, Harvy, it was mostly the pull from your father that brought me back to Canada. He and I had had many nice suppers with his Montreal friends, Vidor and Aras and Celia. He wanted us to spend more time together."

Her voice tightened. "After your father and I had been going out for several months, a funny thing happened. One evening, while I was driving home to the West Island after we had a meal at the Troika, I noticed your father's Mercedes sports car ahead of me." She smiled. "It was hard to miss that spiffy red thing."

At 58 years old, my father drove a Mercedes 450 SLC. I knew Elaine was considerably younger than Dad, but I was surprised to learn that she had been under 35 when she had met him. She was barely ten years older than my brother.

There was a twinge of irritation in Elaine's voice as she recounted the story. "As your father drove west, I saw he didn't turn north to head to the Town of Mount Royal where he said he lived." She pointed. "Instead, he continued west toward Dorval, where your mother lived. Since I lived in Pointe Claire, the next town over, I followed him."

Elaine's eyes became narrow and intense. "I was shocked when I saw him exit the highway in Dorval."

When they first went looking for properties in New York State, Vidor must have told my father about Elaine being good looking and unattached. Dad probably took off his wedding ring when he and Elaine first met, and he removed it from his finger during their nights out.

Elaine took a breath, and her voice rose. "By the time I got home, I was livid. I called both Vidor and Aras, and I yelled at them for lying to me about your father being separated." She turned to me, seething, "They had this little boys' club about keeping such secrets from their wives and other women."

I stayed quiet as she spewed. "I called your father the next day and told him our relationship was off. I told him point blank that I never wanted to see him again."

After a few long seconds, Elaine's tone quieted. She looked past me as if she were looking at an image projected on the wall. "I didn't see your father after that. Vidor and Aras were toast in my mind too."

She took another long breath. "However, I did like Aras's wife, Celia, and we maintained a friendship. She and I had dinner together here and there in the city."

Elaine looked at me with a small smirk. "But you know how your father can be! When he wants something, it's hard to say no to him."

Her voice stayed calm. "About a year after I had blown off Johnny, Celia called me to a supper party at their apartment. Confidentially, she warned me about Johnny being there too. She even told me your father had arranged the whole thing, repeatedly asking her and Aras to have this small gathering for the four of us."

She looked away and then back at me again. "I don't know why, but I agreed to go."

Elaine took a sip from a glass of wine she had poured for herself. "Your father was very nice all evening, his usual charming self. We both had a fair amount to drink."

Her eyes blinked several times. "On the way out, as we headed to the elevators, he cornered me and said, 'Elaine I want to be with you. Please let me come back.'"

She started at the wall and said, "I asked him point blank, 'What about your wife and kids?'

"He said, 'I'm going to leave Anne. I just need time to tell my sons.' He then crossed his heart and said, 'I promise.'"

She glared into the distance. "I said, 'Okay, Johnny, let me know when it's official, and then we can talk.'"

* * *

Acknowledgements

In addition to the usual suspects, Tom, Terri, and Barbara, I'd like to thank my proofreader, Susan Lucker, for her close line-by-line look at my manuscript and catching the little stuff that I and others had missed. I also wish to thank my wife, Beth, for her many big and small story-line suggestions that worked to make the manuscript better than even I could imagine. Lastly, no writer is without their supportive writing group. I want to thank all those aspiring and published writers with whom I have worked over the years, especially Pam Moriarty, who have helped, supported, or cajoled me on my way to becoming an author. It's all the little things that count as much if not more than any one big thing.

About the Author

For too long, Harvy Simkovits followed in the path of his "Just *Lassen* to Me!" patriarch. Harvy's war survivor, communism escapee, Canadian immigrant, business builder, and tax-skirting father told him to complete engineering school, business school, and then law school. The family's flamboyant forbearer wanted his second son to become somebody. He then wanted Harvy to come into the family business where he could tell him what to do. "Just *lassen* to me, son! I have more experience than you," was his brash dad's regular refrain.

Harvy, a loyal and impressionable young man, heeded his predecessor's wily wisdom for a while. After completing bachelor's and master's degrees in engineering at MIT and a stint at Harvard Business School, Harvy realized that he was leading his father's deceitful dream and not his own.

Harvy dropped out of Harvard and discovered his passion in the fledgling field of organization development. After completing another master's degree in that concentration, Harvy had a twenty-five-year career in management consulting and executive coaching. He helped many owner-managed companies and family businesses not to make the same mistakes that his father and family made in their business.

Then, in 2005, years after the death of his patriarch, Harvy felt he had to make peace with his past. He started to write not only about how his charming, hard-driving, and finagling father built his success in Canada, but also about how those qualities had had an insidious impact on their family, the family business, and (of course) Harvy. Harvy had to reconcile the moral and ethical dilemmas he faced with his furtive father and the rest of his thorny family so that he could successfully survive his survivor dad.

Harvy Simkovits has been writing and publishing stories about his Canadian immigrant family and their family's business since 2005. *Just Lassen to Me!* is Harvy's full-length memoir turned book series. He resides in Lexington, MA with his wife, two kids, and two cats.

Visit Harvy at his website:
www.HarvySimkovits.com
to read about the latest news regarding his memoir series.

22190928R00212

Made in the USA
Columbia, SC
27 July 2018